IMMIGRATION, NATIONAL AND REGIONAL
LAWS AND FREEDOM OF RELIGION

IMMIGRATION, NATIONAL AND REGIONAL LAWS AND FREEDOM OF RELIGION

Proceedings of the XXIth Meeting of the European Consortium for Church and State Research

Madrid, 12-15 November, 2009

Edited by
AGUSTIN MOTILLA

PEETERS
LEUVEN – PARIS – WALPOLE, MA
2012

A catalogue record for this book is available from the Library of Congress.

© 2012 Uitgeverij Peeters, Bondgenotenlaan 153, B-3000 Leuven (Belgium)

D/2012/0602/81
ISBN 978-90-429-2483-3

To Prof. Dr. Axel Frhr. v. Campenhausen

TABLE OF CONTENTS

Preface (A. MOTILLA) 1

H. KALB, Immigration and Religion in Austria 3

H. P. BEROV, Immigration and Religion in Bulgaria 17

A. C. EMILIANIDES, Immigration and Religion in Cyprus 27

J. R. TRETERA – Z. HORÁK, Immigration and Religion in the Czech Republic 35

L. CHRISTOFFERSEN, Immigration and Religion in Denmark 45

M. KIVIORG – L. ROOTS, Immigration and Religion in Estonia . 55

S. SIRVA, Immigration and Religion in Finland 69

T. RAMBAUD, Religion et émigration en droit français 75

H. M. HEINIG, Immigration and Religion in Germany 93

C. G. PAPAGEORGIOU, Immigration and Religion in Greece 107

B. SCHANDA, Immigration and Religion in Hungary 115

M. ENRIGHT, Immigration and Religion in Ireland 121

R. MAZZOLA, La religion face à l'immigration dans le système juridique italien 141

R. BALODIS, Immigration and Religion in Latvia 151

A. SPRINDZIUNAS, Immigration and Religion in Lithuania 159

S. VAN BIJSTERVELD, Immigration and Religion in the Netherlands 171

M. RYNKOWSKI, Immigration and Religion in Poland 179

N. PIÇARRA – F. BORGES, Immigration and Religion in Portugal 189

J. MARTINKOVÁ, Immigration and Religion in Slovaquia 199

B. IVANC, Immigration and Religion in Slovenia 209

C. GARCIMARTÍN, Immigration and Religion in Spain............... 229

L. FRIEDNER, Immigration and Religion in Sweden.................... 241

D. McCLEAN, Immigration and Religion in the United Kingdom 247

PREFACE

This volume contains the contributions to the XXI Annual Congress of the European Consortium for Church and State Research. It was held in Madrid on 12-15 November 2009. The issue of the discussion was "Immigration, National and Regional Laws and Freedom of Religion". Nearly fifty people from different countries of the European Union – Consortium members, guests and national reporters- participated in the Meeting.

The issue addressed by the reporters, the repercussion of national immigration laws in the safeguard and exercise of freedom of religion, were prepared following these main points: legal provision currently existing to facilitate or limit immigration; statistics available for recent years about application of residence and religious dimension of this matter; legal requirements placed upon acquisition of citizenship and tests about countries institutions and values; systems respecting the legal regulation of asylum; churches actions in asylum; pastoral assistance to illegal immigrants; religions dimensions of united family policies on immigration laws and practice; and restrictions or quotas for the employment of non-EU citizens and exemptions clauses for clergy or pastors.

The national reports were studied by all the participants at the Madrid Meeting. The discussions in the Meeting were divided into three different sessions. The topics of each session were: the facilitation or promotion of immigration or the granting of asylum and positive steps taken by the States in this regard; the limitation or restriction of immigration, addressing the manner in which the State regulates entry to the country whether for a permanent or temporary stay; and the religious dimension of immigration -for example pastoral care given to asylum seekers, rights of entry for foreign clerics, and church asylum as a means of subverting national law.

We should highlight some common patterns in the national reports about immigration and freedom of religion. Asylum because of religious discrimination in the foreign country is granted if the asylum seeker can prove physical or moral harm for him or for his family in the case of returning to his country. In order to obtain nationality a long stay is required in the European country –between eight and fifteen years depending on the country- and the passing of an examination about the national language, culture and the political system of the European country. Religious beliefs of the person are not taken in account. However, indirectly, some situations allowed by the religious law, such as polygamy, could be proof of non-integration into the European society of the petitioner. Clergy and pastors of recognized religions have special facilities to enter the countries and to obtain a residence card. And, finally, some institutions allowed in Islamic family law, such as polygamy and forced marriages, are commonly considered to be against national public order; so they will impede the family reunification. These common patterns are in stark contrast with the wide range of solutions in national law about religious chaplaincy in the detention centres of illegal immigrants.

Just a few lines to show the reader the variety of issues addressed in the reports of the Meeting and the wealth of information that could be found in this book. Summarizing the volume contents **offers** a comparative view of European immigration laws and their repercussions on religious freedom.

I wish to thank all those who helped to organized the conference in Madrid. First of all, I extend my thanks to the members of the Committee of the Madrid Meeting, Iván C. Ibán, Miguel Rodríguez Blanco, Paloma Lorenzo, David García-Pardo and Marcos González. Without their assistance and advice the Meeting would not have been possible. I am also grateful to the members of the Executive Committee of the Consortium, especially to Lars Friedner because of his active role in collecting the national reports, Brigitte Basdevant-Gaudemet and Norman Doe for the language corrections of the reports and Gerhard Robbers for the edition of the acts of the conference.

I am also grateful for the financial help for the organization of the Madrid Meeting and the edition of this volume of the *Ministerio de Ciencia e Innovación* of the Spanish Government (*Proyectos de Investigación SEJ2007-64106/JURI* and *DER2008/05097,* and *Acción Complementaria DER2009-05614-E)* and Carlos III University of Madrid.

Madrid, April 27, 2010
Agustín Motilla

HERBERT KALB

IMMIGRATION AND RELIGION IN AUSTRIA

1. Preliminary statement

Central components of the Law Concerning Foreigners in Austria are the Act Concerning the Police Department for Foreigners (Fremden-polizeigesetz, FPG), the Act Concerning Settlement and Sojourn of Foreigners (Niederlassungs- und Aufenthaltsgesetz, NAG) and the Asylum Act (Asylgesetz, AsylG), as amended by standards given by the Constitutional Court. The Employment of Foreigners Act (Ausländerbeschäftigungsgesetz, AuslBG) and the Citizenship Act (Staatsbürgerschaftsgesetz, StbG) ought to be mentioned as well.[1]

The law relating to foreigners is regarded as a difficult subject, even among lawyers. This complexity is caused by the dynamics of legislation which obfuscates a clear total conception by detailed, special, and extraordinary regulations.

The constant generation of new statutory provisions on the basis of problematically-led discussions creates legal uncertainties, since it impedes the development of established administrative procedures and adjudications.

Schumacher/Peyrl rightly state that it is hardly possible for the persons affected to answer simple legal questions about migration. By expecting too much of the persons directly affected a feeling of uncertainty is generated. "In the collective mind of migrants who live in Austria the perception is registered, that their legal interests can be interfered with at any time according to the prevailing political situation."[2]

The package of laws relating to the Law Concerning Foreigners of 2005 constitutes an important step in legal development. It fundamentally reforms the treatment of foreigners, by complying with European standards.

---

[1] Muzak/Pinter [Ed.], Fremden- und Asylrecht [Loseblattsammlung]; excellent collection of legal sources, judicature and literature till 2009 by Josef Rohrböck, judge at the asylum court, on the internet asylum online (http://www.asylum-online.at).

[2] Schumacher/Peyerl, Fremdenrecht (2007³), 16.

In January 2010 the "Package concerning foreigners" (Fremdenrechtsänderungsgesetz 2009) came into operation, which aims at an intensification of custody in preparation for deportation, and at a reduction of "consequential applications" (i.e. applications which try to delay an impending deportation). Furthermore, the asylum status, granted after a five-year stay, can be revoked if someone is sentenced with final force and effect.

This package concerning foreigners – as well as the previous legislative projects – were vehemently discussed and severely criticized by Caritas and Diakonie. This discussion has shown that it is important to take into consideration the reference framework as well.

If this discussion is seen in the light of the EU framework, Austria can be given good marks in its policy towards foreigners. The acceptance rate, as regards asylum seekers, is well above the EU average. According to material published by the Eurostat of the 281, 120 asylum applications within the EU, 28.3% were granted as compared with 61,6% of the 13, 705 applications in Austria. Even in appellate proceedings the Austrian rate of 26, 1% is above the EU average rate of 23.7%.

If this discussion is seen however in the perspective of internal discussions and implementations within Austria, the criticism voiced by churches, Caritas, Diakonie, NGOs and others sound plausible.

2. Immigration

Migration in Austria has long been put on a level with temporarily-limited employment of foreign workers. Up to 1993 immigration was directed via the labour market, without legal limitation of the absolute numbers of immigrants. After the collapse of communism in Eastern Europe the situation changed fundamentally. From then on, attention has focused on security policy, combined with a quota-system for long-term immigration (§§12, 13 NAG).

Every year the federal government issues a regulation determining the number of permissions to settle, and the maximum number of employment certificates for foreigners. Every person who wants to stay longer in Austria (on the basis of a visa – area of application of FPG) needs a title of residence (a term including various forms of permissions to stay).

The general preconditions for a title of residence are:

- a travel document
- proof of legal claim for accommodation in conformity with local custom
- proof of secured sustenance
- existence of a health insurance covering all risks
  (for some titles of residence a far-reaching warranty declaration of another person concerning the defrayment of costs for health insurance, sustenance and accommodation is necessary)
- a health certificate
- an integration agreement (obligation to attend a German-integration course within 5 years).

The integration agreement is an obligation for new immigrants to attend a German language course, or even a reading and writing course and to pass the relevant examinations. The integration agreement is separated into two modules:

Module 1: The reading and writing course comprises 75 hours and aims at conveying these skills. This course is a prerequisite for module 2.

Module 2: German-integration course for reaching the A 2 level of the Common European Reference Framework for Languages. This course comprises 300 hours and conveys basic skills in the German language about every-day subjects, with civic elements, and about European and democratic ideas. The Austrian integration fund can ask institutions explicitly named in the integration agreement to implement these courses. Among these rank institutions are the "legally recognised churches and religious communities which are entrusted with advising, supporting and caring for foreigners" (§1 Abs 1 Z 5 of integration agreement regulation).

- no existing residence ban
- no danger to public security
- applied quota system as a rule
- conformity with procedural regulations.

Quota places and utilization 1998-2006[3]

---

[3] Schumacher/Peyrl,, Fremdenrecht, 39. The settlement quota is not identical with the influx quota Thus only 5,569 persons came to Austria within the framework of the influx quota, whereas the figures published by the „Statistik Österreich" registered 108,947persons. (reason: many foreigners do not need permissions to settle; e.g. EU-citizens, relatives of Austrian citizens, temporary stays such as students, illegal migration).

year	total quota	proportional utilization of the quota
1998	8.540	84.32
1999	8.670/9,656[4]	91.28
2000	7.860	98.07
2001	8,338	97.43
2002	8.280	94.26
2003	8.070	75.80
2004	8,050	69.18
2005	7.500	89.39
2006	7.000	69.46

One important difference within the context of the different titles of residence is the differentiation between a temporary stay (more than 6 months, but limited in time), and permanent settlement for establishing one's place of habitual residence or for starting to work. Immigration with the aim of earning money is only possible – apart from some special forms – for so-called "key-workers".

The immigration figures show that "family-uniting" constitutes the major form of migration. The relevant regulations – whose framework is laid out by European norms – have been implemented in a restrictive and complicated manner. Due to constitutional problems, the past 12 years have seen 5 different models for "family-uniting" (implementation of the Directive Concerning the Right of family-unification, RL 2003/86/EG).

It has to be said that the quota-system and restrictive practice have encouraged illegal immigration. This illegal immigration is reflected in different political demands which can be reduced – simplified – to two fundamental tendencies:

• Keeping out strategies

These are characterised by demands for tightening of immigration regulations and extending police competences etc.

• Acceptance strategies

Migration concepts which take immigration as a fact.

---

[4] The quota was increased in order to enable relatives of Albanians living in the Kosovo to come to Austria during the war.

It has to be noted that numerous cases exist in Austria where people, despite a residence ban, cannot be deported, because the relevant home countries refuse to take them back – mainly due to a lack of relevant travel documents. Such persons are excluded from any public social support in Austria, at best they are taken care of by charitable (church) organisations. The fact that these persons – due to their hopeless social situation – sometimes come in conflict with the law is used by supporters of a more stringent Law Concerning Foreigners.[5]

2.1. *Acquisition of citizenship*

The naturalization of foreign citizens is ruled by the Citizenship Act (StbG).

Citizenship is basically acquired in to ways, either by birth or by conferment.

Acquisition by birth: at least one parent must have the Austrian citizenship (jus sanguinis as to nationality), the place of birth is irrelevant.

Acquisition by conferment: in combination with the general prerequisites and the necessary duration of stay, citizenship is conferred as a result of a concluded integration process.

The general prerequisites are:

No imprisonment; no severe administrative penalty; no existing residence ban or pending proceedings for the termination of stay; good conduct of the applicant; secured sustenance; abandonment of hitherto existing citizenship; knowledge of the German language and applied geography.

Necessary duration of stay: citizens of foreign countries can be naturalized after 10 years as a rule, after 15 years of legitimate and uninterrupted stay (sustained personal and professional integration) one has a legal claim for naturalization.

It has to be noted that the numbers of naturalizations have decreased in recent years. After a strong increase in naturalizations in the years 2001 to 2004 (the summit was reached in 2003 with nearly 45,000 people naturalized), the numbers have fallen continuously ever since.

---

[5] General statistic information is exhaustively covered by statistics on asylum and foreigners published by the Ministry for the Interior (BMI); further information in: Biffl/ Bock-Schappelwein, About the Settlement of Foreigners in Austria, Department for Economics Research 2008. It also has to be referred to the "Information of the Austrian Integration Fund" (e.g. numbers, data, facts 2009)

1998: 18,321	2003:45,112
1999: 25,032	2004: 42,174
2000: 24,645	2005: 35,417
2001: 32,080	2006: 26,259
2002: 36,382	2007: 14,041
2008: 10,268	

Since 2004 the number of naturalizations has decreased and the year 2008 with 10,268 cases was less than a quarter of the historical summit reached in 2003. The reason for this summit in 2003 was an influx in migration at the beginning of the 1990, with these persons meeting the naturalization requirements ten years later.[6]

A prerequisite for any conferment of citizenship (general prerequisite) is the proof of knowledge of the German language, and basic knowledge of democracy and the history of Austria and the relevant Austrian province. The proof of knowledge of the German language is basically furnished by the Integration Agreement. The necessary knowledge of the country's institutions and values is examined by way of a multiple-choice-test. (Subject of the test: basic knowledge of the democratic institutions in Austria; basic knowledge of Austrian history; basic knowledge of the history of the relevant Austrian province).

There have been no distinct demographic changes in the religious configuration of the country due to naturalization.[7]

The total strategy presents the following picture: naturalization is primarily a privilege of immigrants with higher income and higher education.

As with the general prerequisites, the proof of a secured sustenance and regular income without making use of social support constitutes a major hurdle. For migrants with low-income professions this prerequisite can hardly be met. The costs of the proceedings are high, a four member family has to consider € 3000 at least.

The required knowledge about a country's institutions and values also aims at people of a certain educational level, since no such courses are

---

[6] Source: Statistik Austria; Österreichischer Integrationsfonds (Ed), zahlen daten fakten 2009, Einbürgerungen.

[7] Remarkable is the increase in the proportion of Muslims living in Austria. The census of 1991showed a share of 2% and in 2004 a share of 4.2% with most Muslims living in the area around Vienna (2001: 7.8%). In addition to that numerous Muslims are living in industrial centres, especially in the centre of Upper Austria and Vorarlberg; cf detailed documentation by Statistik Austria.

legally stipulated. One has to note, fundamentally, that Austria – compared with the other members of the EU – has implemented a severe immigration regime. Since Austria does not see itself as a country of immigration, it has stipulated a very long time (10 years) of necessary stay.[8] Even the naturalization of children born in Austria is referred to naturalization by conferment. Thus one-third of the persons naturalized in 2007 were already born in Austria.

People naturalized in 2007 came mainly from former Yugoslavia (67%) and from Turkey (15%) with hardly any naturalizations of persons from other EU countries (only 3,5%).[9]

The religious dimension is reflected in various xenophobic or anti-Islamic discourses[10] (where the speakers sometimes fulfil the element of the crimes of indoctrination and disparagement of religious teaching, which has even led to the criminal conviction of political functionaries).

3. Asylum

Austria implemented a friendly asylum policy during the time of the cold war. One has to bear in mind the acceptance of more than 200,000 Hungarians after the failed national uprising in 1956, and of 160,000 Czechs after Russia's military intervention in 1967.

In the 1980 this climate changed. Up until then, Austria had been a much-used country of transit (Jewish emigration from Eastern Europe); it now became a target country. At the same time public discussion changed and the image of "economic refugees" was invoked and terms such as "asylum-abuse" – partly politically employed – became dominant. The legal reaction in this double-sense did not fail to cause and tightened restrictions, characterized by the development of asylum law. This culminated in the Asylum Act Amendment 2003, whose restrictive regulations were repealed by the Constitutional Court in 2004. An Asylum-Court was introduced by the amendment of the Federal Constitution Act in 2008 after controversial discussions. Up until then, two administrative instances had been involved – the Federal Asylum Office and the Independent Federal Asylum Panel – in asylum matters, and they were controlled by the Administrative Court or by the Constitutional Court.

---

[8] Cf. Belgium: 3 years; Ireland: 4 years; France, Luxembourg, the Netherlands, Great Britain: 5 years.

[9] Cf FN 6,

[10] Bunzl/Hafez (Ed), Islamophobie in Österreich (2009).

Demands for speeding-up procedures led to a two-tier system: The Federal Asylum Office and the Asylum-Court (AsylGH), with the Administrative Court being excluded as a regular court of appeal in asylum matters; the independent Federal Asylum Panel was transformed to the Asylum-Court. This resulted in an increase of complaints concerning rulings issued by the Asylum-Court to the Constitutional Court.[11]

Three guidelines characterize the Austrian asylum law:

• Austria's incompetence in many asylum proceedings

An application for asylum in Austria is inadmissible if the applicant can find protection from prosecution in another country (third country security), or if another country is obliged to examine the application for asylum, especially according to the competences laid down in the Dublin II Regulation.

In practice, refugees conceal their flight routes. Proceedings at airports gain special importance, where applications for asylum are submitted to airport authorities. If an application for asylum has to be repudiated because another EU-country is in charge (Dublin II – Regulation), consultations have to be instituted within one week. Repudiation because of third-country security or rejection, as regards content is only possible with the consent of High Commissioner for Refugees (UNHCR).

Applicants for asylum detained at a transit room are cared for by the personnel of Caritas Vienna: Social services at Schwechat airport.

• Reduction of legal procedural standards

Aiming at an "acceleration of the asylum procedure" and "struggle against asylum-abuse" the competences of authorities were increased at the expense of the rights of the parties concerned. These findings correspond with international obligations which allow an independent national asylum policy only within a narrow framework such as norms concerning the law of procedure.

• Basic care at a low level

Asylum applicants have a right to basic care during the asylum procedure (subsistence, accommodation and other provisioning services) rendered at a low level. The rules of the Employment of Foreigners Act (AuslBG) correlate with this situation. Applicants for asylum are denied any employment within the first three-months of their application. If no

---

[11] Muzak/Rohrböck, Der Asylgerichtshof (2008).

decision has been taken after this time limit, one can apply for a licence for employment. This licence is difficult to obtain since it is only issued for seasonal employment.

For implementing the provisions the authorities can make use of humanitarian, ecclesiastical or private institutions (§4 Abs 1 Basic Provisioning Act). In order to gain unified provisions and to avoid regional imbalances, a basic agreement has been concluded between the federation and the provinces according to Article 15a of the Federal Constitutional Law for temporary provisions for needy foreigners (applicants for asylum, asylum beneficiaries, displaced or other persons who cannot be deported due to legal or factual reasons). The Basic Provisioning Acts of the various Austrian provinces also provide for the use of humanitarian, ecclesiastical or private institutions for implementing this basic provision.[12]

Once the asylum procedure has been legally terminated the right to stay ends according to the Asylum Act, and the granting of a right to stay according to the NAG is excluded as a rule. Only an attempt could be made to gain a humanitarian licence to stay with reference to Art 8 ECHR, but such attempts have not proved successful as a rule.

The NAG, in its version of 2005, provided for an official granting of the licence to stay for humanitarian reasons – even though some hindrances existed – with the approval of the Minister for the Interior.

In implementing a decision of the Constitutional Court the humanitarian right to stay was newly regulated:

In special cases (degree of integration) a humanitarian right to stay was granted to foreigners who have sojourned in Austria since 1st, May 2004 (licence to settle – limited). The granting needs the approval of the Minister for the Interior, who has established a "preparatory council for the deliberation of special cases". One out of four members of this council appointed by the Minister for the Interior has to belong to humanitarian or ecclesiastical institutions which specialize in the integration and counselling of foreigners.

It has to be mentioned again that Austria's rate of granting the right to stay is well above the EU average despite a decrease in the number of applications.

Applications for the right to stay – affirmative decisions with Europe:

---

[12] Statistics about asylum and foreigners of the Ministry of the Interior; Biffl/Bock-Schappelwein, About the settlement of foreigners in Austria, Austrian department for economics research 2008; organized crimes of people smugglers. Illegal migration, annual report 2008 by the Ministry of the Interior.

Rate of granting the right to stay in 2008

total decisions	affirmative on the first level of authority (%)	affirmative on the second level of authority (%)
EU-27: 281.120	28.3	23.7
Poland: 4.425	65.3	15.8
Switzerland: 13.805	64.0	14.3
Austria: 13.705	61.6	26.1
Denmark: 1.725	58.3	34.3
The Netherlands: 11,725	52.0	51.6
Italy: 20.260	48.2	0
Hungary: 965	43.7	1.8
Germany: 30.405	40.7	25.1
Finland: 1.770	39.1	87.2
Great Britain: 33.525	29.9	31.6
Sweden: 31.220	26.6	49.0
France: 56.115	16.2	25.9
The Czech Republic: 2.880	15.5	3.1
Estonia: 6.250	5.4	1.1
Spain: 260	2.5	0

Austria has granted the special status of protection in 61,6% of applications out of a total of 13,705 according to figures presented by the Eurostat. 3,640 applicants were accepted by the first level of authority and 2,035 by the second level.[13]

People from Chechnya constitute the largest proportion of grants to stay (35.6%), followed by people from Afghanistan (15.4%) and from Serbia (7.6%)

One important element of the term refugee according to international law, which is referred to by the Asylum Act, is the existence of one or more factors of the convention (race, religion, nationality, membership of a special social group, political attitude).

The judicature refers to the handbook of UNHCR as well as to UNHCR directives for international protection: religious prosecution. A summary can be found in the decision of the Administrative Court (VwGH 21.9.2000, 98/20/05557).

Religion is defined by reference to the European Convention on Human Rights and Fundamental Freedoms (ECHR), and to the UN

---

[13] Most asylum seekers were accepted by the following countries in 2008 according to Eurostat figures France, 11,500 persons; Germany, 10,700 persons; Great Britain, 10,200 persons; Italy, 9,700 persons; Sweden, 8,700 persons; the Netherlands, 6,100 persons und Austria 5,675 persons

human rights pacts. Referring to the common point of view of the European Council from 4th, March 1996 concerning the harmonisation of the term "refugee" in Art 1 of the Refugee Convention, the term "religion" is broadly understood and includes "theistic, non-theistic or atheistic confessions, meaning that religious prosecutions can exist even if the person affected is of no religious conviction, is no follower of a religion or refuses partially or completely to submit to customs and rites in connection with a certain religion.

In the Austrian praxis the Geneva Refugee Convention feature "religion" is in the following three constellations of importance.[14]

– Impending or feared prosecution by sects, with the Administrative Court applying a closed metaphysical system of thoughts characterized by some concept of god for the term "religion".
– Conversion especially from Islam to Christianity. Conversions in the asylum country are examined in respect of "pretended conversions".
– Criminal sanctions with the aim of protecting "religious values". Here the frequent connection in the country of origin between state and religion is taken into account and the disparity of state actions because of infringements of moral rules obligatory in the country of origin (examples: handing on of bibles, possession of a book by Salman Rushdie, assistance in the flight of a woman prosecuted for adultery, sexual relationship between a female Muslim and a male Christian, etc).

Some high-profile cases of churches wanting asylum can be registered in Austria also, mostly a close cooperation between dedicated parish members and their priests. The state does neither legally recognize nor support the asylum given by churches and the officially registered churches keep their reserves in such cases and limit their actions to calls for "humanitarian solutions".

Illegal immigrants are taken care of by NGOs and by church organisations (e.g. Caritas). Only the spiritual care for prisoners is legally recognised in Austria (§85 StrafvollzugsG), and in organized form, for the Catholic (Concordat 1933) and Evangelical Church (§§18 und 19 Protestantenpatent). For persons without a licence to stay, persons under detention to be deported, and similar cases, no legal regulations exist.[15]

---

[14] Putzer/Rohrböck, Leitfaden Asylrecht (2007), 38ff
[15] Kalb/Potz/Schinkele, Religionsrecht (2003), 265ff.

So-called "cultural offences" such as murder out of honour, forced marriage, mutilation of genitals etc. are covered by existing criminal facts (murder out of honour: §75 Criminal Law Act – murder; forced marriage: enforcement to marriage as qualifying circumstance for enforcement in general according to §105 Abs 1 Z 3; mutilation of genitals: bodily harm according to §§83 ff Criminal Law Act, whereas §90 Abs 3 Criminal Law Act excludes a legal – and therefore exculpatory – consent to the mutilation of genitals.

During the last election campaign demands for the creation of special "cultural offences" – such as murder out of honour – came up. These simplistic demands are reflected in the government programme under the title "force caused by tradition". But one should not refer to tradition, philosophy of life, or religion in order to justify, to excuse or to mitigate these crimes.

Basically, it can be stated that the theory of criminal law denies the necessity of such "cultural offences", since no additional advantage can be found in such new statutory definitions of criminal offences.

With such cultural facts one has to refer to the general norms concerning mistake of law, and to necessity as an excuse – which are hardly applied successfully in practice – and to the possible taking them into account at sentencing.

"Foreigners regarding their pastoral activities within the framework of legally recognized churches and religious communities" are exempted from the scope of the application of the Employment of Foreigners Act (§1 Abs 2 lit d AuslBG).

Foreign nationals, who work in Austria as pastors of a recognized church or religious community, can obtain a title for staying (licence to stay – special cases of employed work).

The restriction on recognized churches and religious communities is problematic since it does not take into account the so-called "registered confessions". Amendments are necessary due to the judicature of the European Court of Human Rights (ECHR).

To illustrate the situation: The Act about the Legal Personality of Confessions (BekGG) introduced in Austria a second category or religious communities, which were granted no public legal standing in contrast to the legally recognized churches and religious communities. This second category has private law standing, and is subject to a kind of special law of associations. With this BekGG the prerequisites for recognition were tightened which were rightly termed as "prerequisites for preventing recognition" (e.g. the necessary number of members is 2 per thousand, at the moment, about 16,500 members; existence as religious community for 20 years, out of these 10 years as registered confession).

As a result a two-tier system is provided for recognition: 10 years as registered confession, then – if the prerequisites for recognition (16,500 members) are met – gaining of status as a legally recognized church or religious community. The ECHR sees in its judgement of 31.7.2008, Religious Community of Jehovah's Witnesses and Others v Austria, substantial privileges in connection with legal recognition and a lack of "fair opportunity" to gain this status – explicitly mentioned are the requirement of 20 years of existence, out of these 10 years as registered confession – as violation of Art 9 and Art 14 in connection with Art 9 ECHR. These arguments also apply to the required number of members meaning that the whole recognition procedure will have to be a new draft.

Since 1998 two specific legal forms have existed in Austria – i.e. the registered confessions and the legally recognized churches and religious communities, each complementary to the other – the problem arises how the nearly exclusive consideration of legally recognized churches and religious communities by the Austrian legal system (substantive privileges) can be justified. Basically, one has to assume that constitutional civil rights can be exclusively reserved to religious communities with public law standing.

Austria's highest courts have not yet followed this opinion. But change has been initialled by some judgements of the ECHR in connection with the Military and Non-military Service Act. Here the limitation of the exemption from military or non-military service to functionaries of the legally recognized churches and religious communities was considered to be contrary to the Convention[16]

Taking this situation into account, this report of findings also applies to the mentioned provisions of the Employment of Foreigners Act (AuslBG).

---

[16] E.g. Gütl v. Austria, Löffelmann v Austria,, Lang v. Austria, Apl Nr. 49.686/99; 42967/98;28,648/03; Kohlhofer (Ed), Religionsgemeinschaftenrecht und EGMR (ua mit Beiträgen von Kalb/Potz/Schinkele); dies, Österreichisches Religionsrecht in der jüngeren Straßburger Judikatur, öarr 2010.

Hristo P. Berov

IMMIGRATION AND RELIGION IN BULGARIA

1. Introduction

The geographic position and territorial situation of the Republic of Bulgaria in South-Eastern Europe makes it almost a natural bridge between two continents – on the East – Asia and on the West – Europe. In fact, since 2007 several Bulgarian borders are borders of the EU. Therefore the experience of multicultural, multiethnic and multi-religious immigrants should be rich enough to have become a part of the "national" memory[1] of the country. At the same time 20 years since the end of the communist era – a post-communist iron curtain still exists through reactions of some socialist regime generational representatives, who in a sense of a "national" memory still raise "traumatically" – argued topics on demographic catastrophes of Bulgarians as an ethnic group of the population in the country. In a certain way, large parts of the Bulgarian population[2] (mainly from small towns and villages in the provincial parts of the country) remain prejudiced towards the "other" (ethnic, racial and religious) groups. In the bigger cities there are more people who do not regard religious, ethnic or national origin as significant. It appears that they are more interested in the social position of the so-called "others" – including immigrants.

In my opinion, in Bulgaria there is, with small exceptions, almost no serious public discussion on issues such as refugees and asylum. Such phenomenon can surely be disturbing, because of future tendencies, that could appear in Bulgaria in the same way as in other EU-countries.

---

[1] From the so-called first systematic Turkish massacre on Armenians (1894-95) there were officially about 20 000 Armenian refugees in the Bulgarian state.

[2] Actually, the population of Bulgaria is composed of three main ethnical communities – Bulgarians, Turks and Roma (gypsies). Other groups are so small that they are not to be considered in a censure percentage. According to the last censure statistics from 2001, the self-determination was as follows: Bulgarians – 83,6%; Turks – 9,5%; Roma – 4,6%; other – 1,5%; not determined – 0,8 %.

2. Legal provisions on immigration in Bulgaria

First of all, as a prime legal provision, Art (=Article) 27[3] of the *Constitution*[4] from 1991 ought to be mentioned. It is also worth pointing out that the norm of Art 5 Para 4[5] ensures that international treaties, which are ratified, have priority over conflicting domestic law. In such cases it could be theoretically questionable if Bulgaria needs a particular legislation on many issues or should only genuine regulations of international treaties and conventions be followed. Nevertheless the *Asylum and Refugees Act*[6] is the special legal legislative regulation concerning Bulgarian immigration law. It explicitly enumerates in its first provisions (Art 2 and Art 3) international norms such as the *Convention relating to the Status of Refugees* of 1951 and the *Protocol relating to the Status of Refugees* of 1967.

There is no sufficient research material on topics comparing the coherence between Bulgarian legislation and international provisions on this issue, so that it cannot be hereby concluded to what extent the quality of Constitution and special legislation correspond to the Bulgarian obligation in international matters.

The Bulgarian legislation (according to the mentioned *Asylum and Refugees Act*) grants four types of protection in the following legal frames and distinguishes between: 1. *Asylum* granted by the President of the Republic of Bulgaria to aliens who have been persecuted due to their beliefs or activities in support of internationally recognized rights and freedoms; 2. *Temporary protection* granted by virtue of an act issued by the Council of Ministers for a certain period, in the event of a mass influx of aliens who have been forced to leave their country of origin due to an armed conflict, foreign aggression, large-scale violence or violation of

---

[3] *Constitution: Art 27. Para 1* No alien who legally resides in Bulgaria may be expelled there from or surrendered to another State against the will of the said alien, except under the terms and according to the procedure prescribed by statute. *Para 2* The Republic of Bulgaria grants asylum to aliens who are persecuted for reasons of their convictions or activities in defence of internationally recognized rights and freedoms. (3) The terms and procedure for the granting of asylum shall be regulated by statute.

[4] Constitution of the Republic of Bulgaria, promulgated, SG (=State Gazette) No. 56/13.07.1991 last amended SG No. 12/6.02.2007.

[5] *Constitution Art 5 Para 4:* Any international treaty, which has been ratified according to a procedure established by the Constitution, which has been promulgated, and which has entered into force for the Republic of Bulgaria, shall be part of the domestic law of the land. Any such treaty shall take priority over any conflicting standards of domestic legislation.

[6] Asylum and Refugees Act, promulgated: SG No. 54/31.05.2002, last amended SG No. 109/20.12.2007, effective since 1.01.2008.

human rights; 3. *Refugee[7] status* granted by the President of the State Agency for Refugees in line with the criteria set out in the 1951 Geneva Convention and the Law on Asylum and Refugees; 4. *Humanitarian status* granted by the President of the State Agency for Refugees to an alien whose life, security and freedom are threatened due to an armed conflict or danger of torture or other forms of inhuman and degrading treatment, as well as for other humanitarian reasons. Asylum, refugee status and humanitarian status are granted on the basis of individual examination of the case, while temporary protection is determined on a group basis, each member of the group being considered prima facie (i.e. the benefit of the doubt) a refugee. Refugees acquire the rights and obligations of Bulgarian nationals set forth in the Constitution and the laws of the Republic of Bulgaria, with the exception of: right to participate in general and local elections; right to participate in national and regional referendums; right to be a member of political parties; right to hold positions for which Bulgarian nationality is required by law; right to be members of the armed forces.

The main regulation of the *Asylum and Refugees Act* concerning immigration and religion is implied into Art 24 and Art 28 of the same Act. According to them: *(Art 24)* every alien seeking or granted protection shall have the right to profess a religion in accordance with the Constitution and the laws, at the same time aliens seeking or granted protection who reside in the territory of the Republic of Bulgaria are under an obligation to abide by, and observe the Constitution and the laws *(Art 28)*.

There is no serious political discussion in Bulgaria for being a *"country of immigration"* in a formal (or informal) way, such as in the case in Canada or Australia. There is also no Bulgarian tradition of immigration from particular countries, such as in the European states, which had former colonies. In fact, Bulgaria did not have any colonies at all. As a matter of fact, we could mention some other phenomena with immigrants who have Bulgarian origin and are descendants of former refugees from Bulgaria to other countries – actually for most of them seem to come from the so-called Bessarabia (Ukrainian region in the South of Moldova). These immigrants cannot be seen as refugees, because they are originally considered as having a Bulgarian origin, so that they have the opportunity

---

[7] In accordance with the *Law on Asylum and Refugees of the Republic of Bulgaria* "a refugee is an alien who has a well-founded fear of being persecuted due to his/her: race; religion; nationality; membership of a specific social group; political opinion and/or belief; who is outside of the country whose national he/she is or, if stateless, outside the country of his/her permanent residence, and who, for those reasons, cannot or does not want to avail himself/herself of the protection of that country or return thereto".

rapidly[8] to obtain Bulgarian citizenship and be full-righteous subjects of the Bulgarian law. Another particular type of immigrant comes mostly from Macedonia (former Yugoslav Republic of Macedonia). They also obtain Bulgarian citizenship as a result of Bulgarian origin[9] or Bulgarian self-determination. In some cases, they do not stay permanently in Bulgaria but go back to Macedonia to live there even if some of them could have troubles with the Macedonian authorities because of not being the "ancestors of Alexander the Great". At the same time they are able to travel easier abroad with their Bulgarian ID-documents. Such cases are not within the sphere of refugee' law and reflect no religious dimension.

3. Statistics on Bulgarian Immigrations situation

Some statistics on asylum and refugees[10] for recent years since 1993 (01.01.1993-31.08.2009) are available from the *Bulgarian State Agency for refugees*:

Year	Applications submitted	Refugee status granted	Refugee status refusals	Humanitarian status granted	Prolonged humanitarian status	Terminated procedures	Total number of decisions
1993	276	0	0	0	0	0	0
1994	561	0	0	0	0	0	0
1995	451	73	6	14	0	28	121
1996	283	144	28	13	0	132	325
1997	429	145	28	2	0	88	263
1998	834	87	104	7	0	235	436
1999	1349	180	198	380	5	760	1773

[8] Legal base is the *constitutional provision Art 25 Para 2*: Persons of Bulgarian descent shall acquire Bulgarian citizenship according to a relaxed procedure.
[9] Ibidem.
[10] According to the Bulgarian State Agency for refugees – *for the period of 01.01.1993 – 31.08.2009* the top 10 refugees countries of origin were: 1. Afghanistan – 5554 persons; 2. Iraq – 4045 persons; 3. Armenia – 1751 persons; 4. Iran – 817 persons; 5. Serbia and Montenegro – 771 persons; 6. Stateless – 679 persons; 7. Nigeria – 490 persons; 8. Algeria – 376 persons; 9. Turkey – 369 persons; 10. Bangladesh – 296 persons.
According to the same state agency *for the period of 01.01.2009 – 31.08.2009* the top 10 refugees countries of origin were: Iraq – 196 persons; Stateless – 58 persons; Afghanistan – 45 persons; Iran – 24 persons; Armenia – 22 persons; Turkey – 19 persons; Algeria – 16 persons; Syrian A.R. – 16 persons; Nigeria – 12 persons; Georgia – 11 persons; Somalia – 11 persons.
According to the same state agency *for the period of 01.01.1993 – 31.08.2009* the division of the refugees according to their sex was: men 69%; women 14%; children 17%.

2000	1755	267	509	421	65	996	**2275**
2001	2428	385	633	1185	164	657	**3060**
2002	2888	75	781	646	138	1762	**3411**
2003	1549	19	1036	411	7	528	**2021**
2004	1127	17	335	257	2	366	**989**
2005	822	8	386	78	0	478	**952**
2006	639	12	215	83	0	284	**594**
2007	975	13	245	322	0	191	**772**
2008	746	27	381	267	0	70	**745**
2009	525	24	259	160	0	52	**497**
Total	17637	1476	5144	4246	381	6627	18234

At the same time there is no official data on the extent to which in all these cases a certain religious dimension could be the ground for the refugee subject. In my opinion, in most of the cases, the reasons for entering Bulgaria as a refugee were many. Certain political motives could inevitably represent also a religious problem, as well as be generally connected with the matter of freedom of religion and belief, or together with the usual habits of a religious community.

4. Legal requirements upon the acquisition of citizenship

The main regulations on Bulgarian citizenship are the constitutional Art 25 (esp. Para 1) together with the provisions of the Bulgarian Citizenship Act[11]. According to Art 12 Para 5[12] the acquisition of Bulgarian citizenship by naturalization (also refers to refugees and humanitarian status provided by Art 13a[13]) should require comprehension of the Bulgarian

---

[11] Promulgated, State Gazette No. 136/18.11.1998, last amended SG No. 109/20.12.2007; *Art 8*: Any person, whereof at least one of the parents is a Bulgarian citizen, shall be a Bulgarian citizen by descent. Art 9 Any person, who has been filiated by a Bulgarian citizen or whose descent from a Bulgarian citizen has been established by a judgment of court, shall likewise be a Bulgarian citizen by descent. *Art 10* Any person, born within the territory of the Republic of Bulgaria, shall be a Bulgarian citizen unless acquiring another citizenship by descent. *Art 11* Any infant of unknown parentage, found in the territory of the Republic of Bulgaria, shall be deemed to have been born within that territory.

[12] *Art 12 Para 5* [Amended and supplemented, SG No. 41/2001] has a command of the Bulgarian language subject to verification according to a procedure established by an ordinance of the Minister of Education and Science.

[13] *Bulgarian Citizenship Act: Art 13a Para 1* [amended SG No. 52/2007] Any person, who had been granted a refugee status or asylum not less than three years prior to the date of submission of the application for naturalization, may acquire Bulgarian citizenship if he of she possesses the qualifications referred to in items 1, 3, 4 and 5 of Article 12 herein.

language subject to verification according to a procedure established by an ordinance of the Minister of Education and Science. Alongside this there is no other explicitly settled special test which prospective citizens have to pass, in order to demonstrate their knowledge of a country's institutions and values.

An important prerequisite also for foreigners who are seeking, or have received asylum in Bulgaria is the mastering of the Bulgarian language. For instance, the so-called *Integration Centre for Refugees* (=ICR) has developed a program and has organized courses in language training for both adults and children. The training is carried out by part-time lecturers who have written a specialized Textbook in Bulgarian for Children Refugees. Since 2005, the training set has to be completed by preparing a Training Aid in Bulgarian for Children Refugees and a Language Course for Refugees, which will include fundamentals about Bulgaria.

Until now there are no concrete annotations on demographic changes in the religious configuration of the country due to naturalization (last census was in 2001). As a matter of fact, it is noticeable that some differences in the percentage can generally be expected during the next census in 2011, but more due to the Bulgarians (emigrants) who live abroad since 2001, rather than due to immigrants.

5. Legal system on regulation of asylum

It is very subjective to state that the legal system on regulation of asylum could be specified by just being compared to itself or to its legal history. Therefore, if it seems that some of the legal changes in this area in Bulgaria during the last decade were to a certain extent positive, there is still a lot of work to be done – in order to gain the necessary experience for the general development of legislation and practice in the field of human rights, in which the legal system on regulation of asylum is also situated. The general approach to the question of the law mostly includes the lack of experience in certain areas [esp. civil society] rather than deficits in the legal sources [as already mentioned Bulgaria has ratified an important group of international treaties].

There is also no official statistical analysis available on issues that could help to sharpen our understanding of the legal system, on regulation

Art 13a Para 2 [New, SG No. 52/2007] Any person who was granted humanitarian status no less than five years prior to the date when the naturalization application was filed may acquire Bulgarian citizenship if he/she meets the requirements under items 1, 3, 4 and 5 of Article 12.

of asylum in Bulgaria connected with a certain religion. Bulgarian agencies state that the official frame of the regulation of asylum law of the state should be as follows: 1. Aliens who have been granted asylum or refugee status have the same rights and obligations. 2. Aliens who have been granted humanitarian status have the same rights and obligations as aliens holding permanent residence permits in the Republic of Bulgaria. 3. Aliens who have been granted temporary protection are entitled to: reside in the country throughout the duration of the temporary protection; an identity document; social security; food, shelter, medical care and services.

There is not enough official data to objectively analyze the practice of state authorities dealing with asylum procedures themselves. An evaluation of this practice could be done under certain circumstances, in which a concrete criterion should be set as an instrument of measure.

The lack of official statistics on certain causes of immigration does not permit for the precise mentioning of a frequently important feature of an application (valid also for religion). Nevertheless, having in mind that most unacceptable political regimes try to subordinate the sphere of mental freedom (to which also religion belongs) makes it necessary to assume that religion could also be an important feature of immigration in Bulgaria, if at the same time not often important. On the other hand, it is well known that post-communist countries (such as Bulgaria) do not have enough experience (because of the former communist regimes) within religious freedom. The latter probably has some influence on the choice of (esp.) religious refugees as to the exact country to which they apply for asylum. There are no officially known or published examples on this matter in Bulgaria.

The procedure, which allows a humanitarian right of residence and asylum are equally regulated, at least in regard to the identity papers of the applicants[14].

6. Churches and asylum

The Holy Synod of the Bulgarian Orthodox Church, which represents a creed, proclaimed by the Constitution (Art. 13 Para 3) to be a traditional religion and according to the official state statistics embodies the biggest

---

[14] The old *Refugees Act* regulated the procedure for the provision of a status of refugees and humanitarian protection, but did not regulate the procedure and the conditions for the granting of an asylum in the Republic of Bulgaria.

Bulgarian religious community, has absolutely no church policy in immigration matters, and holds that the immigration is within the pre-rogatives of the state.[15] With the rare exceptions of some Evangelical congregations in Bulgaria, there is no other concrete church policy on immigration matters publicly known. A Christian centre called "Pre-lom"; together with its citizen's initiative *"Spravedlivost 21"* were newly engaged in discussions[16] about legislative amendments on the *Foreigners in the Republic of Bulgaria Act*. The mentioned centre took care in supporting refugees through evangelical volunteers supplying immigrants with clothes, bibles and pastoral supervision. There is no information about initiatives of other religious communities dealing with immigrant' problems.

7. Pastoral assistance to illegal immigrants

There is no official information on pastoral assistance to illegal immi-grants. Having in mind the sensitivity of the question, it is to be sup-posed that it is kept away from public life and is a matter of private initiatives because of the obligation of religious communities in Bulgaria to follow the state legislation.

8. Religious family law and immigration

According to Bulgarian Family law (and Constitution) only monoga-mous marriages are allowed. Forced marriages are forbidden. The Bul-garian state has no experience in matters of immigrants and polygamous

---

[15] Compare for instance the synodal decision – cited from: http://www.bg-patriarshia. bg/news.php?id=12878;
"At its meeting on 23.09.2009, Wednesday (Protocol Nr. 8) the Holy Synod [of the Bul-garian Orthodox Church – Bulgarian Patriarchate] in reduced headcount, in the absence for health reasons of His Holiness the Bulgarian Patriarch Maxim opened its session. The synodal prelates, who attended, were: Neophyte of Ruse – chairing the meeting, Gregory of Veliko Tarnovo, Nathanael of Nevrocope, Ignatius of Pleven. […] In an address to the Holy Synod: Report Nr. 686/10.IH.2009 by the Chief Secretary of the Holy Synod – Bishop Naum of Stoby along with an attached letter from Mrs. Vesela Vatseva, Manager of "Advertising Agency B" Ltd., asking that in the campaign for tolerance towards refu-gees who seek salvation in Bulgaria to also include the Bulgarian clergy with a message of peacefulness, respect and mercy to the neighbour in need. The Holy Synod DECIDED: Mrs. Vatseva has to address the State Agency for refugees in Bulgaria."
[16] Representatives of the "Prelom" Centre, NGOs and state authorities had public discussions on terms of administrative procedures on special boarding-houses for immi-grants and the length of stay therein. Two TV broadcastings showed the discussions, seen from a Christian point of view. [TV-Evropa: Christianstvoto-20.07.2009].

marriages. A reference to *EU Council Directive 2003/86/EC* on the right to family reunification, (Art 4 Paras 4 and 5) has not been applied in the practice, so that its effect on particular religious or cultural background is not officially known.

9. Exemption of restriction clauses for clergy or pastors

There are no exclusive (for certain professions) official restrictions on quotas for the employment of Non-EU Citizens. Furthermore, there are also no special legal regulations containing exemption clauses[17] for clergy or pastors. In fact, the regulation for work permits, given to foreigners who have permanent residence within the country is also the same for foreigners who have been granted asylum, refugee status or humanitarian status.

10. Conclusion

On conclusion, it may be said that the Bulgarian legal system on immigration generally attempts to follow international and EU standards. Despite some exceptions[18] this legal area still remains under-researched under academic aspects. It is also a matter of future specification how Bulgarian legislation and judicial practice will deal with the religious dimension on a growing number of immigrants entering to EU (also through Bulgaria) to form appropriate assessment of the questions in some of the upper sections of this report.

---

[17] According to the *Religious Denominations Act (Art 35 Para 2 p. 5)* the *Religious Denominations Directorate as a body of the Council of Ministers* provides opinions on requests for stay in the country of foreign religious officials who have been invited by the management of registered religious denominations.

[18] For instance: *В. Цанков*, Бежанско право, ВСУ, 2006, etc.

ACHILLES C. EMILIANIDES

IMMIGRATION AND RELIGION IN CYPRUS

1. The Framework of Cypriot Immigration Law

Cyprus had historically been a country of emigration, especially to the United Kingdom, but also to Australia, the United States and South Africa. Following the Turkish invasion of 1974, however, and the occupation of the northern part of the island, the Republic begun issuing individual visas to migrant workers for employment, which were short term and restricted to specific sectors. Demand for labour in Cyprus in specific sectors, such as the tourism industry, led to the granting of visas and work permits on the condition that the worker would be attached to a particular employer, without the freedom to change employer, unless the original employer consented to such a change; in any event the duration of the stay of the worker in Cyprus must be of a temporary and limited nature. Employing migrants who do not have a work permit or who do not reside lawfully in the Republic of Cyprus is a criminal offence, with the penalty of imprisonment normally being imposed on wrongdoers.

It should be noted that prior to its accession to the European Union in 2004 the Republic of Cyprus allowed Russian nationals to enter Cyprus without visas, an initiative which aimed to attract businessmen and which resulted in a large number of Russians migrating to Cyprus and establishing offshore companies. Following its accession, the Republic of Cyprus has been forced to adopt a more restrictive policy; however, the number of Russian immigrants continues to be quite large.

The principle legislative instrument concerning immigration law is the Aliens and Immigration Law Cap. 105, as amended. The Aliens and Immigration Law regulates the issue of refusal of entry within the Republic of Cyprus to illegal immigrants and provides an extensive list of such persons. According to Section 6 of Cap. 105 persons who are considered as illegal immigrants include, *inter alia*, poor persons, persons who are mentally disturbed or who suffer from a contagious disease, persons who have been convicted and imprisoned imprisonment as a result of committing murder or any other serious offence, prostitutes, or persons who are expected to behave in a manner contrary to public order or morals, or who are members of illegal organisations. It should be noted that Section 6 of Cap. 105 has not been modified following the Independence of the Republic of Cyprus in 1960 and, therefore, its provisions might seem rather outdated.

In addition to the above, the immigration authorities of the Republic may refuse entry to any person who is not a citizen of the Republic. Therefore, foreigners do not have an absolute right of entry to the Republic and may be refused entry unless they hold a permanent residence permit or a valid immigration authorisation, or unless they are temporary residents and hold a valid entry permit or disembarkation permit. According to Section 9 of Cap. 105 and subject to the discretionary powers of the Chief Immigration Officer, no person shall enter into the Republic of Cyprus without a passport. Failure to do so will lead the immigration authorities to consider such a person as an illegal immigrant. Section 7A of Cap. 105 further provides that if the immigration authorities find out that a fictitious marriage has been performed, then they may prohibit the foreigners from remaining within the territory of the Republic, or they may cancel or refuse to renew the residence permit granted to the foreigner.

Normally, an alien will need a visa to enter into the Republic, namely an authorisation granted by the consular authorities of the Republic. Foreigners may be prohibited from entering into the Republic unless their passport has a Cypriot visa; if no such visa is demonstrated, then the foreigner may be considered to be an illegal immigrant. Nevertheless, the Council of Ministers may from time to time issue Orders prescribing that passports or Cypriot visas are not required for the citizens of a certain country or for any class of persons.[1] It should be noted that while the general rule is that a person should apply for a visa to be issued by the consular authorities of the Republic, such person may, in special cases, apply for a visa at the borders for the purpose of entering or transiting from the Republic; such a person ought in any event to comply with the requirements of Cap. 105 for entering into the Republic; he or she should not have been in a position to apply for a visa beforehand from the consular authorities of the Republic, should file all necessary documents proving the unforeseen and urgent reasons for

---

[1] The Council of Ministers has prescribed that nationals of countries such as Russia, USA, Australia, Canada, Japan, Argentina, Andorra, Bolivia, Brazil, Brunei, Chile, Costa Rika, Guatemala, Honduras, Hong Kong, Liechtenstein, Mexico, New Zealand, Singapore etc. do not require visas for stays up to 90 days.

entering into the Republic, and should prove that the return to the country of origin is secured.

The Aliens and Immigration Law has been recently amended on a number of occasions for the purpose of harmonising the Law with the acquis communautaire. There are no restrictions for European Union citizens entering or residing in Cyprus. The Law Concerning the Freedom of Movement and Residence of Citizens of Member States of the European Union and of Members of their Family has been adopted for the purposes of harmonisation, and provides that citizens of the Union and their family members have a right to move and reside freely within the territory of the Republic of Cyprus.

Section 111 of Law 141(I)/2002 provides that a non Cypriot who resides lawfully in the country may acquire citizenship via naturalisation, so long as he/she fulfils certain criteria. The Minister of Interior may grant citizenship to an adult and fully-able applicant, if he is satisfied that the applicant: a) has resided lawfully in the Republic for the twelve months preceding the submission of the application, b) has resided lawfully in the Republic for a period of at least four years in total during a period of seven years preceding the aforementioned twelve months, c) is of a good character, d) has the intention to reside in the Republic or work in the public service of the Republic. Citizenship via naturalisation may also be granted in special cases by a decision of the Council of Ministers. In principle the Cypriot government follows a restrictive policy with respect to the granting of citizenship to non-Cypriots, because it does not wish to alter the demographics of the island (namely the analogy between Greek Cypriots and Turkish Cypriots), because of the ongoing Cyprus problem.

Ever since the Turkish invasion of 1974, providing precise figures with respect to the population of Cyprus has presented certain difficulties, due to the abnormal situation prevailing in the island. The Statistical Service of the Republic of Cyprus has estimated, however, that by the end of 2006 the population of Cyprus was 867,600, out of which 660,600 (76.1%) belonged to the Greek community, while 88,900 (10.2%) belonged to the Turkish Community. The remaining 118,100 (13.7%) were foreign residents, including mainly Greek and British citizens, as well as citizens of Russia, Philippines, Sri Lanka, Romania, Bulgaria and other countries. Of the members of the Greek community, 2,700 (0.4%) were Armenians, 4,800 (0.6%) were Maronites, while 900 (0.1%) were Roman Catholics. With the exception of a few agnostics, atheists and naturalised foreign citizens, all other members of the Greek

Community adhere to the Greek Orthodox religion. In view of the fact that many non Cypriots, such as mainland Greeks, Russians, Romanians and Bulgarians also adhere to the Orthodox Christian religion, it is estimated that approximately 82% of the total current population of Cyprus are Orthodox Christians. It is further estimated that the number of Roman Catholics residing in Cyprus, if foreigners are also included, is approximately 2%.

According to the Statistical Service, migration towards Cyprus increased by 50% between 2003 and 2005 (i.e. a year prior to EU accession and the year after accession). More specifically, the number of immigrants rose from 16,779 in 2003 to 24,419 in 2005. While a few of those immigrants are repatriated Cypriots (9% for 2005), the biggest majority are individuals who come to Cyprus to live and work (78%). Approximately 69% of those immigrants are from EU countries (mainly Greece and the UK) and 15% are from Asia. The rest are from other European but non-EU states, Africa, America and Oceania. It is worth noting that Immigrants from Sri Lanka, the Philippines, Russia, China and India seem to be increasing more rapidly than any other group.

In any event, it should be noted that pastoral assistance may well be given to illegal immigrants, if requested, although there does not seem to be any formal procedure governing such assistance. In principle the State is willing to provide such assistance to the illegal immigrants on an ad hoc basis.

2. Churches and Work Permits

There have been no cases of a church attempting to give asylum in Cyprus. Nor does the legal framework contain any exemption clauses for clergy or pastors. In the case of *Levantis*, the applicant was a Greek national married to a Greek Cypriot, and resident in Cyprus. He impugned by means of recourse before the Supreme Court of Cyprus, the decision, whereby his application for a permit to work as a Religious Officer of the Church of God of Prophecy, was rejected.[2] It was argued by the applicant that he was prevented from exercising and expressing his religious duties as a Religious Officer of the Church of God of Prophecy in Cyprus, that there was discrimination and unequal treatment against the applicant as a religious officer of the said Church, that his freedom of worship was violated, as well as that the applicant was com-

---

[2] *Levantis v. The Republic* [1988] 3 CLR 2483.

pelled in a manner tantamount to the exercise of moral pressure to change his religion.

The Supreme Court rejected the application and held that article 18 of the Constitution safeguards freedom of religion and not entitlement to work permit, a matter which is regulated specially by the Laws of Cyprus. The applicant was free to profess any religion he wished, while the refusal of a work permit did not prevent him from attending his Church or otherwise manifesting his religion or belief. Thus, it was held that there was no violation of article 18 of the Constitution. While it can be generally accepted that granting work permits to aliens falls within the discretionary powers of the State and that religious freedom does not entail a right to be granted a work permit, it is suggested, on the other hand, that the aforementioned decision of the Supreme Court presents certain problems. The said alien was a resident of Cyprus who had married a Cypriot and who intended to work as a religious minister of a Church; rejecting his application for a work permit should not be arbitrary so as to cause concerns that it was due to his religious beliefs and to the fact that he wanted to work as a religious officer of the particular Church. There seemed to be no justification why the application for a work permit was rejected in the case of *Levantis* and this raises serious concerns of religious discrimination.

3. Asylum and Religion

Article 3 §1 of the Refugee Law 6(I)/2000, as amended, provides that a person may acquire the status of a refugee, so long as he/she is outside his/her country due to a well – founded fear of persecution, and cannot, or is not willing due to such well – founded fear of persecution to, be protected by his/her country; persecution may relate to racial, political, or religious grounds, or to the fact that the refugee is part of a specific social group. A refugee may be persecuted by the State, or groups or organisations controlling the State or a substantial part of the State, or even non – state actors, so long as the state actors – including international organisations – may not, or are not willing, to provide protection from persecution or harm. In 2002 there were 839 applications for asylum in Cyprus; the number increased dramatically in 2003 and reached 4032 applications, while in 2004 it amounted to 9285, in 2005 to 7291, in 2006 to 4286 and in 2007 to 5905. Between 2002-2008 more than 23,000 cases were examined; only 65 applications were accepted, while in another 286 the authorities granted ancillary protection or humanitarian status.

Religious grounds of persecution include, inter alia, according to article 3D of Law 6(I)/2000, as amended by Law 112(I)/2007, the adoption
of theistic, non – theistic, or atheistic convictions, or the manifestation of
such convictions, either individually or collectively, in private or in public, or abstention from such manifestation, or other religious acts or
expression of beliefs, or other types of individual or collective behaviour
based upon religious convictions. When examining a petition on the
basis of Law 6(I)/2000, the authorities may not discriminate on grounds
of religion. The above principles have been applied by the Supreme
Court of Cyprus in the recent cases of *Sarmadi*[3] and *Faramarzian*.[4]

The applicant in the case of *Sarmadi* was of Iranian origin. While his
initial application for being recognised as a refugee within the meaning
of Law 6(I)/00 had been rejected, the applicant requested that his application be reconsidered in the light of the fact that he had subsequently
been baptised as a Christian. The applicant maintained that he had aban-
doned his country due to his political and religious beliefs and that he
had been imprisoned for sixteen months for refusing to co – operate with
Iranian authorities; he argued that when he was in Iran he had some
Christian friends and during his meetings with them, he read the Bible
and was fascinated; he was then baptised as a Christian and attended
religious classes. He further maintained that his life was in danger,
should he ever return to Iran, due to the fact that he had been baptised as
a member of the Christian Community Church; in particular the applicant argued that the Iranian authorities would kill him, because of the
fact that he had converted to Christianity.

The Asylum Authority maintained that the applicant had not proved
genuine Christian convictions, or knowledge. It was further maintained
by the authorities that there was no well – founded fear of persecution
should the applicant return to Iran, since the Iranian authorities had not
been aware of his conversion to Christianity prior to him leaving Iran.
The Supreme Court rejected the arguments of the Government and held
that the conclusion of the Government that the applicant had not proven
well – founded fear of persecution, or genuine Christian convictions,
was fundamentally flawed. It held that the fact that the applicant had not
answered correctly certain specific questions with respect to Christianity

---

[3] *Mozafar Sarmadi* v. *The Republic*, Judgment of the Supreme Court of Cyprus of 3
April 2007 (in Greek). See also *Seyfallah Mozafar Sarmadi* v. *The Republic*, Judgment of
the Supreme Court of Cyprus, 17 December 2009 (in Greek).

[4] *Faramarzian and Hayati* v. *The Republic*, Judgment of the Supreme Court of Cyprus
of 22 May 2008 (in Greek).

was immaterial, since the applicant had correctly answered most of the questions and had in general provided sufficient evidence of his conversion to Christianity; genuine religious feelings are associated not only with theoretical knowledge, but also with the way one has chosen to live, while the evidence showed that the applicant had chosen to live as a Christian. Furthermore, the Court observed that while the authorities had essentially acknowledged that the Christian minority of Iran is persecuted, they incorrectly held that the fact that the Iranian authorities might not be aware of the applicant's conversion meant that his life was not in danger should he ever return to Iran.

The Court also held that each claim requires examination on its merits on the basis of the individual's situation. In this context, the well-founded fear need not necessarily be based on the applicant's own personal experience. What happened to the similarly situated individuals, such as the claimant's friends and relatives, or other members of the same religious group, may well show that his fear that he also will become a victim of persecution is well-founded. While mere membership of a particular religious community will not normally be enough to substantiate a claim to refugee status, there may be, however, special circumstances where even mere membership suffices, particularly when taking account of the overall political and religious situation in the country of origin, which may indicate a climate of genuine insecurity for the members of the religious community concerned.

In the case of *Faramarzian* the applicants – also Iranian citizens- were husband and wife, whose application to be recognised as refugees had been rejected by the authorities. It was maintained on behalf of the applicants that their conversion to Christianity had put their life and fundamental freedoms in danger, should they ever return to Iran. The authorities concluded that the applicants had not been baptised, and had not proven that they had genuine Christian convictions, since their knowledge concerning Christianity was inadequate. The Supreme Court held that the decision of the authorities was flawed; it held that the applicants had in general answered correctly many questions about Christianity and they could not be expected to know all details about their new religion, when they were still in the process of being religiously educated by their church. In addition, the questions concerned the Orthodox Church, while the applicants had adhered to the Protestant Church; thus, many of the questions asked by the authorities did not prove that the applicants' knowledge of Christianity was inadequate as maintained by the authorities.

Jiří Rajmund Tretera – Záboj Horák

IMMIGRATION AND RELIGIOUS IN THE CZECH REPUBLIC

1. Legal regulation of immigration in the Czech Republic

There are several types of legal sources regulating immigration[1] to the Czech Republic. Most of them make immigration possible and facilitate it, some bring small limiting barriers, in accordance with international law, and regulations of European law.

a. Constitutional law and obligations from the international and European law

In the first place, there are provisions of the Czech constitutional law, above all *The Charter of Fundamental Rights and Freedoms*.[2] Secondly, there are provisions of ratified and promulgated *international agreements*. They constitute a part of the Czech legal order. Should an international agreement make a provision contrary to Czech law, the international agreement is to be applied.[3] Some examples of international agreements, which bind the Czech Republic in cases concerning the subject of this article are: the Convention relating to the Status of Refugees (Geneva, 28 July 1951) and the Protocol relating to the Status of Refugees (31 January 1967). Both documents were published under No. 208/1993 Coll.

---

[1] Immigration = the coming into a country of foreigners for purposes of permanent residence, *Black's Law Dictionary*, Abridged sixth edition, St. Paul, Minn., U.S.A., 1991.

[2] *The Charter of Fundamental Rights and Freedoms* is a Czech legal document, which is a part of a constitutional order of the Czech Republic. Originally it was published under No. 23/1991 of the Collection of Laws of Czechoslovakia as an enclosure to the Constitutional Act of the Czech and Slovak Federal Republic, passed by the Federal Parliament on 9th January, 1991. To the date of dissolution of the federal state, 1st January, 1993, the Constitution of the Czech Republic was proclamated as an constitutional Act No. 1/1993 of the Collection of Laws of the Czech Republic (further only: Coll.). This Constitution incorporates the above mentioned Charter in the constitutional order of the Czech Republic. The Charter was published again under No. 2/1993 Coll., and has the same legal effect as the Constitution of the Czech Republic. In reality it has a position of the second part of the Constitution.

[3] The Constitution of the Czech Republic, Art. 10.

And at last, but not least, are the *regulations and directives* of the European Council.

b. Acts of the Parliament

There are two specialized Czech legal acts, which concern immigration. There is the *Act No. 325/1999 Coll., on Asylum*, as amended, because asylum seekers are also immigrants, too. The second one is the *Act No. 326/1999 Coll., on the Residence of Foreigners at the Territory of the Czech Republic*, as amended. This Act regulates not only the granting of permanent residence, i.e. immigration in the real sense of the word, but also granting of temporary residence.[4]

First of all there is the Act on Asylum, which facilitates immigration to the Czech Republic. Asylum is granted to foreign citizens and persons without citizenship, who are in their home countries prosecuted for promoting of political rights and freedoms, or if they have real fear of prosecution for their race, sex, religion, ethnic, adherence to a special social group or political opinions.[5]

Secondly, immigration is facilitated by the provision, according to which the legally specified family members of asylum holder have a right to obtain asylum.[6]

Thirdly, immigration is facilitated by the provision on humanitarian asylum.[7]

Fourthly, we can consider immigrants also as persons who obtain permission for permanent residence.

Foreigners can gain the right to stay in the territory of the Czech Republic according to permission for temporary or permanent residence on the basis of above mentioned Act No. 326/1999 Coll.

Foreigners obtain permission for permanent residence, who have lived in the Czech Republic for at least 5 years,[8] or if they ask (even without previous residence at the Czech territory) for permanent residence for humanitarian reasons.[9] Persons, who have resided for at least 4 years at the Czech territory, after fulfilling some legal

---

[4] Temporary long-time residence concerns the term of more than 90 days, but not more than 5 years.

[5] Act No. 325/1999 Coll., Art. 12 lit. a), b).

[6] Act No. 325/1999 Coll., Art. 13.

[7] Act No. 325/1999 Coll., Art. 14.

[8] Act No. 326/1999 Coll., Art. 68.

[9] Act No. 326/1999 Coll., Art. 66, sect. 1, lit. a).

prescribed conditions, obtain the permission permanent residence, too.[10]

The Charter of Fundamental Rights and Freedoms emphasises that a foreign citizen may be expelled from the territory of the Czech Republic only in cases specified by legal act.[11]

c. Immigration policy of the Czech Republic

Immigration policy is considered not only as an issue of internal Czech State politics, but as a European one. Therefore, members of the Parliament of the Czech Republic and executive power representatives proposed such changes, which are discussed in the European meetings.

Despite the historical tradition of being a country of asylum contemporary political discussion does not tend to consider Czech Republic as a "country of immigration".

After 1918 Czechoslovakia accepted many refugees from Soviet Russia, after 1933 refugees from Nazist Germany. After the communist coup d'état of 1948 thousands of Greek children, orphans from the civil war in Greece, were invited to Czechoslovakia.

After 1945 tens of thousands of Roma-Gipsies settled in Czech Lands, in having moved from Slovakia, Hungary and Romania.

In the late years of the communist totalitarian regime many students from Marxist oriented African and Asian countries (e.g. Libya, Syria, Iraq, Afghanistan) studied at the Czechoslovak Universities. Many of them stayed in Czechoslovakia permanently. At the same time a large number of Vietnamese came to Czechoslovakia as workers.

The tradition of immigration from **Vietnam** goes on today. After the democratic changes in 1989 Vietnamese mostly changed their employment and became small shopkeepers and have began to control the cheap textile market and later also groceries and greengroceries. The number of long-resident members of this minority has grown rapidly owing to new immigrants from Vietnam, and now there are several tens of thousands of people.

After the dissolution of Czechoslovakia (1993) a mutual exchange of inhabitants between the Czech Republic and Slovak Republic has started. It is connected with continuity economical ties, cultural and language similarity. Nowadays **Slovaks** are the largest minority in the

---

[10] Act No. 326/1999 Coll., Art. 67.
[11] Charter of Fundamental Rights and Liberties, Art. 14, sect. 5.

contemporary Czech Republic.[12] The Slovak language is used as the second official one in the Czech Republic.

A new wave of immigration comes from the **Ukraine**. Ukraine is the main supplier of construction workers and hospital auxiliary workers to Czechoslovakia. There is no real language barrier because of the similarity of Ukrainian to Czech. Most Ukrainians come from the Subcarpathian Region of Ukraine, which was part of Czechoslovakia before the Second World War (Ruthenians), another large number of Ukrainians come from West Ukraine (former Galicia), which also has traditional cultural connections with the Czech Lands. Many Ukrainian workers return after a time to Ukraine, but a lot of them ask for permanent residence.

Russian immigration to the Czech Republic is new and somewhat different in background. Russian businessmen own spas in Carlsbad and have not only many guests, but also spa employees who come from Russia. Russian businessmen live also in Prague and other cities. There is a possible source of future immigration.

Since 1989 many **Polish** workers have come to the Czech Republic, but they usually return home. Hundreds of Polish priests have a long-time temporary residence in the Czech Republic helping for Czech Catholics, usually with a 5 year term contract.

Certain number of **Islamic** immigrants includes those, who under the Communist regime (1948-1989) were invited from the befriended Arabic or other Islamic countries to study in Czechoslovakia, and who decided not to return home. One of the frequent reasons for this has been their entering into marriage with a person of the Czech or Slovak nationality and consequent founding a family in the Czech Lands. The number of Muslims in the Czech Republic is not large.

2. Contemporary statistical data in respect to immigration

In 2008 there were 18,743 applications for permanent residence, and 215,676 applications for long-term temporary residence.

Religious belief is not questioned, because it belongs to sensible personal data, which are not relevant in the field of general immigration agenda. For this reason we are not able to report on the precise number

---

[12] See ŠRAJEROVÁ, Oľga, *Slovenská menšina v Českej republike (The Slovak Minority in the Czech Republic)*, in: PETRÁŠ, René, PETRŮV, Helena, SCHEU, Harald Christian (eds.), *Menšiny a právo v České republice (Minorities and Law in the Czech Republic)*, Auditorium, Praha, 2009, p. 189–198, ISBN 978-80-87284-00-1.

of Muslims applicants, but with regard to countries of origin of applicants we can state that Muslims are not a prevailing group among the applicants for residence.

3. Legal requirements placed upon the acquisition of citizenship

Czech citizenship is to be granted[13] to a person, who fulfils all the following requirements:

- permanent residence in the territory of Czech Republic for at least 5 years,
- loss of foreign citizenship (with exception of refugees),
- not sentenced for intentional crime for last 5 years,
- knowledge of Czech language (with exception of Slovak citizens).

Parents can include their children younger than 18 years in the application.

There is no special test which prospective citizens have to take in order to demonstrate their knowledge of a country's institutions and values. Only the language test is required.

Demographic changes in the religious configuration of the country due to naturalization

As for the residence of foreigners in the Czech Republic apparent is the expansion of spiritual care, and number of members of Greek-Catholic Church (because of some immigrants from Eastern Slovakia and majority of immigrants from Western Ukraine) and East-Orthodox Church (because of other Ukrainians and most Russians), and of the Centre of Muslim Communities.[14] Muslim immigration comes from different countries, but has a common religious organization in the Czech Republic till today.[15]

---

[13] Act No. 40/1993 Coll., on Acquisition and Losing of Citizenship of the Czech Republic, as amended, Articles 7–11.

[14] See TRETERA, Jiří Rajmund, *Legal Status of the Islamic Minority in the Czech Republic*, in: Religious Freedom and its Aspects, Islam in Europe, Bratislava, 2005, p. 300-306 (of the English text), ISBN 80-89096-22-0.

[15] According to the finding of the Czech Statistical Office from 2001 there were 3.699 Muslims in the Czech territory, but this data is out-of-date. Nowadays the number of Muslims is estimated on about some 11.000 among 10,3 million inhabitants of the Czech Republic. The leadership of Muslim communities remains in the hands of Czech Muslims and some naturalized Arabs or Afghanis (see above). What is interesting, is almost the absence of Turks at the Czech territory.

4. Legal regulation of asylum

The Charter of Fundamental Rights and Freedoms grants "… asylum to citizens of other countries, persecuted for asserting political rights and freedoms" and sets down that "asylum may be denied to a person who acted contrary to fundamental human rights and freedoms."[16]

The Convention relating to the Status of Refugees (Geneva, 28 July 1951) and the Protocol relating to the Status of Refugees of 31 January 1967 contain international obligations. In the Czech Republic both documents were published under No. 208/1993 Coll.

The source of law of asylum is *Act No. 325/1999 Coll., on Asylum*, as amended. This Act was transformed in connection with entry of the Czech Republic to the European Union. The Act on Asylum contains material and procedural rules on this question. In the Czech Republic there is a system of "international protection", which contains only two types of protection – asylum and subsidiary protection. The Czech Republic also recognizes refugee status granted by another state or by the United Nations High Commissioner for Refugees (UNHCR), and so not granted by the Czech state authorities.[17]

As for European law, there are for example the following provisions on asylum:

Council Regulation (EC) No 343/2003 of 18 February 2003 establishing the criteria and mechanisms for determining the Member State responsible for examining an asylum application lodged in one of the Member States by a third-country national (so called Dublin Regulation),

Council Directive 2003/86/EC of 22 September 2003 on the right to family reunification,

Council Directive 2004/83/EC of 29 April 2004 on minimum standards for the qualification and status of third country nationals or stateless persons as refugees or as persons who otherwise need international protection and the content of the protection granted, and

Council Directive 2005/85/EC of 1 December 2005 on minimum standards on procedures in Member States for granting and withdrawing refugee status.

---

[16] No. 2/1993 Coll., Art. 43.
[17] Act No. 325/1999 Coll., Art. 90.

a. Legal changes introduced during the last decade

According to Act No. 2/2002 Coll. the judicial examination of administrative decisions of the Ministry of Interior in asylum cases was introduced.

From 1st September 2006 the system of international protection was created, either by granting of asylum (political, for family reunification, humanitarian), or subsidiary protection. Subsidiary protection concerns persons, who are not entitled for to be granted asylum, but cannot be expelled for other reasons (the principle of non-refoulement).

b. Available statistics

The Czech Statistical Office publishes data on the above mentioned material on the websites www.czso.cz, according to years. The main states from which *asylants* came to the Czech Republic in last 10 years, were *Afghanistan, Mongolia* and *Kazakhstan*.[18]

As for the year 2008:

1,656 foreigners asked for international protection in the Czech Republic. They came from 59 countries.

Asylum was granted to 157 applicants, the most numerous group were refugees from Burma (Myanmar) – 26, Belarus – 19, Russia – 18, Ukraine – 17, Kazakhstan – 14, Iraq – 10, without citizenship – 11.

132 persons obtained subsidiary protection. The most numerous group came from Cuba – 62.[19]

c. The practice of state authorities dealing with asylum procedures

A foreigner makes a statement about his intention to apply for international protection, mostly at the boundary or other place of his first contact with State authorities of Czech Republic. Then the application for granting of international protection is mostly written in the Accepting Centre, which is the beginning of the international protection procedure. The applications for international protection are submitted to the Department of Asylum and Migration Politics of the Ministry of Interior. The application for international protection is not accepted if another EU member State is competent according to the Dublin Regulation (in such a case applicant is transported to a competent State).

---

[18] See websites of the Czech Statistical Office www.czso.cz.
[19] See websites of UNHCR (United Nations High Commissioner for Refugees) in the Czech Republic http://www.unhcr.cz.

The Ministry of Interior decides to grant the international protection, or to deny it.

d. The religion of the applicant

The religion of the applicant is not often an important feature. The question on religious affiliation is usually not posed to applicants. Such a question is not allowed, because of neutrality of the Czech Republic in relation to the atheism or religion.

Only if the reason of the application is prosecution for religion, is such a question relevant. Then it is inquired, if the applicant's religion is really prosecuted in his country, and if he is really member of this religion.

Examples can be given: the last time such an inquiring was held was in cases of "pure" islamists from Kazakhstan, and of the Chinese Roman Catholics in obedience to Pope.

e. A process which allows a humanitarian asylum

The Act No. 325/1999 Coll., on Asylum, regulates in its article 14 granting of humanitarian asylum, when according to a strict interpretation of the law asylum could not be granted. There is larger administrative discretion in this procedure.

In addition, Act No. 326/1999 Coll., on the Residence of Foreigners at the Territory of the Czech Republic, contains permission of permanent residence for humanitarian reasons (article 66, section 1, and article 67, sections 2, 3, 7).

5. Church asylum

There is no legal basis for church asylum in the Czech Republic. The Czech legal order does not take Church asylum into account. No legal or political propositions in such a direction are known. There is no experience of "civil disobedience" in this regard, either.

6. Pastoral assistance given to illegal immigrants

Pastoral assistance is given to illegal immigrants in cases of pending determination of their application to remain, as well as in cases after they have been ordered to be expelled from the country. Such assistance is in the competence of the prison chaplains of the Czech Republic, and of the Civil Association for Prison Spiritual Care, whose members can be members of all religious societies, even of those not yet registered. According to the constitutional provisions individual spiritual care must not be refused to anybody. The religious details of foreigners should be taken into account also in the detention facilities, where they stay before they are expelled from the country (Act No. 326/1999 Coll., on the Residence of Foreigners at the Territory of the Czech Republic, art. 141).

Available chaplaincy services

According to the Agreement of Pastoral Service in Prisons between the Prison Administration of the Czech Republic, Ecumenical Council of Churches in the Czech Republic and the Czech Bishop's Conference the Corps of Prison Chaplains was created. The first agreements were signed in 1994, then in 1999, and the last one in 2008. Pastoral care according to this Agreement is provided not only in favour of prisoners, but all persons in some form of detention. Chaplains, who are nominated according to the above mentioned Agreement, are paid by State.

There are 21 churches and religious societies, which are entitled to send their ministers to the detention facilities, because they are registered "with special rights" according to the Act No. 3/2002 Coll., on Churches and Religious Societies, as amended. The representatives of the Civil Association for Prison Spiritual Care can enter the detention facilities, too. These representatives can be members of other registered churches and religious societies or even members of not yet registered ones. Ministers or Association representatives in all such "pro persona" provided services are not State employees and, therefore, they are not paid by State.

7. Immigration and principle of the united family

Principle of united family is respected in both procedures, on granting of asylum and granting of residence permission. The Acts define the family. The polygamous marriage is not recognized. Religious differences between members of the family do not play any role.

In cases of polygamous marriage asylum can be granted only to one marriage partner, who lives with the asylant on the territory of Czech Republic, according to the EU Council Directive 2003/86/EC on the right to family reunification, art. 4 sect. 4. Cases of forced marriage are not regulated by the law; marriages with minor persons are not recognised.

8. Employment of Non-EU Citizens, especially of pastors

There are no quota for the employment of non-EU Citizens. But according to the Act No. 435/2004 Coll., on Employment, as amended, the Czech employment seekers have precedence before non-EU Citizens. This restriction does not concern spiritual ministers of registered churches and religious societies from abroad, as to the Act No. 435/2004 Coll., art. 97 lit. c).

LISBET CHRISTOFFERSEN[1]

IMMIGRATION AND RELIGION IN DENMARK

1. Socio-historical context

Questions regarding the possible religious dimensions of migration to Denmark have been central to the formation of the Danish political scene since the elections in 2001, after which the Danish Peoples Party formally became the parliamentary basis for (without being members of) the government; after two later elections they are still in charge. In particular, the immigration of Muslim groups into Danish society has caused political changes and brought questions about religion and values to the centre of social debates. There are, however, signs that the latest change of leadership in Prime Minister Lars Løkke Rasmussen (who came to power without public elections, because the former Prime Minister Anders Fogh Rasmussen, who, among others, was the prime minister during the Cartoons Crisis, became the Secretary General of NATO) has changed the focus to making it more orientated towards economy and the welfare organization of the Danish society.

Denmark has 5,5 million inhabitants. Recent statistical information shows that 9.5 % of the population ($\frac{1}{2}$ million people) are migrants and their descendents. 2/3 of these are from non-western countries (350.000). Of the total number of migrants, the old EU-countries represent 18 % (90.000), the new EU-member states 10 % (50.000) and the Nordic countries 25.000.

The biggest groups of migrants are Turks (ca 58.000); Germans (30.000); and people from Iraq (29.000). These three groups also portray the main root of immigration to Denmark:

Turkish citizens came to Denmark throughout the 1960's and -70's in order to work and then return to Turkey, but Europeanization and changed living conditions established instead a situation of immigration to Denmark which also included families. They represent a larger number of (culture)-Muslim groups in Denmark and as in other European

[1] Professor in Law, Religion and Society; Department of Society and Globalisation; Roskilde University; lic@ruc.dk

countries they therefore are also very often at the centre of the cultural-political discussions; very often, however, they are focused more on other Muslim groups (stateless Palestinians; Sudanese; people from Morocco and Afghanistan).

Germans (and the citizens from other Nordic countries), on the contrary were always part of the Danish picture (Østergaard 2007). Actually the Danish law on citizenship was already decided upon in the late 18th century in order to remove Germans from and to give Danes a better chance in state administration. Nordic migrants are welcomed as immigrants, as is fitting with the cultural scheme of the country, and given long-standing notions of resentment especially towards Germans there is tendency in Danish society not to see European citizens in Denmark as a problem, but just as – immigrants.

People from Iraq represent the newer wave of refugee-based migration from countries with a different culture, some of whom are also Muslims (more or less engaged), whereas others are Christians, secular or of other religious traditions. As refugees they are expected to be given asylum for a period, but due to political circumstances in their home countries and to the formulation of the legislation, their status can often change from refugees to a right to permanent stay, as a step towards citizenship.

Denmark has no official statistics on religious commitment or belonging, and it is, therefore, difficult to determine about the size of different religious groups. Based on tax payments it is, however, known that 82 % of Danes are members of the Danish Lutheran national church. Sociologists of Religion (Warburg et al 2007) think that Muslims, as a broad group, (including many internal confessional, cultural and country-of-origin distinctions) form the second biggest religious group, numbering around 200,000, being the second biggest present religious group in the country. Catholics, who used to be the second biggest group have now numbers around 30,000; whereas Jews number less than 10,000 and other Christian denominations each number less than 5,000.

In the 1960's Muslims were seldom seen in Denmark, with less than 1000 inhabitants of Muslim faith. This rather sudden change in the religious picture, from the national church having a practical monopoly in public life, along with very small jewish-christian groups, to the current practical religious pluralism with a rather large Muslim group, is the sociological background for the political debates concerning immigration and religion in Denmark during the past 15 years (see also the articles in Christoffersen et al 2010).

2. Main Legal Framework

Following Adamo 2009 I use the concept 'migrants' as a common concept, covering asylum-seekers; people with a right to stay, based on refugee status; EU-citizens and others with a right to stay, based on their status as workers or students; family members and their descendents. The concept 'immigration' is used to describe people with a permanent right to stay, or people who have Danish citizenship. These distinctions are based on distinctions in the field of Danish legislation.

Migration to Denmark is legally regulated by the *Aliens Act,*[2] originally introduced in 1983. The general scheme of legislation has since the early 1970's been that of controlling flows of migration. The regulation distinguishes between basically four different groups of (lawful) migrants:

- Asylum seekers and refugees, who are treated in accordance with the Geneva-convention, of which some arrive spontaneously whereas others are invited from UN-refugee-camps;
- citizens of EU-countries or Nordic countries, who are treated in accordance with EU-legislation (even though Denmark has an opt out, all rules, including the Schengen agreement and the Dublin convention, are implemented on inter-governmental basis);'
- Third Country Nationals (immigrants), who can only acquire lawful residence if one among a list of specific conditions in the law is fulfilled. This list of conditions include a) family reunification (with many sub-requirements to which I return below). The list also includes residence permits on the basis of employment in relation to a green card scheme; a positive list of professional fields where there is a shortage of qualified labour; a pay limit scheme; a corporate residence permit; labour market ties; or, where necessary, employment or business considerations make it appropriate to grant the application. The possibilities also include grants of residence permits in cases of humanitarian aid (outside the concept of asylum); of 'exceptional reasons' including regard for family unity; a possibility for previous Danes; a special rule regarding religious practice (I also return to this below) and some other possibilities.

---

[2] Aliens Consolidation Act, LBK nr 785 of 10 August 2009, hereafter 'aliens act'. Information regarding legislation and statistics can be found, most of them in English, on the website of the Ministry of Refugees, Immigrants and Integration, www.nyidanmark. dk; New to Denmark – the Official Portal for Foreigners and Integration.

- Visa for short period stay. The general rule is 3 months within a 6-month period, but people from certain groups of countries may only be granted a visa for much shorter periods in cases of business relations or rare close-family visits, and then only if their departure is guaranteed by the resident. This, of course, causes trouble among other religious groups and requires international cooperation. Religious groups have, therefore, tried to change this rule, but with no results.

The granting of residence permits for refugees on the basis of asylum is decided upon by an independent boarder. The matter of religious backgrounds regarding persecution is dealt with in relation to analysis of country background; the relevant religious groups etc.

3. The Family and its bearing on the rules

As can be seen, the idea of keeping the family together and giving families possibilities of living together has an impact on the Danish rules of residence permits. On the other hand, experience within the authorities shows that many 'families' are established on a fake basis in order to acquire the right to stay. There are also many reports of more or less forced marriages between relatives from the home country in order to acquire residence permits, but with little benefit for the integration of foreigners in the country. These experiences and observations may have to do with the very easy means of divorce in the Danish system: not only are there no social problems related to being a divorced person, but the legislation grants a person divorce on demand after a 1 year wait, with no requirement to provide special argumentation. The possibility of Danes selling a marriage to people wishing for a European residence permit was, therefore, foreseen together with the malpractice of young 2nd or 3rd generation immigrants being married to persons from their countries of origin not knowing the language, the culture etc.

These practices formed the background for a very detailed set of conditions for getting a right to stay based on family reunification, for a married couple. The rules were established after 2001. The rules for residence permits for spouses, registered partners and cohabitant partners are as follows:

- The marriage or registered partnership must be recognized by Danish law. This rule means e.g. that it is not possible for a man to get a residence permit for more than one wife; and that the spouses must have been present at the time when their marriage was performed

- The marriage must have been entered into voluntarily, that is: without any force and according to the wishes of both spouses
- The marriage must not have been entered into solely for the purpose of obtaining residence permits
- Both partners must be over the age of 24
- Both partners must live at the same address in Denmark when the residence permit is granted
- The combined attraction of the couple must be greater to Denmark than to any other country.
- The Danish partner must be a Danish or Nordic citizen, or hold a Danish residence permit granted under the status of asylum, or have held a permanent Danish residence permit for the past three years or more
- The Danish partner must further, reside permanently in Denmark; have accommodation of an adequate size at his or hers disposal; must be able to support both partners, that is: not receive public assistance for at least the previous 12 months. In order to secure the economic background for a residence permit for partners, the Danish partner must have around 10,000 euro deposited in a bank. Finally the Danish partner must not have been convicted for violence against a former spouse/partner within the previous 10 years prior to the application.

The meeting of all these requirements is normal procedure. There are, however, situations, where these demands give rise to problems in relation to ECHR art 8 on the protection of family life. That is in particular the situation, if the residence permit in Denmark is based on asylum; if the Danish partner already has a child here; or if the Danish partner is elderly; has a serious illness or debilitating handicap. Finally, the rules mention the circumstances, where a mother must be afforded protection while under parental leave; and situations regarding security problems; both resulting in different decisions. It is however necessary to emphasize, that these circumstances do not automatically establish a basis for exceptions.

4. Immigration from the Nordic countries and from EU and its impact on the family reunification practices

Nordic citizens (citizens of Norway; Iceland; Sweden and Finland) can freely reside and work and also bring their families to Denmark.

EU-citizens can, according to EU-legislation, also stay with their families for up to three months. If they apply for work: for up to six months.

This rule covers family members, who themselves are EU-nationals or Third Country nationals. If the spouse finds employment in Denmark, the family member can be granted a right to reside on this basis. There are many rules regarding who can be defined as a family member; which types of employment are regulated; that the residence must be genuine and effective, and so the marriage; combined also with rules about the ability to self-support; however, these rules as with rules about prior lawful residence in another EU-country are common to all member states.

The rules, also apply, count to Danish nationals who have exercised the right to free movement within EU, whereas Danish nationals who have stayed under Danish law, or have moved outside EU are not covered by the EU-regulations, but only under national law.

5. Special religious clauses as grounds for a residence permit

The Danish Aliens Consolidation Act has a specific rule on granting a residence permit based on religious grounds:

"(1) Upon application, a residence permit may be issued to:

(i)   An alien who is to act as a religious preacher in Denmark;
(ii) An alien who is to act as a missionary in Denmark;or
(iii) An alien who is to act within a religious order in Denmark.

(2) It must be made a condition for a residence permit under subsection (1) that the alien proves that he has ties with the Danish national church or a recognised or approved religious community in Denmark. It is a condition for the issue of a residence permit under subsection (1) that the number of aliens holding a residence permit under subsection (1) within a religious community is reasonably proportionate to the size of the religious community.

(3) It must be made a condition for a residence permit under subsection (1) that the alien proves that he has the relevant background or training to act as a religious preacher or missionary, or to act within a religious order.

(4) It must be made a condition for a residence permit under subsection (1) that the alien, and persons issued with a residence permit as a result of family ties with the alien, do not receive any public assistance for their maintenance during their stay in Denmark.

(5) A residence permit under subsection (1) cannot be issued if there is reason to assume that the alien will constitute a threat to public security, public order, health, morals or the rights and duties of others.

(6) A residence permit under subsection (1) must be obtained before entry into Denmark. After entry, such application cannot be submitted, or examined, or be allowed to suspend enforcement of any decision in Denmark unless particular reasons make it appropriate."

The rules on special possibilities for a person to get a residence permit in relation to being a preacher, or missionary, or member of a religious order were formally implemented into the law about five years ago. It had, however, been a longstanding practice and the government, as well as researchers, found it very appropriate to have these rules directly implemented into the law. The idea behind the rules is to secure the right for religious communities in Denmark to decide for themselves who should be their preachers or missionaries etc; and also to secure freedom of religion across borders. On the other hand, it also follows from the formulation of these rules, that freedom of religion is limited in accordance with general public order requirements. It can be added, that religious preachers must also pass a test in the Danish language etc, see below.

6. Permanent residence, Integration and Naturalization

The Aliens Consolidation Act also includes rules on how to obtain a permanent residence permit in Denmark. These rules are now (again) changed in order to limit the possibilities for foreigners who do not integrate, whereas foreigners who are considered to be well-integrated can obtain the right to permanent residence easier. The rules on integration are formulated in a separate Act on Integration of Aliens in Denmark.[3] The rules on integration include rules on introductory programmes; an individual contract specifying Danish courses (3 year courses in the Danish language, but also courses in Danish history and society), and offers on guidance, upgrading and job-training schemes which are compulsory for the alien in order to integrate into Danish society and, not least, into the Danish labor market.

It must also be stated, that a permanent right to reside in Denmark can be withdrawn in relation to a committed crime, as well as for people who have a permanent residence permit as refugees if they travel to their country of origin. This rule is of course based on the very idea behind

---

[3] Consolidation of the Act on Integration of Aliens in Denmark, Consolidation Act No. 839 of 5 September 2005 of the Danish Ministry of Refugee, Immigration and Integration Affairs. This law was formulated at first in 1999 (the first integration law in the world) and it will be changed in 2010.

being a refugee, that is: being a person who seeks asylum in another country until the possibilities of returning to the country of origin reappear.

Danish nationality is acquired automatically by birth if one of the married parents is Danish; if the unmarried mother is Danish; or if the unmarried father is Danish and the child is born in Denmark after 1 February 1999. There are special rules for children of unmarried, and later married couples; for adopted children; and for originally Nordic nationals. Others can be granted nationality after application.

Such naturalization is granted by law under the condition that the applicant

a. Signs a declaration in swearing allegiance and loyalty to Denmark and the Danish society and declaring a willingness to observe Danish legislation and respect fundamental Danish principles of law. The applicant must also provide information on any criminal offences committed, in the form of a solemn declaration. In that connection, the applicant must solemnly declare not to have committed any offence contained in Parts 12 and 13 of the Criminal Code (offences against national independence and security).

b. Normally the applicant must also renounce his or her former nationality

c. There are further rules on public debt and on the possibility to self-support; and finally the applicant must

d. Prove a knowledge of Danish society and of Danish culture and history, by presenting a certificate of a special citizenship test.[4]

7. Churches and Asylum

Focusing on the religious dimensions of migration to Denmark it is also worth reflecting on a couple of episodes where churches and religious groups have been active in supporting refugees, asylum seekers or others, who have wanted to stay here and have also been active in questioning Danish politics in this field.

In the middle of the 1990's a rather large group of asylum seekers from the Palestinian areas with no nationality applied for status as refugees. However, they did not fulfill requirements and were to be returned to the camps they came from. Confronted with this possibility, they went

---

[4] For further information on the citizenship test, see http://www.nyidanmark.dk/en-us/citizenship/danish_nationality/citizenship_test.htm

into a church in Copenhagen and applied for *Church Asylum*. This concept is not a part of Danish law; but, on the other hand, Danish law recognizes that churches are special spaces. Since the relevant church ministers supported the presence of the asylum seekers in the church, nobody wanted to interfere by sending in the police. The outcome of this long (about 4 months) period of stay was that a special act was passed in parliament giving the group asylum outside the normal rules.

During the past 10-15 years many groups supporting refugees and asylum seekers have based their support on religious norms, referring especially to the gospel and the Christmas story with formulations like: there was no space for Christ to be born, and his family – will there be space for refugees in Denmark currently? Church ministers among others have supported their actions by preaching strongly in relation to specific persons who have been sent out of the country on the basis of the interpretation of the laws, questioning whether or not Denmark is still a country showing mercy.

During the summer of 2009 young students (many of whom were from Roskilde University) organized a group called Church Asylum.[5] They were supporting a group of Iraqi asylum seekers who had been refused asylum but who had, on the other hand, not been returned to their home country due to rules on non-refoulement. After agreements between the Danish and the Iraqi governments in the spring of 2009, they were, however, now to be sent to Iraq, even though they still feared for their lives and even though they had been in Danish asylum camps for very many years.

Kirkeasyl organized housing for them in a church, but this time the attitude of both church leaders and politicians were 'cooler' and the action led nowhere – resulting in the police emptying the church (in the middle of the night, which was unnecessary) and sending a group of them to Iraq by force, whereas others were granted a right to residence based on other grounds.

8. Trafficking and other forms of illegal immigration and illegal residence

Denmark, like other EU countries, has seen an increase in illegal immigration and illegal residence very often connected with trafficking, which is of course prohibited in Denmark. The rules try to support victims of

---

[5] http://kirkeasyl.dk/english/

trafficking, and different church groups try to search for them and support them. The religious dimension here again is more related to diaconia than to freedom from religion rules.

9. To conclude

Danish politics on migration is an area where religious norms confront legal norms, very often with the result that religious norms trying to support human beings in their suffering cannot withstand what can be seen as cold legal norms.

On the other hand Danish politics on migration is also an area, where different types of religious norms internally confront legislation: one group would, as I have shown, argue, that robust politics hindering the access to Denmark of 'aliens' is against the Christian gospel. Others, also active politicians, however argue the opposite, that the Good Samaritan lead to a plea to love one's neighbour as oneself – not to open one's country to people from the whole world. Thus, this part of politics has given rise to renewed discussion on the basic norms in Danish society.

Bibliography

Silvia Adamo 2009: *Citizenship Law and the Challenge of Multiculturalism. The Case of Denmark*; thesis defended for the Ph.d.-degree in Law, Faculty of Law, University of Copenhagen

Lisbet Christoffersen, Hans Raun Iversen, Hanne Petersen, Margit Warburg (ed) 2010: *Religion in the 21st Century. Challenges and Transformations*; Aldershoot: Ashgate

Margit Warburg og Brian Jacobsen (red) 2007: *Tørre tal om troen. Religionsdemografi i det 21. århundrede* [How to count faith. Demography on Religion in the 21st Century]. Aarhus: Forlaget Univers

Bent Østergaard 2007: *Indvandrerne I Danmarks historie. Kultur- og religionsmøder* [Immigrants in the Danish history. Cultural and religious encounters]. Odense: Syddansk Universitetsforlag

MERILIN KIVIORG[1] – LEHTE ROOTS[2]

IMMIGRATION AND RELIGION IN ESTONIA

1. Introduction

Estonia does not consider itself a country of immigration. There are two main reasons for this. Firstly, since the end of the Soviet occupation (1991) Estonia has not been a country of extensive immigration. On the contrary, it experiences a quite troubling net out-migration. This means the loss of an educated and skilled labour force and a decrease in its native population, which currently is approximately 1.3 million.[3]

Secondly, due to the extensive in-migration administered by the government of the Soviet Union after the Second World War, Estonia is left with a considerably large Russian speaking minority.[4] From the total population, approximately one-third are from an immigrant background. However, the exact numbers are debatable and depend on what is taken as a basis for determining the immigrant background today.[5] Neverthe-less, this large minority has had, and does have, an effect on demograph-ics and politics in Estonia. Three characteristics of this minority need to be mentioned: a higher fertility rate compared to the native population, a higher rate of marriage, and very few mixed marriages between the two. Population growth since 1945 is entirely attributable to immigration, with a profound influence on the age and ethnic structure of the population. The children of immigrants are highly segregated. It also needs to be noted that there is an uneven regional distribution of the immigrant popu-lation, with up to 90% concentrated in urban areas. These factors make integration of this minority into Estonian society more complicated. However, as Rannut has pointed out, the main dividing factor has not been ethnicity as such, but rather the mother tongue, representing the

---

[1] Max Weber Fellow, European University Institute (Florence).
[2] Doctoral Researcher, European University Institute (Florence).
[3] According to the Estonian Statistics Office the Estonian population on 1 January 2010 was 1 340 000 inhabitants. Available at www.stat.ee (24.01.2010).
[4] Main groups are from diverse origins from regions of the former USSR: 74% Russians, 18% Ukrainians and Byelorussians.
[5] Some figures will be given later on in this article, under the subheading "Statistics".

main source of information and opinion and value creation (also through media). Language has been the main filter to various societal goods and values, and the channel to societal mobility and economic well-being. Soviet language policy promoting monolingualism in Russian created a barrier based on language use. 'This language barrier was not broken by political changes leading to the restitution of Estonia's sovereignty.'[6]

Currently, immigration to Estonia is discouraged although all forms of immigration are possible like, family reunification, immigration for work and study purposes, asylum and protection from inhuman treatment. According to research carried out by the Estonian Migration Foundation the prevailing political view seems to be that as Estonia has already a significant number of immigrants (as a result of the administered migration during the Soviet occupation) it needs to deal with the integration problems of this group before liberalising its immigration rules.

Thus, Estonia steers, although somewhat reluctantly, towards integration of the existing community into Estonian society. The reluctance is evident in quite strict language policies and requirements set up for acquiring citizenship. There is very slow access to citizenship for people of an immigrant background. This policy seems to be directly related to controversial concerns about loyalty of the immigrant population to the State, but also to preservation of the Estonian language.

However, there have been debates about liberalising immigration rules and reducing exam requirements for citizenship, because of the ageing population and the emigration shortage of skilled labour which emerged during 2006/2007. Nevertheless in 2009 the unemployment increased to 15.2% in Estonia compared to the 5.2% unemployment rate in 2008.[7] It is not clear yet what kind of effect these developments will have on citizenship and immigration rules and policy.

As to religion in this debate, it needs to be mentioned that before 1940 Estonia was more or less religiously homogeneous. In the 1920s and 1930s, most of the population (ca 76%) belonged to the Estonian Evangelical Lutheran Church.[8] The second largest Church was the Estonian

---

[6] M. Rannut, 'Estonian Language Strategy in Progress', World Congress on Language Policies, Barcelona 2002, Available at http://www.linguapax.org/congres/taller/taller3/article22_ang.html (08. 01. 2010).

[7] Estonia (6.5% to 15.2% between the third quarters of 2008 and 2009), http://epp.eurostat.ec.europa.eu/cache/ITY_PUBLIC/3-08012010-AP/EN/3-08012010-AP-EN.PDF (28.01.2010).

[8] According to the national census 1934, there were 874 026 Evangelical Lutherans in Estonia of a total population of 1 126 413. See http://www.estonica.org/culture/religion (28.01.2010).

Apostolic-Orthodox Church (consisting mostly of ethnic Estonians). Today, the majority of believers still belong to the Lutheran Church. However, some new data suggests that the Orthodox community may have grown in numbers, and have become a fraction bigger.[9] Currently, the Orthodox community in Estonia is divided between the Estonian Apostolic Orthodox Church and the Estonian Orthodox Church of Moscow Patriarchate. The relations between the two Orthodox Churches, one under the canonical jurisdiction of the Ecumenical Patriarchate, and the other under the canonical jurisdiction of the Moscow Patriarchate are complicated due to historical, legal/canonical and ethnic reasons. Most orthodox believers belong to the latter church. It also needs to be mentioned that most members of this church are Russian-speaking, which indicates that the majority have an immigrant background. In 1990s there were heated debates and legal battles concerning registration of the "Russian" Orthodox Church. There were controversial accusations about this church being a "fifth column" with the potential to undermine Estonian territorial integrity. All the above, however, needs to be set against the background that Estonia can be considered as one of the least religious countries in Europe. Most people in Estonia do not belong formally to any religious organisation. Today, only approximately 30 % of the Estonian population is officially connected to any Christian Church. It also needs to be mentioned that religious organisations are not obligated to provide the Ministry of Internal Affairs with statistical information of their membership. Religious organisations have voluntarily informed state officials about the number of their adherents. Although, presented figures leave considerable room for any kind of interpretation they hopefully reflect to some extent the objective reality of religious life in Estonia.

Currently, religion seems to play a minor role in questions relating to integration, immigration or asylum. Estonia does not yet have any of the challenges related to the growing Muslim communities, as experienced in other European countries.

2. Legal Framework

Estonia has several acts that regulate immigration. The main legal provisions regulating the field are contained in the State Borders Act,[10] Aliens

---

[9] Information about current membership of religious organizations is based on data from the Ministry of Internal Affairs. Available at http://www.siseministeerium.ee/37356 (27.10. 2009).

[10] Riigipiiri seadus, RT I 1994, 54, 902 (has been amended several times).

Act,[11] Act Granting International Protection for Aliens (AGIPA)[12] and Obligation to Leave and Prohibition of Entry Act.[13] Other acts relevant in this field are the Citizen of European Union Act,[14] and Citizenship Act.[15] Additionally, there are several government regulations that deal with residence permit issues.

The main government body dealing with immigration and asylum is the Police and Border Guard Board, under the supervision of the Ministry of Internal Affairs. Before 1 January 2010 the Citizenship and Migration Board dealt with immigration and asylum questions. There was also the Estonian Migration Foundation, which was established by the order of the Government of the Republic of Estonia on 10 June 1992. The Ministry of Internal Affairs was appointed as the executor of the right of the founder. The main purpose of the Foundation was to support the migration, return and integration processes and to raise funds so as to undertake these tasks. From 7 October 2005, the Estonian Migration Foundation was the contact point of the European Migration Network in Estonia. At the end of 2009 the Foundation was closed and the tasks were divided between other government institutions. The contact point for the European Migration Network is the Estonian Public Service Academy.

From time to time there are discussions in the media about the immigration policy, but in most cases it confirms the restrictive approach and unwillingness to open up the borders. Estonia definitely does not consider itself a country of immigration like Canada or Australia. Only since 1997 is it possible to apply for asylum in Estonia as the country joined up to the 1951 UN Refugee Convention and introduced its first Refugee Act. In 2006 the Refugee Act was replaced by the Act Granting International Protection for Aliens.

When the voluntary resettlement program for refugees was agreed upon at the European level, the Estonian Minister of Foreign Affairs announced that Estonia was not going to take part in that action. It was also stated that under the voluntary burden sharing scheme Estonia

---

[11] Välismaalaste seadus, RT I 1999, 44, 637; RT I 2009, 62, 405 (New Aliens Act will come into force 1 October 2010, RT I 2010, 3, 4. The information provided on the basis of the Aliens Act currently in force will largely still be accurate after that date (except paragraph numbers).

[12] Välismalastele rahvusvahelise kaitse andmise seadus, RT I 2006, 2, 3 (has been amended several times).

[13] Väljasõidukohustuse ja sissesõidukeelu seadus, RT I 1998, 98/99, 1575, RT I 2009, 62, 405.

[14] Euroopa Liidu kodanku seadus, RT I 2002, 102, 599.

[15] Kodakondsusseadus, RT I 1995, 83, 1442 (has been amended several times).

would not be taking any refugees from Malta.[16] It shows a very limited willingness on the part of the state to cooperate at the EU level regarding immigration or asylum.

In order to get a residence permit to work in Estonia, it is necessary to have an offer of work that no local person has accepted or taken up. A residence permit for work purposes is issued only if the wages of an alien ensures his/her subsistence in Estonia. An employer must pay an alien a salary which is at least equal to the wage of the recent average yearly wages in Estonia published by the Statistical Office of Estonia, and adding the coefficient 1.24. The amount of remuneration paid by an employer must be in line with the latest data valid at the start of the processing of an application for a temporary residence permit.[17]

3. Statistics

The statistics are normally collected by the Estonian Statistics Office (Statistikaamet).[18] Statistics about immigration, asylum, residence and citizenship are collected and maintained by the Police and Border Guard Board (previously Citizenship and Migration Board).[19] As mentioned previously, approximately 30% of Estonian inhabitants are from an immigrant background. However, the number of residence permits issued is decreasing every year, because people with an immigrant background become naturalised and became Estonian citizens. Between the years 1992-2008 there were 149, 351 naturalisations.

Some groups of persons, like previous KGB workers or Soviet Army officers, do not have the possibility of naturalisation. They would have to submit an application for a residence permit. The total number of applications submitted for permanent or temporary residence is not recorded and is not available, but the number of permits granted is recorded and is available on the website of the Estonian Police and Border Guard Board.[20]

The new immigration following the dissolution of the Soviet Union is not remarkable in Estonia. Between 2000-2009 approximately 290 000

---

[16] Kukk, K., *Eesti põgenike ümberasustamise projeketis ei osale*. Available at http://uudised.err.ee/index.php?06181286 (28.01.2010).

[17] http://www.pol.ee/et/teenused/elamisluba/tahtajaline-elamisluba/tootamiseks/index.dot (27.01.2010).

[18] Available at www.stat.ee (27.01.2010).

[19] http://www.politsei.ee/et/organisatsioon/avalik-teave/statistika/ (28.01.2010).

[20] Estonian Police and Border Guard Board, www.pol.ee

temporary and permanent residence permits were granted by the office of Citizenship and Migration Board (Now called Police and Border Guard Board). However, these residence permits include the permits of those persons who moved to Estonia during the Soviet period and who had to renew their residence permits. There is no official information about how many applications were refused or how many new immigrants have applied for a residence permit.

In 2009 there were 214 829 persons living in Estonia with residence permits.

Of this number, 25 300 persons held a permanent residence permit, and 189 529 were temporary residence permits.[21] The highest number of permits 107 638 was held by persons with undefined citizenship, 97 572 persons were Russian Federation citizens and 9619 were citizens of other states (Ukraine, Byelorussia, USA, China, Armenia, Azerbaijan, Kazakhstan, India, Israel etc.).

The number of asylum seekers is not significant. Estonia receives around 10-40 asylum applications per year. Asylum seekers and immigrants come from various countries and various religious groups including Islamic, Hindu and Buddhist. Usually, there are no statistics collected in relation to the religious background or beliefs of immigrants. Applicants for asylum have to declare their religion, as this is part of the asylum-recognition process, and might be a basis for persecution and a reason to give protection and a residence permit. These statistics are not publicly available, but are collected for the purpose of investigation of the asylum application. The Personal Data Protection Act[22] regulates data collection, use and storage, and applies to all data collections including those of foreigners and citizens.

4. Citizenship

Acquiring citizenship in Estonia is a long process. Any alien who wishes to acquire Estonian citizenship by naturalisation has to comply with the conditions, and follow the requirements provided for, by the Citizenship Act. In 2008 a government regulation was introduced explaining the rules of the exams.[23] According to the Citizenship Act, any alien can

---

[21] All the statistics on residence permits are from 2 July 2009.

[22] Isikuandmete kaitse seadus, RT I 2007, 24, 127.

[23] Kodakondsuse taotleja Eesti Vabariigi põhiseaduse ja «Kodakondsuse seaduse» tundmise eksami läbiviimise kord, Vastu võetud Vabariigi Valitsuse 25. septembri 2008. a määrusega nr 143 (RT I 2008, 43, 245), enforced 1.03.2009.

submit an application for acquisition of Estonian citizenship by naturalisation if:

- he or she has settled in Estonia before 1 July 1990, and holds a residence permit at the time of submitting his or her application; or
- he or she holds, at the time of submitting his or her application, a residence permit of a long-term resident, or has a permanent right to residence.

If one of these preconditions is fulfilled, an alien who wishes to acquire Estonian citizenship must, before the application is submitted:

- be at least 15 years of age;
- have a general knowledge of Estonian, as needed in everyday life;
- have resided in Estonia on the basis of a residence permit, or the right of residence for at least eight years, and the last five of them permanently;
- have knowledge of the Constitution of the Republic of Estonia and the Citizenship Act;
- have a registered place of residence in Estonia;
- have a permanent legal income which ensures his or her own subsistence and that of his or her dependants;
- be loyal to the Estonian state;
- take an oath: "Taotledes Eesti kodakondsust, tõotan olla ustav Eesti põhiseaduslikule korrale" [In applying for Estonian citizenship, I swear to be loyal to the constitutional order of Estonia."

In order to apply for Estonian citizenship a person has to pass an exam on his or her knowledge of the Constitution and the Citizenship Act of the Republic of Estonia, as well as an exam on knowledge of the Estonian language. Some groups of people are exempted from passing the examination. They are adults with restricted legal capacity and persons who, due to their state of health, are not able to partly or fully pass the examination.

Persons who have acquired a basic, secondary or higher education in the Estonian language are exempted from the Estonian language exam, but still need to take the exam regarding knowledge of the Constitution and Citizenship Act.

The demographic change in the religious configuration due to naturalization in Estonia is not remarkable. As the number of refugees and persons with other types of international protection is small, (and most of them simply keep their residence permit or their refugee status), there is no increase in religious configuration from this group of migrants, due

to naturalization. None of the recognized refugees in Estonia has applied
for Estonian citizenship. There has always been a small Muslim, (persons from previous Soviet Union Countries), or Jewish community in
Estonia.

5. Asylum

In 1997 Estonia acceded to the 1951 Geneva Convention Relating to the
Status of Refugees of 1951 and its New York protocol of 1967, which
means that Estonia has gained an international obligation to protect
aliens who meet the requirements set out in the document. In 1997, also,
the Refugee Act was introduced which was itself replaced in 2006 by
another called the Act Granting International Protection for an Alien. It
contains principles arising from the aforementioned convention and also
requirements arising from European Union directives. Before 2010
application for asylum had to be placed with the Refugee department of
the Citizenship and Migration Board and Board of Border Guards. After
the restructuring of government offices, the Police and Border Guard
Board became responsible for asylum applications. The applicant is
interviewed several times and has to define his religion, as it is part of
the asylum recognition process. The background of the applicant including his religion and beliefs are studied carefully during the asylum procedure since it could form the basis for giving asylum. After the interview, applicants stay in the open reception centre until they receive the
decision. A negative decision rejecting asylum may be appealed against
to the Tallinn Administrative Court.

The number of asylum seekers in Estonia is not significant compared
to the numbers in Europe. The total number of asylum applications
between 1997-2009 was 147. Most applications (25) were filed by Iraqi
citizens, 21 by Russians, 17 by Turks, 11 by Byelorussians, and 10 by
Georgians.[24] There were a small number of applications from a wide
variety of other countries including Africa and Asia.

Before entry into Estonia an application for asylum can be submitted
to a border guard official at any border point of the Republic of Estonia.
This opportunity should be used if a person does not have a valid visa,
travel documents, or a residence permit in Estonia; if a person is already
in Estonia he or she should contact the office of the Police and Border

---

[24] Kodakondsus- ja migratsiooniamet. http://www.mig.ee/index.php/mg/eng/statistics
(accessed 19 June 2009).

Guard Board in Tallinn to apply for asylum. Asylum applications are processed by the Police and Border Guard Board.

Complementary residence permits were introduced into Estonian legislation in order to transform the EU directives on subsidiary protection and temporary protection. According to Estonian legislation, a person enjoying subsidiary protection is an alien who does not qualify as a refugee, but in regard to whom there is a reason to believe that his or her expulsion or return from Estonia to the country of origin may result in a serious threat to his or her well being, including:

1. implementation or execution of the death penalty; or
2. torture or other cruel, inhuman or degrading treatment; or
3. violence due to an international or internal armed conflict.

Estonia also makes provision in cases of mass influx of immigrants. In such cases, persons can be granted a temporary residence permit with a one year limitation.

6. Freedom of Religion, Churches and Asylum

No examples can be given on churches giving asylum. There are no known cases. There is no legal basis or exemptions from generally applicable laws in this regard.

As to pastoral assistance for illegal immigrants if the asylum seeker or illegal immigrant wishes he or she can always contact the church for pastoral assistance. According to the §5 (1) of the Aliens Act aliens staying in Estonia are guaranteed rights and freedoms equal to those of Estonian citizens (incl. freedom of religion or belief protected by Art 40 of the Constitution) unless the Constitution, Aliens Act, other Acts or international agreements of Estonia provide otherwise (e.g. set restrictions to the manifestation of this freedom). Aliens are also guaranteed the rights and freedoms arising from the generally recognised rules of international law and international custom (Aliens Act §5 (2)).

The recognition of religious freedom in public institutions is regulated by §9 (1) of the Churches and Congregations Act.[25] This article stipulates that: 'Persons staying in medical institutions, educational institutions, social welfare institutions and custodial institutions and members of the Defence Forces have the right to perform religious rites according to their faith unless this violates public order, health, morals, the rules

---

[25] Kirikute ja koguduste seadus, RT I 2002, 24, 135.

established in these institutions or the rights of others staying or serving in these institutions'. The general conditions for religious assistance in public institutions are regulated by the §9 (2) of the Churches and Congregations Act. §9 (2) provides that a religious association shall conduct religious services and religious rites in a medical institution, educational institution or social welfare institution with the permission of the owner or the head of the institution, in a custodial institution with the permission of the director of the prison, and in the Defence Forces with the permission of the commanding officer of the military unit, and in the National Defence League with the permission of the chief of the unit.

The army and prison chaplains are civil servants and are fully-paid by the state budget. Only people from the member churches of the Estonian Council of Churches are entitled to serve as chaplains. Members of other religious organisations (including non-Christian) do have access to these institutions upon the request of the people staying there. The institution of the chaplaincy is meant to be inter-denominational and ecumenical. Since 1997 there is a chaplain in every prison, and since the year 2000 the work of prison-chaplains is coordinated by the Adviser-Head Chaplain at the Department of Prisons of the Ministry of Justice.

7. Family Reunification and Immigration

Family unity is generally respected in Estonia by law. The Council Directive 2003/86/EC on family reunification was transformed to the Aliens Act. This act regulates the family reunification of Estonian citizens and foreigners living legally in Estonia. The family reunification of a refugee or a person in need of other international protection is regulated by the Act Granting International Protection for an Alien. Family reunification of European Citizens is regulated by the Citizens of the European Union Act. The applicable rules depend mostly on the status of the sponsor who applies for family reunification.

Polygamy in principle is not recognised in Estonia. It is only possible to live with one wife in Estonia. As regards children, it is possible to invite all the children of a sponsor to cohabit, including the children of a second or third wife, but not the wives themselves. The husband has to choose which wife he wants to join him in Estonia. Only official marriage is recognised and partners who are not officially married cannot benefit from family reunification. In family reunification cases, immigration officials check that there are no marriages of convenience. Both partners are questioned, and also their neighbours can be interviewed.

An alien who applies for family reunification must have lived in Estonia at least for two years according to art 12[1] of the Aliens Act.

A family member can get a temporary residence permit for the purpose of settling with his/her spouse. Spouses have to share close economic ties and must have a psychological relationship. The family has to be stable and the marriage not fictitious. In these cases a residence permit for the purpose of family reunification can be justified. In order to benefit from family reunification, the spouse has to reside permanently in Estonia. The permanent residence requirement does not apply to the Estonian citizen who wants to invite his/her spouse in order to settle together in Estonia. Similar types of rules apply to descendent relatives. In some cases the ancestral relatives can join the sponsor also.

The Act Granting International Protection for Aliens regulates the residence permit application of a family member of a refugee, or person who holds subsidiary protection or temporary protection. The Act says that a refugee or a person who has subsidiary protection or temporary protection may apply for family reunification within a 3 month period after he or she has got a residence permit for Estonia. In cases where the application is made later than the 3 months, the person can be asked to submit additional proof. The person has to prove that he or she has a permanent legal income to ensure that the family is maintained in Estonia; the family must have an actual dwelling in Estonia; and the family member of the alien must have valid health insurance during the period of validity of the residence permit. [26]

According to information from the Population Department, the Department of Gender Equality Commissioner and Department of Religious Affairs of the Ministry of Internal Affairs there is no information about forced marriages.[27] As the Population Department records only registered marriages, they do not have any information on other forms of marriage. The Citizenship and Migration Board does not have relevant statistics either.[28] Equally there is no debate in

---

[26] Member States may require the refugee to meet the conditions referred to in Art 7(1) if the application for family reunification is not submitted within a period of 3 months after the granting of the refugee status. See art 12 section 1 last sentence of directive 2003/86/EC.

[27] M.Kiviorg communication/interview with Mr. Ringo Ringvee, Ministry of Internal Affairs (7 Jan 2008 at 08:54).

[28] Now renamed as Police and Border Guard Board. Communication Registered in Citizenship and Migration Board: M.Kiviorg, Information Request No 15.6-06/11710-1, Anneli Viks, Reply No 15.6-06/11710-1.

society, or media coverage as regards these issues. The Estonian
Women's Associations Round Table, does not have any information
on forced marriages.[29] One of the possible conclusions from this is that
the Estonian population is still fairly homogeneous as regards traditions concerning marriage. Estonia has not yet become a destination
for extensive new immigration. It seems probable that this is a reason
why forced marriages have not become an issue yet. However, all the
above information from different institutions seems to rely on the
assumption that there is no such thing as forced marriages in Western/
Eastern European society/Estonia. This kind of assumption seems to
rely on a narrow, culture specific definition of forced marriage. A
broader definition may reveal some interesting data. There are currently no studies or statistics available. Gender studies in Estonia, for
example, focus more on equal pay for men and women, homosexual-
ity, and domestic violence.

Regarding forced marriage among asylum seekers, refugees and their
family members, Estonia has no recorded information. As there are very
few asylum applicants, the problem of forced marriages has not yet
emerged in society, or at least, is not known by officials dealing with
asylum applications.

8. Quotas for Employment of Non-EU Citizens

There are immigration quotas in the case of residence permits (majority
of which are applied for employment purposes). There are no separate
provisions (or exemptions) for clergy or pastors.

According to the §6 (1) of the Aliens Act, the annual immigration
quota should not exceed 0.1 per cent of the permanent population of
Estonia annually. Thus it is approx 1300 persons per year. Within the
limits of the immigration quota, the Minister of Internal Affairs may
distribute the immigration quota according to the grounds for application, and the basis for issuing the residence permit, and the annual
schedule. In 2009 the residence permit quota was reduced to 1002 persons per year, and only 721 were issued.[30]

---

[29] http://www.enu.ee; M. Kiviorg, communication/interview with Mrs. Ilvi Jõe (6 Mar
2008 at 14:31:01).
[30] 2009. aasta sisserände piirarvu kehtestamine. Vabariigi Valitsuse 30. detsembri
2008. a korraldus nr 537, RTL, 07.01.2009, 1, 25 and see also P. Pullerits, *Eesti sõnum
võõrastele: te ei ole siia teretulnud!* Postimees (16.10.2009).

The quota is not applied to ethnic Estonians who wish to settle in Estonia,[31] and to family members of Estonian citizens or foreigners who already live in Estonia on the basis of a residence permit.[32] The quota system also does not apply to the citizens of Japan and the United States of America. They do not fall under the quota calculation system.

9. Conclusion

Religion does not yet play a significant role in relation to immigration or asylum. Law and policy relating to immigration are more influenced by the fact that Estonia has a large Russian speaking minority, which emerged in Estonia during the Soviet era. Most importantly, law and policy are related to the integration problems of this minority. New immigration is still insignificant, but has also been discouraged. There appears to be a tendency for new immigrants to treat Estonia as a country of transition from where they try to move on to other wealthier European states. Growing numbers of immigrants in other European states, and economic factors may put pressure on Estonia to open up to immigration in the future.

---

[31] §6(2) Aliens Act. It needs to be noted that in some cases the law refers to „Estonian nationality" and not to „Estonian citizen". Nationality and citizenship in the Estonian context are two different terms. Nationality refers to ethnic belonging, and citizenship to the political term. The law does not provide a clear answer how to determine who has Estonian nationality it only determines Estonian citizen.

[32] Aliens Act §6(2). Persons who have the right to settle in Estonia outside of the immigration quota or to whom the immigration quota does not apply are not included in calculating fulfilment of the immigration quota.

SARI SIRVA

IMMIGRATION AND RELIGION IN FINLAND

1. The Legal Provisions governing immigration

The central legal provision governing immigration is the *Aliens' Act* (30.4.2004/301). All the European Council's directives and legislative instruments concerning the Common European Asylum System, together with the directive on family reunification have been incorporated into the prevailing Aliens' Act.[1]

The Aliens' Act has been amended since 2004 and there is currently a debate about introducing into the asylum procedure a new accelerated procedure in order to deal with manifestly unfounded applications in a more speedy manner.

Section 9.4 of the Finnish Constitution Act includes the principle of *non refoulement*: no one shall be sent back or extradited to a country where he or she may face the death penalty, torture or inhuman treatment. The Aliens' Act also includes the principle of *non refoulement* in its provisions on refusal of entry and expulsion.

The former Cabinet, Matti Vanhanen I, announced in its 1997 programme that Finland will, in the future, be a country of immigrants owing to demographic factors and the need to expand the skills matrix. This has not, however, led to any programmes for immigrants to gain a residence permit more easily and expediently. The programme of the Cabinet focuses mainly on integration.

---

[1] Council Directive 2005/85/EC of 1 December on minimum standards of procedures in Member States for granting and withdrawing refugee status; Council Directive 2004/83/EC of 29 April 2004 on minimum standards for the qualification and status of third country nationals or stateless persons as refugees or as persons who otherwise need international protection and the content of the protection granted; Council Directive 2001/55/EC of 20 July 2001 on minimum standards for giving temporary protection in the event of mass influx of displaced persons and measures promoting a balance of efforts between Members States in receiving such persons and bearing the consequences thereof; Council Directive 2003/86/EC of 22 September 2003 on the right to family reunification; Council Directive 2003/109/EC of 25 November 2003 concerning the status of third-country nationals who are long-term residents; Council Regulation (EC) No 343/2003 of 18 February establishing the criteria and mechanisms for determining the Member States responsible for examining an asylum application lodged in one of the Member States by a third-country national.

There is no distinct tradition of immigration from former colonies as Finland has never been a colonising country. However, immigrants from the Ingermanland are subject to special rules concerning their return as they are considered returnees if they, both, or their parents or grandparents have held Finnish nationality prior to the WWII.

2. Statistical issues

The Finnish Migration Service produces statistics, based on grounds of application. They separate asylum applications from migration-related applications. Migration related applications are broken down into various grounds of application, such as family, work and studies. The first permit is always temporary, although all A-status permits become permanent after four years. Since the local police grants permanent residence permits, the Migration service does not produce any statistics on them.

The Finnish migration service also produces separate statistics on grounds of refusal and acceptance of applications. They also count the percentage of all accepted/rejected from the total number of applications.

There is no religious dimension to these matters irrespective of the applicant's religion.

3. Acquiring Citizenship

Pursuant to Section 13 of the Finnish Nationality Act the general requirements for naturalisation are as follows:

(1) An alien is granted Finnish citizenship on application if, when the decision is made on the application:
  1) he or she has reached the age of 18 years or has married before that;
  2) he or she is and has been permanently resident and domiciled in Finland (*period of residence*);
     a) for the last six years without interruption (continuous period of residence); or
     b) for eight years after reaching the age of 15 years, the last two years without interruption (accumulated period of residence);
  3) he or she has not committed any punishable act, nor has a restraining order been issued against him or her (*integrity requirement*)

4) He or she has not materially failed to provide maintenance, or to meet his of her pecuniary obligations under public law;

5) he or she can provide a reliable account of his or her livelihood; and

6) he or she has satisfactory oral and written skills in the Finnish or Swedish language, or instead of oral skills similar skills in the Finnish sign language (*language skills requirement*).

There is no special test required in order to demonstrate the applicant's knowledge of the country's institutions and values.

According to statistics by the Finnish statistics centre the percentage of inhabitants in Finland confessing other than the Lutheran or Orthodox faith has changed very little. Between 2000 and 2008 there was growth of 0.2 % from 1.1% to 1.3 % of the total population.[2]

4. The Legal Requirements on Asylum

The Aliens' Act of 2004 provides criteria for granting asylum and also procedures. These are in conformity with the respective EU legislative documents. The application is left either at the frontier or at the police station. The police fingerprint all applicants, questions their travel routes and identities, and the Migration Services interview applicants on the merits of any decision. The decision is served on the applicant by the police, and, if it is positive he or she can settle in the country. A negative decision can normally be appealed against to the Helsinki Administrative Court, with a suspensive effect.

The Aliens Act has been amended approximately 14 times during the past decade partly because of EU legislation, partly because of the debate on the need for accelerated procedures to deal with fraudulent applications.

The Migration Services keeps statistics on all asylum and residence related matters. They are available in English on www.migri.fi.

Finland, as described above, has a system whereby the decision maker directly interviews the applicant. The average processing time has been anything between 6 to 24 months during the last decade. The length of the procedure is a constant problem. Detention is also used in most instances where a person has previously lived in another EU country, and would be sent back (the so-called Dublin procedure).

---

[2] Finnish Statistical Centre, 2008

Religion, as a ground for seeking asylum, has been an issue to varying degrees. Iranian Baháls and Christians have been the most successful. Although Finland has had very few asylum seekers from Eritrea, those of them whose applications, are based on their Pentecostal faith, have been successful. In general, religion is not the most important factor for seeking asylum in Finland.

The asylum application includes a residence permit application, so the procedure combines both. Pursuant to section 52 of the Aliens' Act of 2004 a residence permit can be issued for individual humanitarian reasons when rejection of the application would be unreasonable given the state of health, ties with Finland or other individual humanitarian reason, and in such circumstances he or she would end up in his or her home country or would be in a vulnerable state.

5. Church asylum and its Legal Basis

The Finnish Lutheran Church, the Pentecostal Church and the Finnish Orthodox Church have all given asylum to failed asylum seekers pending deportation. There are no legal provisions for this and, legally-speaking, the police have a right to deport the person who is enjoying sanctuary in the church. However, the practice has been that the whereabouts of the person is made clear to the police who, in the few cases there have been, have respected the terms. The asylum seeker is given an opportunity to seek asylum again and receives moral and financial support from the church.

The Finnish Ecumenical Council has published in 2007 guidelines ("Church as Asylum") for church working. It defines its own terms and urges them to contact the local police and inform them that a person has been given asylum in the church. It, then, encourages a working-together with the asylum seeker and his or her lawyer in order to gather new evidence to build a stronger case. The guidelines emphasize that they are not legally binding. The cases since 2007 have numbered less than ten.

6. Pastoral assistance Given to Illegal Immigrants

(a) pending determination of their application to remain.

Churches are open to illegal immigrants who are welcome to join regular services and can also make personal appointments with the parish priest. Parishes also organise recreational events and offer spiritual and psychological support. Personal discussions with a priest and other personnel is available. Asylum seekers are also entitled to material assistance upon request, as customers of the churches deacon services.[3]

(b) after they have been ordered to be expelled from the country.

The Finnish Lutheran Church has since the 1990's offered counselling to those who are to be deported. They also try and establish some network for the returnee in the country of return, through the international network the church has. In some cases contacts have been kept with the returnee by telephone. The purpose of the counselling is to offer emotional and spiritual support for the returnee in starting work to sort-out his or her life on return.[4] Churches can also offer asylum, as described in question number 5.

There are no chaplaincy services. The church and the state are separate, so the government does not fund church activities.

7. Principle of Family Unity and Asylum Law

Pursuant to the Aliens' Act of 2004 the families seeking residence permits or asylum, are processed together. The head of the family usually determines what status the family will get:- that is, other family members have a derivative status depending on the residence permit status granted to the head of the family, be it a mother or a father. Married couples are interviewed separately in asylum hearings and children over 12 along with their parents, if necessary. The length of the residence permit depends on the principal applicant- the dependent applicants receive residence permits with the same duration.

In application of family unity religious aspects play no role.

Family reunification is granted on different grounds depending on whether the sponsor has a refugee or supplementary protection status. In this case he is exempted from the responsibility of maintain the family. Other applicants must secure a livelihood and home for of their dependent family members. Health insurance is not required.

Family members are defined along the notion of the nuclear family: married or cohabiting parents with their minor, unmarried children.

---

[3] Telephone discussion with ms. Maija-Liisa Laihia, the secretary of the churches immigration services, Thursday 3 September 2009
[4] ibid.

Polygamous marriages are not recognised pursuant to EU Council Directive 2003/86/EC on the right to family reunification (Art 4 paras 4 and 5). Therefore, polygamy accepted by a certain religion will not be respected, but for the first spouse. Cultural sensitivity is respected in a sense that fully dependant parents of adults may be given residence-permits on the grounds of family reunification if they are fully dependent on their children in Finland and they have together as a family unit lived until the separation and it is the intention to continue living together as a family in the same household.

Forced marriages do not constitute a basis for family reunification. Pursuant to Finnish marital law marriage is a consensual legal act. The rationale behind the EU Council's directive to protect children and women is accepted in the Finnish Aliens' Act.

8. Employment of non –EU Citizens

There are no quotas for employment of non-EU citizens in Finland.

There are no direct restrictions, either. It should be mentioned, though, that EU-Citizens benefit from freedom of movement and for them it might be easier to travel to Finland for three months and find work.

There are certain professions who require legalisation in order to be able to practice, such as health professionals. This may limit, in practice, their ability to find employment.

There are no legal regulations to regulate the employment of clergy or pastors.

Thierry Rambaud

RELIGION ET ÉMIGRATION EN DROIT FRANÇAIS

La délicate question des rapports entre la religion et l'immigration[1] ne peut être envisagée indépendamment des évolutions récentes qui affectent le droit français.

Le droit français des étrangers, qui concerne l'entrée sur le territoire, le séjour et le départ des étrangers[2], est un droit mouvant, qui évolue au gré des différentes alternances politiques[3].

Depuis le vote de la première loi Sarkozy relative au contrôle des flux migratoires en 2003, la politique de la France en la matière se construit autour du cap fixé par le ministre de l'Intérieur, puis Chef de l'Etat, Nicolas Sarkozy, cap qui est de poursuivre le rééquilibrage entre une immigration professionnelle et une immigration familiale, en faveur de celle-là.

Il l'écrit, notamment, dans sa lettre de mission à Eric Besson, le nouveau ministre de l'Immigration et de l'Identité nationale, le 30 mars 2009.

Les grands axes de la politique gouvernementale, depuis la réélection de Jacques Chirac en 2002, en matière de gestion des flux migratoires, se concentrent autour des points suivants:

- le développement des accords de gestion concertée sur les migrations;
- un renforcement de la lutte contre les abus et la fraude, notamment contre les mariages de complaisance permettant au conjoint immigré d'obtenir un titre de séjour;
- une meilleure intégration des migrants en situation régulière. Cela présuppose que les nouveaux arrivants sur le territoire français connaissent et respectent certaines des valeurs essentielles de la République française au premier rang desquelles figurent le principe de l'égalité entre les hommes et les femmes et le principe de laïcité. Il est ainsi intéres-

---

[1] Le terme immigrer vient du latin *in* = dans et *migrar* = voyager.
[2] En droit, l'étranger est l'individu qui n'a pas la nationalité du pays dans lequel il réside.
[3] F. Julien-Laferrière, *Droit des étrangers*, Paris, PUF, Collection Droit fondamental, 2000.

sant de noter comment une des évolutions récentes du droit français des étrangers a conduit à introduire l'exigence de laïcité comme élément permettant d'évaluer la capacité de l'étranger à s'intégrer en France. On voit ici comme le droit des religions rejoint le droit des étrangers.

1. Des dispositions destinées à faciliter l'intégration des immigrants

Le concept de nation en France est davantage assimilateur qu'intégrateur. En effet, la nation française est à l'opposé du *melting pot* américain, où les différentes communautés d'origines ethniques ou nationales différentes coexistent sur un même territoire. En France, la nation tend à fondre les populations d'origines différentes dans un cadre unique, le «creuset républicain», qui ne reconnaît ni les races, ni les ethnies, ni les religions[4]. Le Conseil constitutionnel, dans sa décision du 15 décembre 2007, a même condamné la pratique de statistiques dites «ethniques». *Le modèle français d'assimilation* repose, notamment, sur les principes constitutionnels d'égalité de tous devant la loi et de la laïcité. Au-delà de ces principes, la cohérence nationale repose sur l'instruction publique, ainsi que sur l'apprentissage de valeurs et la pratique d'une langues commune: le français. En pratique, le modèle français d'assimilation est souvent mis à mal par le maintien de nombreux freins, d'ordre économique, social ou culturel. Certaines communautés, d'origines, nationales, religieuses ou ethniques, subsistent sur le territoire français. Face à cette situation, le législateur a élaboré certains instruments visant pallier les dangers résultant de certaines dérives, dont le contrat d'accueil et d'intégration qu'a mis en œuvre l'Office français de l'immigration et de l'intégration (OFII).

a. La mise en place d'un contrat d'accueil et d'intégration

Un tel contrat est obligatoire depuis le 1er janvier 2007. Il constitue le témoignage d'une politique migratoire désireuse d'améliorer l'intégration des étrangers sur le territoire national. A certains égards, cette politique s'inspire des exemples nords-américains.

Le contrat d'accueil et d'intégration est conclu pour une année[5] entre l'Etat, représenté par le Préfet, et le migrant souhaitant s'installer sur le

---

[4] C. Nicolet, *Histoire, nation et République*, Odile Jacob, 2000; P. Nora (sous la direction de), *Les lieux de mémoire*, Gallimard «Quarto», 3 volumes, 1998. Voir également, J-C. Barreau, *De l'immigration en général et de la nation française en particulier*, Le Pré-aux-clercs, 1992.

[5] Eventuellement renouvelable pour une durée identique.

territoire national. En vertu des dispositions de l'article L 311-9 du Code de l'entrée et du séjour des étrangers, «l'étranger, qui est admis pour la première fois au séjour en France et qui souhaite s'y maintenir durablement, prépare son intégration républicaine dans la société française. A cette fin, il conclut avec l'Etat un contrat d'accueil et d'intégration».

L'Etat, aux termes de ce contrat, prend en charge les prestations suivantes:

– une formation civique d'une journée comportant une présentation des institutions françaises et des valeurs de la République, notamment le principe de l'égalité entre les hommes et les femmes et **la laïcité.**
– une session d'information sur la vie en France, destinée à sensibiliser les nouveaux arrivants au fonctionnement de la société française.
– un accompagnement social si la situation personnelle ou familiale du signataire le justifie.

Il a été mis en place à titre expérimental le 1er juillet 2003 dans 12 départements, puis rendu obligatoire à compter du 1er janvier 2007. **Du 1er janvier 2007 au 31 décembre 2008, il a été signé par 439 409 personnes représentant 150 nationalités.** En 2007, les signataires du contrat sont majoritairement francophones ou ont une connaissance du français jugée suffisante pour se voir dispensés de formation linguistique lors de leur passage sur la plate-forme de l'accueil de l'ANAEM.

Par ailleurs, sous forme d'un carnet personnel que les immigrés peuvent utiliser pour valoriser leurs parcours d'apprentissage du français, le livret «Vivre le Français» constitue un *vade-mecum*. Ce document doit leur permettre de faire consigner, étape après étape, leur progression dans la connaissance et la pratique de la langue française.

Ce livret, qui est délivré, aux personnes étrangères primo-arrivantes, ainsi qu'aux migrants installés en France depuis plusieurs années, mentionne:

– des informations personnelles sur le détenteur (son identité, son adresse, son niveau de connaissance du français...)
– l'ensemble des formations d'apprentissage du français qu'il a reçues et le niveau de français atteint à l'issue de ces formations.

Ce livret est remis en mains propres au migrant par un organisme d'évaluation et de prescription linguistique retenu par l'OFII ou l'ACSE dans le cadre de marchés publics mis en place et financés par l'un de ces opérateurs.

Ce document n'emporte aucune conséquence sur le droit au séjour de l'intéressé. Ce n'est donc pas un élément de preuve de la régularité du séjour de l'étranger. Selon les dispositions de ce contrat, la réalisation de celui-ci «fait l'objet d'un suivi administratif et d'une évaluation par l'OFII», portant, notamment, sur la réalisation effective des actions de formation ou d'information qui y sont inscrites. A l'issue de cette vérification, une «attestation nominative récapitulative qui précise les modalités de leur évaluation» est transmise au préfet.

Les étrangers, qui arrivent en France, se voient remettre un «Livret d'accueil» qui consacre des développements aux institutions françaises et aux droits fondamentaux.

Dans le même sens, les pouvoirs publics, par la loi du 24 juillet 2006, relative à l'immigration et à l'intégration, ont décidé de généraliser les cérémonies d'accueil dans la citoyenneté, moment trop longtemps négligé[6], permettant de célébrer l'entrée dans la nationalité française, qu'elle soit acquise par voie de naturalisation ou par voie de mariage. Il s'agit de consacrer le «vivre ensemble» autour des principes fondateurs de la république française, mentionnés et protégés par la Constitution: liberté, égalité, fraternité, laïcité et démocratie au sein de la communauté nationale. Rappelons qu'en droit constitutionnel français, comme en droit allemand, la qualité de citoyen est conditionnée par la nationalité. Est citoyen français, l'individu qui dispose de la nationalité française.

Sur la question de l'intégration et de la religion, il importe de dire également quelques mots de la question de la réception des droits religieux dans l'ordre juridique interne français.

b. Dans le cadre de la politique du regroupement familial

Depuis le 1er décembre 2008[7], le membre de la famille, qui demande à rejoindre la France, bénéficie d'une évaluation de son degré de connaissance de la langue française et des valeurs de la République.

S'il s'avère qu'un tel apprentissage est nécessaire, l'étranger suit une formation gratuite d'une durée maximale de deux mois avant la délivrance de son visa. La délivrance du visa par l'autorité diplomatique ou consulaire est subordonnée au constat du suivi effectif de la formation prescrite. Néanmoins, la délivrance d'un visa ne dépend pas des

---

[6] Contrairement aux Etats-Unis ou au Canada.

[7] Ce dispositif a été introduit par la loi n°2007-1631 du 20 novembre 2007, relative à la maîtrise de l'immigration, à l'intégration et à l'asile. Cette loi fut mis en oeuvre par un décret n?2008-1115 du 30 octobre 2008.

résultats à un examen. L'office français d'immigration et d'intégration (OFII) est responsable de ce dispositif en relation étroite avec la représentation française dans le pays d'origine. Sont ainsi concernés par ce dispositif:

– les ressortissants étrangers âgés d'au moins 16 ans et de moins de 65 ans pour lesquels le regroupement familial est sollicité;
– les conjoints français âgés de moins de 65 ans sollicitant le visa.

La loi dispense de cette formation:

– les personnes qui ont déjà acquis les compétences requises par une scolarité d'au moins 3 ans dispensée en langue française à l'étranger ou d'un an d'études supérieures en France;
– celles qui résident dans un pays dans lequel le suivi de ces formations est rendu difficile, voire impossible en raison de troubles majeurs (guerre, catastrophe naturelle…)
– celles pour qui le suivi d'une formation entraîne des contraintes incompatibles avec leurs capacités physiques ou financières.

On constate actuellement en France une diminution marquée de l'admission au séjour de membres de familles de Français, baisse amorcée en 2004 et qui s'est amplifiée par la suite. Cette diminution s'explique particulièrement par la baisse du nombre d'admissions au séjours de conjoints de Français (2003: 49544; 2007: 38054).

2. Le statut des droits religieux dans l'ordre juridique français

Pour illustrer ce thème, nous avons choisi deux exemples qui permettent de mieux saisir les enjeux juridiques soulevés par l'implantation de populations immigrées, de confession majoritairement musulmane, sur le territoire français: la réception des règles de statut personnel dans l'ordre juridique interne français et l'implantation des dispositifs de droit financier islamique en droit intene. Ces deux exemples témoignent de l'importance des questions qui se posent et en même temps du degré de réception et d'ouverture dont peut témoigner le droit français.

a. Une question controversée: Le statut des Droits personnels

S'agissant du statut personnel en droit musulman, la question qui se pose, dans le cadre des ordres juridiques des Etats membres du Conseil de l'Europe, est celle la prise en considération des droits fondamentaux

par le droit international privé. Il peut s'agir d'institutions comme la
répudiation, la polygamie ou l'inégalité successorale[8].

Les internationalistes, à ce sujet, se partagent en plusieurs courants:

– l'application directe des droits fondamentaux selon une méthode
  proche de celle des lois d'application immédiate;
– en assurer le respect au moyen traditionnel de l'ordre public après
  éviction de la loi compétente;
– élaborer des clauses spéciales d'ordre public au regard du contenu des
  droits fondamentaux.

Si l'on opte pour le mécanisme classique de l'exception d'ordre public,
est-il nécessaire de faire application d'un ordre public européen spéci-
fique[9] ou de l'ordre public au sens du droit international privé, enrichi
des principes d'ordre public de sources internationale?[10]

Les arrêts de la Cour de Cassation de 2004, dans cinq espèces, ont
refusé la reconnaissance d'une répudiation en raison de son essence dis-
criminatoire et inégalitaire rompant ainsi avec une jurisprudence anté-
rieure hésitante. La solution de la Cour de cassation se rapproche de
celle en vigueur en Grande-Bretagne depuis une loi de 1986. En effet, la
loi sur la famille de 1986 a mis un terme à la reconnaissance de la répudiation ou du divorce musulman par consentement mutuel (*tehul'a*) par
le droit britannique alors qu'auparavant dès lors que ces dissolutions du
lien matrimonial étaient prononcées selon la loi du domicile du mari à
l'étranger, elles étaient valides en Grande-Bretagne[11]. Pour qu'une telle
reconnaissance puisse néanmoins avoir lieu, il faut prouver l'existence
d'un lien étroit avec le lieu où est intervenue la dissolution et que
l'époux ou l'épouse n'ait pas résidé de manière régulière en Grande-Bretagne durant les douze mois précédant la dissolution.

De telles solutions se rapprochent également de celles de la Cour
européenne des droits de l'Homme qui considère, au regard de l'arrêt du

---

[8] T. Rambaud, "Les institutions traditionnelles du droit musulman à l'heure de la
mondialisation du droit: quelques remarques sur l'avenir des statuts personnels confron-
tés à la dynamique des droits fondamentaux", *Revue de la Fondation pour l'Innovation
politique, Revue 2050*, n°10, pp 96-105.

[9] F. Sudre, «Existe-t-il un ordre public européen?», *Quelle Europe pour les droits de
l'Homme*, Bruxelles, Bruylant, 1996, pp 39-80.

[10] M-L Niboyet,??Regard français sur la reconnaissance en France des répudiations
musulmanes?, art. précité, p 30.

[11] S. Poulter,??Les systèmes juridiques en Europe et les populations musulmanes?,
Familles, Islam, Europe. Le droit confronté au changement, Marie-Claire Foblets dir.,
Paris, L'Harmattan, Musulmans d'Europe, 1996, pp 47-56.

3 mai 2005 précité, que le statut personnel ne peut l'emporter sur l'ordre public européen. De la même manière, la Cour européenne des droits de l'Homme rappelle la nécessité d'accorder les mêmes droits successoraux aux enfants adultérins qu'aux enfants légitimes. Dans l'arrêt *Mazurek* du 1er février 2000, la Cour a condamné la France pour discrimination fondée sur l'article 760 du Code civil entre un enfant adultérin et un enfant légitime[12]. Aux termes de l'article 760 du Code civil, la part successorale de l'enfant adultérin est égale à la moitié de celle de l'enfant légitime.

Cette prise en considération d'une exigence de non-discrimination en matière successorale est également susceptible de soulever des difficultés au regard des dispositions du droit musulman en matière successorale[13].

Dans le contexte actuel des difficultés nées de l'application de la *Chari'a* dans les systèmes juridiques occidentaux, notamment en matière de statut personnel, le professeur Sélim Jahel esquisse deux pistes de réflexion pour réaliser cette harmonie[14]:

– la rédaction d'un Code à l'usage des musulmans d'Europe qui serait inspiré largement de la *chari'a* dans son interprétation contemporaine la plus conciliable avec les principes de valeur universelle;
– l'adaptation du droit musulman de la famille au contexte européen par l'insertion généralisée dans les contrats de mariage conclus entre musulmans de clauses matrimoniales qui permettent de déjouer les règles de la *chari'a* pouvant heurter l'ordre public comme la polygamie, la répudiation, l'interdiction pour la mère de voyager sans autorisation de son mari ou d'être tutrice de ses enfants mineurs.

b. *Le respect plus facile des prescriptions religieuses en matière financière: la Finance islamique sur la place financière de Paris*

La finance islamique, qui représente un segment important de la finance mondiale, constitue un secteur en pleine évolution. La finance islamique correspond à «l'exercice d'une activité financière qui se réalise en conformité avec les règles et principes de la Loi islamique, la *Charia*».

Le secteur de la finance islamique est apparu récemment. En effet, il ne prend forme qu'à compter des années 1970 à partir des pays

---

[12] Cour EDH 1er février 2000, *Mazurek c/France*, JCP 2000-II-10286, note A. Gouttenoire-Cornut et F. Sudre.

[13] L. Milliot et F-P. Blanc, *Introduction à l'étude du droit musulman*, Paris, Dalloz, 2ème édition, 2001, p 475 et ss.

[14] *Chari'a et convention européenne des droits de l'Homme*, Une certaine idée du droit, Mélanges offerts à André Decocq, Litec 2004, pp 355-367.

musulmans du Moyen-Orient dans le contexte de la décolonisation[15] et la volonté non seulement de développer des institutions nationales, y compris des institutions bancaires, mais aussi la revendication de restaurer une culture authentique dont relève la référence à l'Islam. En effet, la recherche d'une alternative au prêt à intérêt s'inscrit également dans le cadre d'une réflexion élargie visant à former une idéologie alternative au capitalisme et au communisme: une «économie islamique».

La finance islamique ne se confond pas avec l'ensemble de l'activité financière, telle qu'elle est exercée dans le monde musulman, c'est à dire au sein des pays dont la population est à majorité de religion musulmane. De la même manière, elle ne se réduit pas à l'activité bancaire islamique, mais s'analyse comme un marché où se confrontent une offre et une demande de produits financiers islamiques. Comme dans le cas de la finance conventionnelle, ce marché est régulé par des autorités de tutelle et tend à s'organiser et à se complexifier avec l'intervention d'acteurs para-financiers. La formation de ce secteur s'opère en interaction avec l'environnement extérieur (concurrence des banques conventionnelles, poids de l'opinion publique...)

La finance islamique, qui constitue donc un segment de la finance mondiale, peut se présenter comme une alternative à la finance conventionnelle, car elle cherche à se différencier de cette dernière en proposant des mécanismes financiers et extra-financiers spécifiques, qui privilégient une certaine éthique (prohibition de l'alcool, du commerce des armes, de la pornographie...)

Cela justifie l'attention qui est actuellement portée par les gouvernements nationaux à l'arrivée de la finance islamique comme source de financement de grands projets industriels qui nécessitent des investissements très importants. Outre les mesures édictées par l'actuel Ministre français des finances, des formations spécifiques ont été récemment créées comme un Diplôme d'Université à l'Université Paris Dauphine ou un autre diplôme d'Université à l'Ecole de management de l'Université de Strasbourg, qui vient compléter le Master d'Islamologie-Droit musulman porté par la faculté de droit de l'Université. L'Université

---

[15] La première institution à insérer dans sa raison sociale l'adjectif islamique est la Banque islamique de développement créée par les Etats membres de l'Organisation de la Conférence islamique en s'inspirant de l'architecture institutionnelle des Nations-Unies, avec la Banque mondiale, et des institutions équivalentes à vocation régionale, comme la Banque asiatique du développement. Les premières banques islamiques commerciales font leur apparition au Moyen-Orient à partir de 1975, date de création de *Dubaï Islamic Bank*, suivie en 1977 par la création du *Kuwait finance House* et *Faysal Islamic Bank of Egypt*.

Paris 2 a également lancé un projet de formation sur la finance islamique, mais qui a connu quelques difficultés liées au montant demandé
des droits d'inscription.

Le recours à la finance islamique soulève en France, pays de forte
immigration musulmane, d'importants enjeux tant juridiques que financiers.

Sur un plan juridique, trois points majeurs peuvent être soulignés:

- l'identification des cinq prescriptions posées par le Droit musulman
  qui viennent encadrer le déroulement des opérations financières et
  commerciales: la prohibition de l'intérêt (*riba*), l'interdiction de l'in-
  certitude (*maysir*) et de la spéculation (*gharar*), l'interdiction des secteurs illicites (*haram*), le partage des pertes et des profits, ainsi que la
  contrainte de l'adossement de tout financement à un actif tangible;
- l'utilisation d'institutions ancestrales du Droit musulman pour
  construire une «finance islamique» adaptée au monde économique
  moderne;
- le développement de la finance islamique sur la Place de Paris et la
  transposition de concepts de Droit musulman dans l'ordre juridique
  interne français. Ce dernier peut-il accueillir des institutions juridiques
  élaborées dans la perspective d'une conformité à la *Charia*?

Depuis la fin de l'année 2007, les autorités publiques françaises ont
commencé à se pencher sérieusement en France, sur les possibilités d'at-
tirer les investisseurs des pays du Golfe sur la place de Paris. En fait,
depuis la visite du Président français, Nicolas Sarkozy, en Arabie Saou-
dite en janvier 2008, la question de la position de la France à l'égard de
la finance islamique est devenue omni présente.

Pour les autorités publiques françaises, il s'agit en effet de rattraper la
faible part de pénétration des grandes banques françaises dans la finance
islamique, ainsi qu'un retard dans le développement des produits
conformes à la *Charia*. *Par ailleurs, il n'existe pas en France de banque
islamique de détail, alors que vit sur le territoire français une importante communauté musulmane.*

Selon l'agence Moody's, le secteur de la finance islamique affiche,
depuis 2003, un taux de croissance annuel de 15%. La plus grande partie
de ces capitaux est répartie entre les pays du Golfe (60 %) et l'Asie du
Sud-Est (20 %). Cette zone est caractérisée par une forte abondance de
liquidités avec un montant d'épargne disponible estimé à 5000 milliards
de dollars. Cette croissance est soutenue par l'augmentation régulière du
prix du pétrole et par l'afflux continuel des pétrodollars émanant de cette

région du monde. L'accumulation des liquidités s'est également accélé-
rée ces derniers mois. Les banques des pays du Golfe ont l'habitude de
placer leurs capitaux auprès de banques anglo-saxonnes. Compte tenu du
contexte actuel, elles les ont rapatriés et privilégient désormais les place-
ments auprès d'établissements plus sûrs, comme les banques gouvernementales.

Face à de telles performances, la France ne pouvait ignorer encore
longtemps l'importante poche de liquidités dont disposent les pays du
Golfe. En effet, ce secteur présente un levier de croissance significatif
pour la place de Paris et les banques françaises. Le champ des applications possibles en France est très vaste: investissement en actions dans
les *blue chip companies*, mais également dans les PME, financements de
projets de l'Etat, des collectivités territoriales, financement d'actifs…

Le développement de la finance islamique en France doit respecter
trois principes[16]:

– il doit s'agir d'un processus soutenu par les professionnels concernés;
– ce développement doit respecter le principe de neutralité budgétaire.
  Ainsi, s'agissant de l'émission de «sukuk», il apparaît qu'aujourd'hui
  une telle opération aurait un coût supérieur à une émission d'obligations classiques;
– ce développement doit s'opérer par la voie d'ajustements successifs.

Plusieurs ajustements, tant sur le plan juridique que fiscal, sont ainsi
nécessaires pour accélérer le développement de la finance islamique en
France. Ainsi en janvier 2008, *Paris Europlace* a mis en place une Commission «Finance islamique» chargée d'identifier les obstacles juridiques et fiscaux au développement de la finance islamique en France. *A
cet égard, il importe de rappeler, dans un premier temps, que le droit
français dispose d'institutions équivalentes aux cinq principes posés par
la Charia: la prohibition de l'intérêt (riba), l'interdiction de l'incerti-
tude (maysir) et de la spéculation (gharar), l'interdiction des secteurs
illicites (haram), le partage des pertes et des profits, ainsi que la
contrainte de l'adossement de tout financement à un actif tangible. C'est
la raison pour laquelle l'insertion de la finance islamique dans l'ordre
juridique français ne devrait pas provoquer de bouleversements majeurs,
mais de simples ajustements, notamment en matière fiscale.*

---

[16] Voir l'intervention de Thierry Francq, chef du service du financement de l'économie à la Direction générale du trésor et à la politique économique lors de la table ronde
au Sénat sur la finance islamique qui s'est tenue le 13 mai 2008.

En France, des assouplissements en vue de soutenir les opérations de banque et d'assurance islamiques (*takaful*), ainsi que des incitations nécessaires à l'émission d' obligations conformes aux principes islamiques (*sukuk*) sont ainsi à l'étude.

Une Commission de *Paris Europlace*, spécifiquement consacrée à la finance islamique, travaille actuellement sur ces questions. Des aménagements à certains textes seront donc prochainement apportés, sans toutefois modifier le Code monétaire et financier, *ni créer un cadre législatif spécifiquement dédié à la finance islamique*. En octobre 2009, le législateur a néanmoins voulu consolidé le support normatif voué à l'accueil de la finance islamique sur le marché financier français. Il s'agissait d'une adaptation de la législation relative à la fiducie en vue de permettre le développement de la finance islamique en France.

Précisons à présent quelles sont les principales étapes de l'adaptation du cadre juridique et financier français en vue d'un meilleur développement des produits islamiques sur le marché français.

L'autorité des marchés financiers (AMF) a annoncé, le 2 juillet 2008, une mesure visant à faciliter l'émission des obligations islamiques sur la Place de Paris. Celle-ci s'ajoute à l'autorisation déjà accordée à un organisme de placement collectif en valeurs mobilières (OPCVM) répondant aux critères de la finance islamique (Easy ETF DJI Titans 100 de BNP Paribas). Cette autorisation, publiée le 17 juillet 2007 par l'AMF, permet aux OPCVM d'utiliser des critères autres que financiers pour sélectionner les titres dans lesquels ils investissent. Cette note autorise donc les OPCVM à recourir à des critères extra-financiers de sélection et à faire appel aux services d'un conseil de *Charia* (*sharia board*), à condition qu'il n'y ait pas de transgression de l'autonomie de la société de gestion.

Dans le même sens, en décembre 2008, la Direction générale du Trésor publie des fiches doctrinales pour préciser les aménagements apportés en faveur de la finance islamique en France. Les instructions fiscales portent sur l'absence de prélèvement à la source, la déductibilité de la rémunération versée par les *sukuk* (obligations islamiques), ainsi que la neutralité fiscale lors des opérations de *murabaha* (achat-revente plus marge).

Revenons un instant sur l'instruction fiscale édictée en 2009 par la Direction de la législation fiscale (DLF) au sujet du traitement fiscal de la *Murabaha*.

Aux termes de cette dernière opération, un vendeur transfert des actifs à un financier islamique, il peut s'agir d'une banque islamique ou une SPV *ad hoc* créée par elle, qui les revend à un tiers moyennant un prix, qui comprend une marge couvrant notamment la charge financière de l'intermédiaire financier, payable à terme. Ce tiers emprunteur peut décider, s'il n'a pas besoin de cet actif, de le revendre au comptant à une tierce personne se procurant ainsi une liquidité immédiate pour les besoins de son exploitation. Ce type de schéma repose juridiquement sur un double transfert de propriété et sur l'intermédiation d'une banque ou d'une SPV en qualité de propriétaire de l'actif.

Au sujet de cette opération, l'instruction fiscale publiée par la DLF contient quatre propositions:

- l'absence d'imposition immédiate du profit réalisé grâce à l'opération de *Murabaha*;
- l'exonération de retenue à la source;
- la limitation des droits d'enregistrements en matière de *Murabaha*;
- l'exonération de droits d'enregistrements en matière de *Murabaha* sur titres d'une société à prépondérance immobilière.

Le législateur proposait d'aller plus loin en modifiant le droit de la fiducie en vue de permettre une meilleure implante de la finance islamique en France. Un amendement adopté par le Sénat et l'Assemblée nationale lors des travaux préparatoires à la loi tendant à favoriser l'accès au crédit des PME, et qui était devenu l'article 16 de la loi n°2009-1255 du 19 octobre 2009, se proposait de modifier la notion de fiducie afin de permettre son utilisation pour accueillir la finance islamique et émettre des *sukuk* sur le fondement du droit français.

A priori, la démarche suivie par le législateur paraît simple et logique, dans la mesure où elle s'inspire pour partie de la méthode choisie en Grande-Bretagne. Rappelons que, dans ce pays où les autorités gouvernementales ambitionnent de faire de Londres la première place financière européenne pour la finance islamique, le développement de la finance islamique se fonde sur le respect de deux principes: le respect du droit anglais applicable en la matière[17] et la conformité de l'activité des banques islamiques à la réglementation applicable aux banques exerçant en Grande-Bretagne.

---

[17] Il y a eu cependant quelques interventions législatives pour lever des obstacles fiscaux en faisant émerger de nouveaux concepts comme les «produits financiers islamiques». On peut citer trois réformes importantes: le «*Finance Act*» de 2003 qui a, notamment supprimé le double droit de timbre sur les transactions immobilières islamiques, le «*Finance Act*» de 2005 qui a consacré la notion de «prééminence de la réalité économique sur l'apparence» et le «*Finance Act*» de 2007, qui a défini un régime applicable aux «*sukuk*». Ces trois réformes peuvent inspirer les futures modifications fiscales françaises.

Le Royaume-Uni a accueilli les *sukuk* en utilisant la technique du *trust*, car cela permet de donner au souscripteur une *equitable ownership* sur les actifs sous-jacents et ainsi de respecter l'un des principes de la *Charia* qui veut que les porteurs de *sukuk* aient un droit réel sur ces actifs et qu'ils participent ainsi au risque de l'activité financée.La législation britannique tient compte de la taxation des opérations de financement islamiques afin d'éviter un effet de double taxation. Les montages de financements des banques islamiques sont généralement structurés de telle manière à ce que plusieurs transferts de propriété sont nécessaires (la banque ou sa filiale achète un bien qu'elle revend avec une marge ou loue avec une option d'achat), chaque transfert de propriété supposant un droit de mutation.

L'autorité financière britannique FSA a facilité l'intégration de banques islamiques en Grande-Bretagne. En 2004, l'*Islamic Bank of Britain* a été agréée par les autorités britanniques (voir le site de la *Financial Service Authority*).

En droit français, la fiducie est la technique juridique qui ressemble le plus au *trust*, mais elle présente l'inconvénient de ne conférer aucun droit réel à son bénéficiaire sur les biens qui figurent dans le patrimoine fiduciaire. Dès lors, la solution la plus simple semblait être de modifier la réglementation de la fiducie pour conférer un droit réel à son bénéficiaire et permettre ainsi l'émission de *sukuk* sur le fondement du droit français. C'est la raison pour laquelle l'article 16 de la dite loi ajoutait un alinéa 2 à l'article 2011 du Code civil affirmant que: «le fiduciaire exerce la propriété fiduciaire des actifs figurant dans le patrimoine fiduciaire (sic), ou au profit des bénéficiaires, selon les stipulations du contrat de fiducie». Il s'agissait de permettre au détenteur de *sukuk* de pouvoir se prévaloir d'un droit de propriété des actifs supports afin d'être en conformité avec la règle interdisant de s'enrichir sans risques, ce qui impliquerait un droit de propriété. On s'interrogera au passage sur la qualité d'une rédaction où figure dans la même phrase à quatre reprises le mot «fiducie» ou «fiduciaire». Cette solution a été contestée en doctrine par les professeurs L. Aynès et P. Crocq qui estiment qu'il n'est pas nécessaire de bouleverser le droit commun de la fiducie, alors que le droit spécial des instruments financiers permettait de trouver une solution adéquate[18]. Pour ces auteurs, il est regrettable que la loi nouvelle, pour répondre aux seuls besoins

---

[18] Note de L. Aynés et P. Crocq, «La fiducie préservée des audaces du législateur?», *Recueil Dalloz*, 2009, n°38.

particuliers de la finance islamique, se propose de modifier la nature juridique de toutes les fiducies, les fiducies-gestions, comme les fiducies-sûretés?[19].

Une telle interrogation est susceptible de se poser dans des domaines parallèles, notamment dans le régime juridique applicable aux cultes. Convient-il de déroger au principe de non-subventionnement des activités cultuelles posé par l'article 2 de la loi du 9 décembre 1905 pour favoriser la construction de nouveaux lieux de culte en faveur des religions plus récemment implantées sur le territoire national, et qui, dans ces conditions, sont dans une situation objectivement défavorable par rapport aux religions traditionnelles d'implantation plus ancienne, comme les religions chrétiennes ou la religion juive? La réponse est délicate et ne saurait se cantonner à une vision strictement technique des choses[20]. Bien au contraire, il importe de réfléchir en profondeur sur les choix que sous-tend une telle interrogation.

3. La protection particulière du droit d'asile

«Tout homme persécuté en raison de son action en faveur de la liberté à droit d'asile sur les territoires de la République».

Cette formule du Préambule de la Constitution de 1946 témoigne de l'attachement de la France au droit d'asile. Le droit d'asile a valeur constitutionnelle (décision des 12-13 août 1993 du Conseil constitutionnel: «Considérant que le respect du droit d'asile, principe de valeur constitutionnelle, implique d'une manière générale que l'étranger qui se réclame de ce droit soit autorisé à demeurer provisoirement sur le territoire jusqu'à ce qu'il ait été statué sur sa demande».

En aucune manière, le droit s'asile ne doit donc être la variable d'ajustement de la politique d'immigration.

Une personne qui sollicite la protection de la France peut obtenir deux types de statut:

- **le statut de réfugié qui est octroyé**, conformément à l'article L. 711-1 du Code de l'entrée et du séjour des étrangers et du droit d'asile:
- en application de la convention de Genève du 28 juillet 1951 sur le statut des réfugiés;

---

[19] F. X. Lucas,??La fiducie au Pays de l'Or noir?, Bull. Joly Sociétés 2009. 825.

[20] On pourra se reporter utilement à J-P. Machelon (sous la direction), *Les relations des cultes avec les pouvoirs publics*, La Documentation française, 2006.

- à toute personne persécutée en raison de son action en faveur de la
  liberté;
- à toute personne sur laquelle le Haut Commissariat des Nations-Unies
  pour les réfugiés exerce son mandat aux termes des articles 6 et 7 de
  son statut.
- **la protection subsidiaire**, qui est accordée à la personne qui ne rem-
  plit pas les critères ci-dessus, mais qui établit qu'elle est exposée dans
  son pays à la peine de mort, à la torture, à des peines ou traitements
  inhumains ou dégradants, ou, s'agissant d'un civil, à une menace
  grave, directe et individuelle contre sa vie ou sa personne en raison
  d'une violence généralisée résultant d'une situation de conflit armé
  interne ou international.

Sur les dispositifs relatifs au droit d'asile, la dernière loi adoptée est la
loi dite Villepin du 10 décembre 2003. Elle développe les procédures
prioritaires et crée une Cour nationale du droit d'asile. La demande
d'asile s'est effondrée entre 2003 et 2007 pour revenir à un niveau comparable à celui de 1997. La question qui se pose est celle de la situation
des demandeurs d'asile qui sont évincés du système. La consultation des
statistiques d'interpellation d'irréguliers révèle qu'en 2007 sur près de
70 000 procédures, 31823 se cristallisent dans le Nord et 26353 dans le
seul Calaisis. On dénombre 8889 Irakiens, 6706 Erythréens, 5268 Ira-
niens qui, pour l'essentiel, allaient en??direction des îles britanniques et
vers les pays scandinaves. En octobre 2009, le Ministre de l'Immigration
et de l'identité nationale, Monsieur Eric Besson, a promis de faire dispa-
raître la célèbre «jungle de Calais».

L'organisation de ces cérémonies revient dans chaque département au
préfet ou, lorsqu'ils en ont obtenu l'autorisation, aux maires, en leur
qualité d'officier d'état civil.

4. La réaction des autorités religieuses aux réglementations étatiques en matière de droit des étrangers

Le 6 février 2002 a été rendue publique la déclaration épiscopale,
L'asile en France, état d'urgence. Cette déclaration a été signée par
Monseigneur Olivier de Berranger, président du Comité épiscopal des
migrations, Monseigneur Lucien Daloz, qui est le Président de Justice et
Paix-France. Cette déclaration condamne sévèrement la politique du
gouvernement français en matière de droit d'asile. Elle dénonce un dispositif «totalement inadapté et défaillant». Elle invite les citoyens à

transformer le regard qu'ils portent sur le droit d'asile et les responsables politiques à adopter des mesures d'urgence :

- réduire la durée des procédures et les délais d'attente afin que les demandeurs d'asile sachent rapidement si leur demande est agréée ;
- renforcer les moyens de l'OFPRA ;
- accorder aux demandeurs d'asile le droit de travailler lorsque le délai de réponse à leur demande dépasse six mois ;
- rendre plus transparent les procédures et les critères d'attribution de l'asile territorial (loi de 1998) ;
- prendre en considération les droits sociaux et l'hébergement des demandeurs d'asile.

L'Eglise s'inscrit dans la longue tradition de l'asile religieux. A l'époque, il consistait en une immunité territoriale de lieux sacrés, de plus en plus largement conçus (cimetières, presbytères, monastères, hôpitaux, simple croix ou même l'anneau placé à la porte des églises). Puis, il va devenir un instrument de protection personnelle contre une justice séculière jugée arbitraire emportant des effets juridiques au-delà même du lieu d'asile, comme par exemple l'extinction de la dette d'un débiteur ou l'affranchissement d'un esclave. L'essor de l'asile religieux témoigne de l'Eglise qui sera à son apogée au XIIème siècle, mais les résistances que suscitent quelques abus, ainsi que la revendication d'un pouvoir royal qui s'affermit d'une plénitude de souveraineté sur son territoire, conduisent à sa mise en cause. Il va être aboli en matière civile par l'ordonnance de Villers-Cotterêts de 1539. Il n'en reste pas moins que la doctrine de l'Eglise catholique est l'héritière de cette prestigieuse histoire et de cette tradition d'attention à l'égard de ceux qui demandent à l'Eglise sa protection. L'Eglise catholique, comme les églises protestantes, sont très attentives à ce qu'un traitement conforme au principe de la dignité de la personne humaine soit réservé aux migrants et aux réfugiés.

Néanmoins, l'Eglise n'appelle pas à se substituer aux pouvoirs et autorités publics pour accorder l'accueil. Dans des cas extrêmes, les chrétiens peuvent être conduits à désobéir aux autorités civiles. Bien entendu, comme le rappelle Eric Besson, «l'action humanitaire en direction des étrangers en détresse, quelle que soit leur situation au regard du droit au séjour, est parfaitement légale»?. Mais, aux yeux du ministre, l'action humanitaire n'est légitime à ses yeux qu'à condition de n'impliquer aucune critique excessive de la politique menée. En ce sens, dans sa lettre du 7 avril 2009, aux associations mobilisées contre le ??délit de solidarité?, le ministre Brice Hortefeux rappelle que 20 millions d'euros par an de subventions sont versés aux associations venant en aide aux immigrés en situation irrégulière.

On mentionnera ici l'arrêt *Perrégaux*, par lequel le Conseil d'Etat avait validé l'expulsion d'un pasteur suisse d'une association marseillaise d'aide aux réfugiés et aux travailleurs migrants en raison du manquement au devoir de réserve. (CE, Assemblée, 13 mai 1977, Rec. P 216). Cette jurisprudence semble dorénavant appartenir au passé. Et ce d'autant plus que dans cette affaire le Conseil d'Etat avait jugé qu'un comportement politique n'est pas à lui seul de nature à justifier l'expulsion. A l'époque, le Ministre de l'Intérieur lui reprochait plus largement des atteintes graves à la neutralité politique par le fait d'avoir prêté les locaux de son association à des organisations d'extrême gauche et d'animer des manifestations tendant à obtenir la régularisation de tous les sans-papiers.

HANS MICHAEL HEINIG*

IMMIGRATION AND RELIGION IN GERMANY

1. General legal framework and political discussion in Germany

After being a country of emigration in 19th century and in the first half of the 20th century, Germany became one of the most important European countries for immigration in the mid-1950s. Thereby one can distinguish between several types of immigration: recruitment of guest workers, immigration for family reunification, the influx of repatriates of German origin (Spätaussiedler) and the reception of asylum seekers.

German Alien law has been subject to a steady change over the past decades. Since the beginning of the 1990s when the immigration of asylum seekers and resettlers reached its maximum, migration became an important topic again in political discussions. The Alien Act (Ausländergesetz) of 1990 was replaced in 2002 by the Residence Act (Aufenthaltgesetz), which was part of a whole complex of new rules pertaining to the Immigration Act (Zuwanderungsgesetz). After the Constitutional Court judged that the Immigration Act was not in conformity with the Basic Law (Grundgesetz) because of formal issues, a new Immigration Act came into force in 2005. Regulations regarding residence, free movement of EU citizens and asylum procedures in this amendment did not last long as there was a deeper need for change due to eleven migration and asylum related directives by the EC. German legislation on migration came to a temporary end after the transformation of these directives into national law in 2007.

Germany has two important acts dealing with immigration besides the right of asylum laid down in the constitution: 1) The Freedom of Movement Act/EU (Freizügigkeitsgesetz/EU) and 2) the Residence Act (Aufenthaltsgesetz).

* Executive Director of the Institute for Public Law (Chair for Public Law and Ecclesiastical Law), Law Faculty, Georg-August-University Göttingen and Director of the Institute for Ecclesiastical Law of the Protestant Church of Germany (EKD). Special thanks for assistance go to Stefan Kirchner, Katrin König, Anya Lean and Dr. Hendrik Munsonius.

The Freedom of Movement Act deals with the migration of EU citizens. The position of the latter is almost equal to that of German citizens. EU citizens are allowed to enter, live and work in Germany without restrictions.

The Residence Act deals with the migration of third country nationals. These nationals when wanting to stay in Germany need a title of residence. Residence titles are given in the form of a visa, residence permit, settlement permit or EC long-term residence permit.[1] To obtain one of these residence titles the following general preconditions have to be fulfilled: 1) secured livelihood 2) established identity 3) no grounds for expulsion 4) no intention to compromise or jeopardize state interests 5) valid passport.[2] Furthermore, the Residence Act gives information about the reasons for residency in Germany: 1) for the purpose of education, such as study, language course or school visit[3] 2) for the purpose of employment, especially for highly qualified persons, researchers and self-employed persons[4] 3) reasons in accordance with international and humanitarian law as well as political grounds[5] 4) for the purpose of family reunification, especially the influx of spouses depending on an obligatory language proof [6] 5) prohibition of deportation and other asylum related regulations.[7]

There is no real tradition of immigration from particular countries. Nevertheless Turkish and Italian immigrants constitute the most important sections of the alien population in Germany.[8] The reason for this is, that in the days of recruitment of guest workers, it was mostly Turkish and Italian citizens who came to Germany on account of special agreements Germany had with these countries. As the groups became settled in Germany, a phase of family reunification followed. Nowadays the search for work and family reunification are still the most common reasons for immigration to Germany.

Another special immigration group are the repatriates of German origin, who come from Middle and East Europe and former states of Soviet

---

[1] Cf. §4 AufenthG.
[2] Cf. §5 AufenthG.
[3] Cf. §16 ff. AufenthG.
[4] Cf. §18 ff. AufenthG.
[5] Cf. §22 ff. AufenthG.
[6] Cf. §27 ff. AufenthG.
[7] Cf. §60 AufenthG.
[8] 2008: Turkish immigrants: 25.1 %; Italian immigrants: 7.8%; Statistics are available at: http://www.bamf.de.

Union. But the number of immigrants has declined rapidly because of the restrictions operative since the mid-1990s – such as a certificate of knowledge of the German language.

2. Statistical data

After the above-mentioned change in the law concerning residence in 2005, the first official statistic considering the new permits were contained in the migration report (Migrationsbericht) of 2007.

The following chart of 2008 lists the different permits and the reasons for which they are grated:

Foreign nationals according to legal status (12/31/2008)

Legal status	Number of foreign nationals
Total	6 727 618
Legal status according to old law (Ausländergesetz 1990)	
Temporary residence permit	314 245
Permanent residence permit	1 712 776
Legal status according to new law (Aufenthaltsgesetz 2004)	
Temporary Residence permit	1 287 174
For educational reasons	141 236
For reasons of employment	86 736
Humanitarian and political reasons and reasons according to international law	169 782
Familial reasons	768 270
Special residence permit	121 150
Permanent residence permit	1 121 280
Others	174 999
EU law, EU residence permit, permit of free movement	1 522 861
Tolerated	103 218
No legal status	465 811

Regarding applications for asylum, there has been a significant decrease in applications since 2005:

	Number of applicants	Refused
2005	48102	17529 (36%)
2006	30759	11027 (35%)
2007	28572	7953 (27%)

3. Requirements for the acquisition of citizenship

The legal requirements placed upon the acquisition of citizenship are regulated in Art. 8-16 Citizenship Act (Staatsangehörigkeitsgesetz-StAG):

Art. 8:

Citizenship can be acquired upon application, if the applicant has his regular residence in Germany and fulfils the criteria listed under Art. 8 I-IV StAG.

Art. 9:

Spouses or life partners of German citizens are to be granted German citizenship under the conditions of Art. 8 StAG

(1) if they lose or give up their other citizenship or if a reason exists to accept multiple citizenship.
(2) if it is warranted that they will integrate into German living circumstances.

They must have sufficient knowledge of the German language.

Art. 10:

Foreign nationals that have lived for eight years in Germany are to be granted German citizenship if they fulfil the following conditions:

1. They have to avow themselves to the free and democratic basic order of the German Basic Law and declare that they do not intend to cause any threat to this order.
2. They have to demonstrate that they can afford living expenses for themselves and their family.
3. They are not convicted for an illegal act.
4. They have sufficient knowledge of the German language.
5. They have knowledge of German law and society.

Art. 11:

The granting of citizenship is impossible if there is evidence that the applicant is, or has been, trying to endanger the free and democratic order, or if a ground for extradition exists.

The Federal Ministry for the Interior introduced nationally a naturalization test by order of August 5th 2008 (Einbürgerungstestverordnung) that came into force on September 1st 2008 – a questionnaire testing knowledge of the legal and social circumstances in Germany. Persons under 16, disabled persons and those impaired by sickness or age are exempted from the test. The test totalling 33 questions comprises thematic areas such as "life in democracy" "history and responsibility" as well as "the human and the society".

One year after introducing the naturalization test, 98% have succeeded at the first attempt. On failing, the test can be repeated.[9]

Since the test was only introduced in 2008, there is no data concerning specifically the changes in the religious configuration of the country due to naturalization. Generally, the number of people granted citizenship has decreased.

4. Legal regulation of asylum

There are four steps as far as national and international refugee protection is concerned:

1) The constitutionally-guaranteed right of asylum is laid down in Art. 16 a (1) GG, and is limited by a "third-country regulation" codified in Art. 16a (2) GG.[10] Because of the strongly-enhanced protection in

---

[9] http://www.migration-info.de/mub_artikel.php?Id=090101

[10] Art. 16a GG: (1) Persons persecuted on political grounds shall have the right of asylum.

(2) Paragraph (1) of this Article may not be invoked by a person who enters the federal territory from a member state of the European Community or from another third state in which the application of the Convention Relating to the Status of Refugees and of the Convention for the Protection of Human Rights and Fundamental Freedoms is assured. The states outside the European Communities to which the criteria of the first sentence of this paragraph apply shall be specified by a law requiring the consent of the Bundesrat. In the cases specified in the first sentence of this paragraph, measures to terminate an applicant's stay may be implemented without regard to any legal challenge that may have been instituted against them.

(3) By a law requiring the consent of the Bundesrat, states may be specified in which, on the basis of their laws, enforcement practices, and general political conditions, it can be safely concluded that neither political persecution nor inhuman or degrading punishment or treatment exists. It shall be presumed that a foreigner from such a state is not

§60 (1) AufenthG and its complete recognition of refugee protection, the constitutional right of asylum will hardly play a decisive role in practice in the future. However, this right still entails an extensive symbolic meaning. The legal doctrine developed by the jurisdiction concerning asylum will continue to play an important since recourse to it reveals that the protective effect developed by the jurisdiction will not make this constitutional right obsolete.

2) The international refugee protection by prohibition of deportation according to §60 (1) AufenthG,[11] and the adjudication of granting

persecuted, unless he presents evidence justifying the conclusion that, contrary to this presumption, he is persecuted on political grounds.

(4) In the cases specified by paragraph (3) of this Article and in other cases that are plainly unfounded or considered to be plainly unfounded, the implementation of measures to terminate an applicant's stay may be suspended by a court only if serious doubts exist as to their legality; the scope of review may be limited, and tardy objections may be disregarded. Details shall be determined by a law.

(5) Paragraphs (1) to (4) of this Article shall not preclude the conclusion of international agreements of member states of the European Communities with each other or with those third states which, with due regard for the obligations arising from the Convention Relating to the Status of Refugees and the Convention for the Protection of Human Rights and Fundamental Freedoms, whose enforcement must be assured in the contracting states, adopt rules conferring jurisdiction to decide on applications for asylum, including the reciprocal recognition of asylum decisions.

[11] §60 (1) AufenthG: (1) In application of the Convention of 28 July 1951 relating to the Status of Refugees (Federal Law Gazette 1953 II, p. 559), a foreigner may not be deported to a state in which his or her life or liberty is under threat on account of his or her race, religion, nationality, membership of a certain social group or political convictions. This shall also apply to persons who are entitled to asylum and to foreigners who have been incontestably granted refugee status or who enjoy the legal status of foreign refugees on other grounds in the Federal territory or who have been granted foreign refugee status outside of the Federal territory in accordance with the Convention relating to the Status of Refugees. When a person's life, freedom from bodily harm or liberty is threatened solely on account of their sex, this may also constitute persecution due to membership of a certain social group. Persecution within the meaning of sentence 1 may emanate from

a) the state,

b) parties or organisations which control the state or substantial parts of the national territory, or

c) non-state parties, if the parties stated under letters a and b, including international organisations, are demonstrably unable or unwilling to offer protection from the persecution, irrespective of whether a power exercising state rule exists in the country, unless an alternative means of escape is available within the state concerned. Article 4 (4) and Articles 7 to 10 of Council directive 2004/83/EC of 29 April 2004 on minimum standards for the qualification and status of third country nationals or stateless persons as refugees or as persons who otherwise require international protection and the content of the protection granted (Official EU Journal no. L 304, p.12) shall additionally be applied in establishing whether a case of persecution pursuant to sentence 1 applies. Where the foreigner cites the ban on deportation pursuant to this sub-section, the Federal Office for Migration

refugee protection according to the Geneva Refugee Convention (§3 (1) AsylVfG), which is significantly determined and covered by the Qualification Directive 2004/83/EC since 2007.

3) The subsidiary protection by declaration of non-refoulement (§60 (2) (3) (4) and (7) AufenthG) and the adjudication of subsidiary status of protection included in the Qualification Directive. The possibility of exclusion is laid down in §60 (8) AufenthG.

4) The "national" subsidiary protection in §60 (5) AufenthG in conjunction with the ECHR and the prohibition of deportation of §60 (7) as well as an absolute prohibition of deportation, which is guaranteed beyond the Qualification Directive by constitutional and humanitarian principles.

The guidelines according to international refugee protection law were stimulated in large measure by the Immigration Act and the transformation of several EC-directives into national law. In particular, an explicit reference to the Geneva refugee convention was adjusted in §60 (1) AufenthG. Furthermore, central grounds for granting asylum – such as recognition by non-state actors and gender – were newly integrated. At the same time, a change in perspective regarding the guidelines of the Geneva Refugee Convention is expected to entail corresponding legal changes.

Statistics regarding asylum are available. The Federal Office for Migration and Refugees edits a booklet every year, which deals with such data. The booklet is available online free of charge.[12] A total of 22,085 asylum applications were submitted in the year of 2008 – a slight increase in comparison with 2007 when there were 19,165 applications. Most applications were made by persons with the following countries of origin: Iraq, Turkey, Vietnam, Kosovo, Iran, Russian Federation, Syria, Serbia, Afghanistan and Nigeria.

Of all applications for asylum, Muslims constitute the largest group with 42.2 %. They are followed by the members of Zarathustra with 21.2 %, of which 99.7% confess to the Yezidian belief. Thus, about two thirds (63.6%) of the applicants belong to these two religions. Christians are in third place with 19.7% of all applications.

---

and Refugees shall establish in an asylum procedure whether the conditions stated in sentence 1 apply and the foreigner is to be granted refugee status, except in cases covered by sentence 2. The decision by the Federal Office shall only be appealable subject to the provisions of the Asylum Procedure Act.

[12] http://www.bamf.de/cln_153/nn_442496/SharedDocs/Anlagen/DE/DasBAMF/Publikationen/broschuere-asyl-in-zahlen-2008.html

The Federal Office for Migration and Refugees is responsible for decisions regarding asylum applications and recognition of refugee-status (§5 (1) AsylVfG). An asylum application is regarded as the expression of intent by an alien in written, oral or in other form, and documentation that the person is seeking protection against political persecution or that he or she claims protection against deportation to the country of origin in which he or she is threatened by a mischief listed in §60 (1) AufenthG.

The recognition of refugee-status on religious grounds is frequently and hotly discussed in Germany, involving serious disagreements – especially as to jurisdiction – since the coming into force of the Qualification Directive. The refugee-status was only recognized when a so-called "religious margin of subsistence" of the person in question was violated before the directive came into force. This margin referred to freedom of belief as well as to religious practice in private. Public religious practice was not included. Today there is a discussion about whether this jurisdiction can still be applied. There is disagreement as to whether resort may be made to the previous jurisdiction after the coming into force of the Qualification Directive. In view of the Geneva refugee convention and the guidelines of the UNHCR to this convention it is highly questionable.

It is mostly Iranian Muslim coverts to Christianity who have been seeking protection from German courts in recent years. Another case, concerning a Chinese woman of Christian belief, was dealt with by the Federal Court of Administration in March 2009.[13] The claimant was a member of one of the officially non-registered Christian underground churches. These churches are regarded as illegal by the Chinese authorities, because they avoid state control with regard to questions of faith. The woman was observed repeatedly attending church services and – amongst other things – subsequently lost her job as a teacher at a public school. The Federal Court of Administration remanded the case to the court of appeal because it had not been made clear by the court whether the claimant would have to face imprisonment because of her religious activities, if she were to return to China. Regarding the judicial criteria the court maintained the following: In evaluating an already-practiced religious belief, it is relevant whether the return to the country concerned constitutes a danger for body, life or physical freedom. If this danger does not exist, recognition of refugee-status can still be considered if the claimant on return to his or her

---

[13] BVerwG, DÖV 2009, p. 726ff. = NVwZ 2009, p. 1167ff.

home country would be hindered in the practice of his or her faith because of prevailing restrictions to such an extent that his or her right of freedom of religion would be substantially violated. From the viewpoint of European law the question of whether only the "religious margin of subsistence" or also public religious activities – and if so under what conditions – are included in the protection has to be decided ultimately by the ECJ.

5. Sanctuary (asylum in churches)

There are some cases of churches giving asylum to prevent people from being deported or arrested in preparation for deportation. Protagonists are Protestant or Roman Catholic parishes and their clergymen. Cases of granting asylum by other religious corporations are not reported. Data about the number of cases differ between 15 and 50 cases a year.

The churches justify the legitimacy of granting asylum with the Christian duty to assist the hunted. On the other hand, the legitimacy of public order should not be challenged. Therefore the churches granting asylum do not intend to provide a permanent habitation but a reconsideration of governmental decisions.

The legal requirement is controversial. A justification for giving asylum is found in freedom of religion (Art. 4 Abs.1 and 2 GG) and the right of self-determination of churches (Art. 140 GG in conjunction with Art. 137 (3) WRV), restricted by the legislation on asylum and aliens as "für alle geltendes Gesetz".

Courts assume that churches are not allowed to give asylum, but in most cases administrative authorities dispense with enforcing action in cases of asylum granted by churches and seek a peaceful settlement with the church representatives.

By establishing commissions for cases of hardship ("Härtefallkommissionen", §23a AufenthG) a procedure is created to meet concerns raised by the churches. An appeal may be made to these commissions when an alien is obliged to depart. When there are special grounds of hardship, permission to remain may be granted, delaying the duty to depart. This rule is time-limited until 31.12.2009. A prolongation has not been decided yet.

6. Family reunion

The principle of the unification of families is a fundamental of German immigration law. Due to the protection of marriage and family life under Art. 6 *Grundgesetz* (Basic Law, GG) §27 (1) AufenthG allows in principle foreigners to immigrate to Germany for the purpose of establishing or continuing family life, unless it is certain that the marriage or familial relationship has only been created for the purpose of allowing the foreigner to immigrate to and to reside in Germany, §27 (1a) no. 1 AufenthG, or that the spouse in question has been forced into the marriage. A residence permit can be denied if the family member already residing in Germany is dependent on welfare, §27 (3) AufenthG.

Non-German citizens who marry a German citizen have the right to immigrate to Germany and can apply for a residence permit for a maximum of three years. Prior to immigration they need to demonstrate a minimum degree of German language skills. Art. 6 (1) GG, guarantees the right to found a family, yet it does not automatically provide the right to residence in Germany upon marriage for foreigners who marry a German citizen or a foreign citizen who lawfully resides in Germany.[14]

The view expressed by the legal situation in Germany that the right to family life does not entail an unconditional right for the non-EU spouse to immigrate is in conformity with Art. 6 GG[15] and the interpretation of Art. 8 of the European Convention on Human Rights by the European Court of Human Rights.[16]

Although the right to found a family (Art. 6 GG) applies equally to Germans and non-Germans, a distinction is made between foreigners who are married to German citizens and those who are married to non-Germans living in Germany. Non-EU citizens who are married to a foreign citizen legally residing in Germany can immigrate only if the spouse who is already residing in Germany is able to provide sufficient living space, §29 (1) No. 2 AufenthG – a requirement which does not exist in cases in which the spouse is a German citizen. Also, the question of whether family life is possible outside the EU, particularly in a country to which the spouse who intends to immigrate has close ties with, is an issue which had been raised prominently in the European Court of Human Rights in *Berrehab v. The Netherlands*,[17] which only applies to cases in which the spouse who is already residing in Germany is not a

---

[14] Verwaltungsgericht Berlin, 30th Chamber, Judgment of 10 March 2009, joined cases 30 V 55.08 and VG 30 V 55.08, para. 39.

[15] Ibid.

[16] Ibid., para. 57.

[17] European Court of Human Rights, *Abdellah and Rebecca Berrehab v. The Netherlands*, Application No. 10730/84.

German citizen.[18] German citizens, on the other hand, do not have to fear being moved abroad in order to live with their family members there. The most important difference between immigrating to live with a German or with a non-German citizen, is that the spouses of foreigners living in Germany have to pass a language test prior to immigrating to Germany, §30 (1) No. 2 AufenthG. The factual background to this requirement is the experience that a large number of male non-German residents in Germany marry women in their home country and bring them to Germany. Facing the difficulty of distinguishing between arranged marriages – common in many countries – and forced marriages, German authorities have found it equally difficult to determine whether women were "brought" to Germany against their will. Although the primary purpose of the rule is to increase integration of foreigners into German society, this rule also provides an indirect tool against forced marriages.

This is particularly necessary since German law to this day does not provide adequate protection against forced marriages. German criminal law punishes coercion with the aim of marriage under §240 (4) no. 1 of the Criminal Code (*Strafgesetzbuch*, StGB) as a particularly severe case of coercion with imprisonment between six months and five years. Forced marriages between foreign citizens abroad are usually outside the scope of German criminal law.[19] Therefore, according to §27 (1a) no. 2 AufenthG, the right to immigrate to Germany for the purposes of establishing or continuing a family under §27 (1) AufenthG does not extend to cases in which there are indicators that one of the spouses has been forced into the marriage. Legislative efforts to create a new law against forced marriages (the proposed *Zwangsehen-Bekämpfungsgesetz*) have been stalled in parliament since 2006,[20] but the new German government has declared its willingness to support the proposed law.[21]

Although some religions may allow for multiple marriages, polygamy is not allowed under German law. Accordingly, foreign citizens who are

---

[18] Cf. §29 (2) No. 2 AufenthG.

[19] Under §§7 (1) and 240 (1) and (4) *Strafgesetzbuch*, foreigners can be punished for coercion in forced marriage cases if the perpetrator later becomes a German citizen and forced marriage is also criminally punishable in the country in which the crime occurred. The latter requirement already indicates that such cases will be rare.

[20] Cf. also Karin Schubert / Isabelle Moebius – Zwangsheirat – Mehr als nur ein Straftatbestand: Neue Wege zum Schutz der Opfer, ZRP 2006, pp. 33-37.

[21] Bernd von Heintschel-Heinegg – Schwarz-Geld will Zwangsheirat unter Strafe stellen, http://blog.beck.de/2009/10/14/schwarz-gelb-will-zwangsheirat-unter-strafe-stellen, 14 October 2009.

married to several spouses and already live with one spouse in Germany are banned by §30 (4) AufenthG from bringing an additional spouse to Germany. §30 (4) AufenthG implements Art. 4 (4) sentence 1 of Directive 2003/86/EC. Similarly, the German legislator has made use of Art. 4 (5) of the same directive by requiring a minimum age of 18 years for spouses to be allowed to immigrate to Germany, §30 (1) No. 1 AufenthG.

7. Restrictions and Quota for the employment of non-EU Citizens

There is no quota as such, although there are a number of obstacles for non-EU Citizens to obtain a work permit. Between 2000 and 2004, the German Green Card model under the *Verordnung über Aufenthaltserlaubnisse für hoch qualifizierte ausländische Fachkräfte der Informations- und Kommunikationstechnologie* (Ordinance concerning residence permits for highly qualified foreign information and communication technology specialists, IT-ArGV) provided relaxed requirements for highly qualified IT experts from Non-EU states. Initially the green card model was limited to 10,000 applicants, later the number was increased to 20,000 but the latter number was never reached. Today the immigration law (*Zuwanderungsgesetz*), which came into force on January 1st 2005, allows e.g. highly trained professionals to obtain a permanent residence permit immediately. While university-educated clerics can be considered highly trained professionals, the law is aimed more at technical experts or scientists, which seriously limits the benefits of the law for non-EU clergy. Foreign citizens who studied in Germany, e.g. to become clerics, now profit from relaxed requirements and can obtain residence and work permits for the first year after graduation more easily. Residence and work permits can be requested by non-EU Citizens for the purpose of working in Germany as an employed cleric as for other qualified jobs. Also asylum seekers can, if given a dispensation to this effect, work as clerics. Working as a cleric does not affect the legal status of a foreigner in Germany.

In some cases clerics work as de facto expatriates in Germany. They are employed by institutions in their home country and affiliate to their home-community even in Germany. This applies primarily to Islamic clerics working for DİTİB (*Diyanet İşleri Türk İslam Birliği* – Turkish-Islamic Union of the Institution of Religion). DİTİB is a *Verein*, an association under German private law, but for all practical purposes it is subordinate to the *Diyanet İşleri Başkanlığı* (the Executive Committee of Religious Affairs – *Diyanet* for short) and is therefore indirectly subordinate to the Prime Minister of the Republic of Turkey. DİTİB operates mosques and serves as an association representing immigrants vis-á-vis the German government. Also, under the auspices of DİTİB, hodjas are sent from Turkey to Germany. Although DİTİB is an association under German law, their hodjas are employed by the Turkish government and are supervised by the local Turkish consulate. In a similar manner some states, such as Portugal, send teachers to Germany and other countries. These teachers are employed by the Portuguese government and supervised by the consulate and teach Portuguese e.g. to the descendants of Portuguese citizens who emigrated to Germany after World War II. This indicates that this model is by no means exclusively used by minority religions, although many clerics of minority religions come to Germany from abroad.

Constantinos G. Papageorgiu

IMMIGRATION AND RELIGION IN GREECE

1. Introduction

Up until the end of the 1980's, the number of immigrants in Greece was so small that the State neither focused nor showed an interest in whether their stay in Greek territory was legal or not. This was also the case with public opinion. However, at the beginning of the 1990's, Greece was overwhelmed by an immigration 'chaos' due to the fact that a large number of "non-community" immigrants entered the country, while the State was not in a position to contain this phenomenon. The events of this period triggered the creation of a legislative mechanism, which has been evolving ever since. This endeavor has not been easy, due to the fact that immigration is essentially long-term; thus, it has an impact on all sectors of the host country. The problem is substantially exacerbated by the fact that Greece, which is situated at the European Union borders, is heavily affected by the repercussions of this 'immigration explosion'.

2. The legal framework on inmigration

Law 1975/1991, entitled *"Entry – Exit, Stay, Work, Deportation of Immigrants and Recognition Process of Foreign Refugees"*, constituted the first attempt to design an immigration policy. A large number of bodies (ministries, law enforcement bodies, etc.) were involved in its implementation. Subsequently, the control and handling of the entry and stay of foreigners in the country became a complex task. Indeed, this law sets out a series of processes which are considerably time-consuming and complex, with regard both to the acquisition of a temporary permit as well as a residence permit; each requires an endless list of supporting documents obtainable from numerous bodies. The inefficiency of this defensive–type restrictive policy, whose law-enforcement measures and bureaucratic mechanism resulted neither in the exit of immigrants from the country nor in the prevention of new immigrants, from entry forced the state to adopt the First Legalization Program.

For the purpose of implementing the *First Legalization Program 1997*, Presidential Decrees 358/1997 and 359/1997 were issued, which initiated the process of legalizing the, until then, illegal foreigners. The First Legalization Program set forth on a first level the census of immigrants, and their partial legalization, on a second level. During the first stage, 370,000 illegal foreigners filed applications for temporary residence permits (a white card, with a three-month validity period). Out of the 370,000, 213,000 obtained a temporary residence permits and proceeded with the process of legalization by moving on to the second stage. At this stage, they could obtain a "green card", provided that they had completed a certain number of working days; the validity period of the green card ranged from one to three years, depending on the case concerned.

Law 2910/2001 paved the way for the *Second Legalization Program*, offering foreigners, who already resided illegally in Greece, a second chance to become legal. Furthermore, Law 2910/2001 laid down a series of rights, such as access to education for all immigrant children, equal rights between Greeks and third country foreigners regarding legal employment and social insurance, assistance with family reunification processes, etc. Finally, xenophobic or racist attitudes attained the status of criminal offences for the first time. Within three months, 351,000 foreigners filed applications in order to obtain, at a first stage, a temporary residence permits, with a six-month validity period.

Law 3304/2005, entitled "Equal Treatment at Work, Employment and the Provision of Goods and Services" was introduced next; it incorporated the European Directives 2000/43/EC and 2000/78/EC[1] into the Greek legislation. According to Article 16 of Law 3304/2005, whoever infringed the prohibition of discrimination on the grounds of ethnic or racial origin or religious or other beliefs, would be punished with 6-month to 3-year imprisonment, and a fine amounting to 1,000 to 5,000 Euros.

Finally, Law 3386/2005 introduced a *Third Legalization Program* and laid down new requirements for the acquisition of a residence permit. A residence permit could be granted to third country foreigners (on condition that they did not pose a danger to the country's public order and

---

[1] Directive 2000/78/EC insists on combating all forms of discrimination in employment and occupation which may be based on religious beliefs, disability, age and sexual orientation, while Directive 2000/43/EC foresees protection from discrimination as a result of ethnic or racial origin or religion with regard to the provision of goods and services.

security) who had been residing in Greece up until the 31ˢᵗ of December 2004. Law 3386/2005 excluded the possibility of legalization for those who had been residing in Greece for years but did not possess certain documents, such as a passport or identity card. Moreover, foreigners who entered the country after the 31ˢᵗ of December 2004 were also excluded from this process. With regard to family reunification, the applicant, having submitted the documents providing evidence of the fact that he or she had been residing in the country legally and continuously over the past two years, was to submit a form of tax return which would prove that he or she had a stable income, sufficient to maintain the members of his or her family. Chapter XII of Law 3386/2005, entitled "Social Inclusion", reiterates the right regarding the "equal participation of third country foreigners in the economic, social and cultural life of the country…in conjunction with the maintenance of their national identity"; meanwhile, it sets out an "Integrated Action Program" which provides for the following: (a) certified knowledge of the Greek language, (b) successful attendance of introductory classes regarding the history, culture and the way of life within the Greek society, (c) integration into the Greek labour market and (d) active social participation. It is true that the current Law 3386/2005 has obvious advantages in comparison with the previous process, since it foresees simpler procedures regarding legalization.

On November 12ᵗʰ, 2007 the Ministry of Interior, Public Administration and Decentralization published the "Integrated Action Program for the sound adjustment and social inclusion of third country nationals residing in the Greek Territory", entitled "ESTIA Program". The completion of the Program was accompanied by the establishment of the General Directorate for Immigration Policy and Social Inclusion of the Ministry of Interior. Its responsibilities were to participate in policy-planning with regard to issues pertaining to the social inclusion of third country citizens/nationale, and other vulnerable social groups. The ESTIA Program aimed at fostering social cohesion by accepting differences and fully respecting Human Rights.

3. Pastoral care for inmigrants

As a result of the inflow of a large number of economic immigrants with different views and religious beliefs, the Orthodox Church, which includes about 93-95% of the Greek people, was faced with an unprecedented reality. On the one hand, the Orthodox Church, could of course, not remain insensitive to the severe survival problems faced by these people, who would on a daily basis, and especially during Sundays, gather outside churches and beg for money or for a job. On the other hand, many members of the Orthodox Church, both clergy and secular, were skeptical about this wave of immigration, since they began to realize that the different racial and religious identity of immigrants paved the way for a profound change in the structure of Greek society, which until then, by virtue of its solid racial and religious uniformity, had constituted a significantly favorable ground for the Orthodox Church. Eventually, despite the fact that incidents of xenophobia and racism were not absent within church circles, the Orthodox Church has generally responded in many instances to the financial needs of immigrants either occasionally or more systematically, by providing food, clothes, medication, feeding, psychological support and generally with any form of assistance for their initial settlement, job–finding or repatriation. There are parishes where thousands of food portions are offered to refugees and immigrants every day. Economic immigrants reside in, are treated or work at church institutions for the elderly, orphans, unemployed people etc. More than five thousand priests, seculars and volunteers have been sensitized and mobilized for the provision of these services.

In the context of its organized efforts, the Church of Greece has also established the *Special Synodical Committee for Immigrants, Refugees and Repatriates*, which operates under the provisions of the Church Regulation 172/2006. This Committee, which comprises 9 members (clergy and secular), is an advisory body of the Church of Greece on issues regarding the pastoral response to problems of survival, coexistence and social, cultural and religious inclusion of immigrants or refugees. The aim of the Committee is to ensure that the Church contributes to the social and cultural inclusion of immigrants through "fundamental principles and values, such as mutual tolerance, recognition and respect towards other human beings which also constitute the basic principles of Christian teaching".

We certainly believe that an inter-church or inter-religious body would assist much more effectively in attaining the aforementioned goals.

At this point it should be noted that the Muslim religion constitutes a special issue case in point. Misunderstandings and insulting comments regarding religion and the holy texts should not be allowed to arise. On the other hand, because of the fact that these people are highly devoted to their rigid religion, it goes without saying that they should be assisted by the state in terms of worship. Thus, mosques need to exist. However, there should be no interference whatsoever from foreign states, and Islam should not be taught by people who consistently disrupt public order.

4. Sociological data

Nowadays, about 80% of immigrants to Greece belong to the age group 15-64, which means that they are a potentially active population in economic terms. According to a recent survey, 90% of foreigners work on a contract of employment basis, and only 6.5% of them are self-employed. About 25% of immigrants are employed in the building sector, 20% usually in the field of home services, elderly- and child-care, 17.5% in the agricultural sector, and a little more than 15% in the field of tourism and commercial services.

Out of the 762,000 registered foreigners, more than half (438,000, 57% of the total number) are Albanian citizens. They are followed by Bulgarians (35,000), Georgians (about 20,000), Romanians (about 20,000), Russians (17,500), Ukrainians, Pakistani, Indians, Polish, etc.

In several surveys Greeks are depicted as xenophobic and distrustful people, over 80% of whom are negative towards immigrants in their country while 79.2% believe, that any foreigner committing the slightest offence should be immediately deported. 82.2% of them prefer a country where almost everybody shares the same customs and traditions, while 57.9% think that cultural life is undermined by the presence of foreigners and 61.7% that foreigners worsen living conditions within the country. At the same time, the importance of religion as a life-value amounts to the highest average European-wide (83%, with the Portuguese next with 58%). The findings of the survey can be explained. Over the past 180 years, our country's primary national vision has been national integration; this vision was based (as has been the case in the rest of the Balkan Peninsula) on nationalism. Of course the threats we were faced with in the past were real, and the dangers substantial; this may in part explain the fear and caution towards "the other". However, Greek expatriates have had no difficulty in adapting to different cultures, cooperating with other nationalities, adopting practices and customs different to their own and eventually enriching their own, experiences and culture.

5. Conclusions

In Greece we find ourselves at a stage where we are trying to smooth the relations between the State and immigrants; as is well-known, this is a stage marked by numerous problems. Immigrants are excluded for reasons associated with the State; for instance, immigrants experience instability and fear in their lives, they have no access to information, the law is very strictly enforced in terms of their obligations, while their rights are frequently ignored, they are not protected from employers and there is a host of other problems. All these turn immigrants into vulnerable unprotected persons and this eventually leads to marginalization and exclusion on the one hand, and exposes them to forms of exploitation on the other.

The European society does not seem to have come up with a clear viewpoint on the issue of immigration. We could probably say that there are certain discrepancies in the attitude and stance both of the official bodies of the European Union, as well as the so-called civil society: on the one hand, everyone is aware of the fact that Europe needs immigrants for a number of reasons, while, on the other hand, a mindset of xenophobic is fostered; the presence of immigrants is interpreted by many as a potential social, economic and cultural threat; thus, a policy of "closed borders" is followed.

In particular with regard to Greece, the uncontrolled inflow of foreigners, along with growing financial problems, are expected to lead to serious social conflicts. For this reason, it is deemed essential that an effective immigration policy be put in place. The Greek authorities are called upon to: (a) clarify the number and expertise that the country can absorb, and (b) clarify whether the country is an assimilation or host country, namely whether we accept foreigners for a certain period of time or for permanent residence.

For their part, immigrants should also understand that within the Greek society that hosts them, they need to respect the values and customs of the host country rather than impose their own on it. Whoever is not fond of this idea may always return to his other country of origin (it should be noted at this point that the "shariah", namely the holy Muslim law, is not applied in Greece). Therefore, any protests or vandalism on the grounds of violation of certain rules or symbols which may be considered holy, constitute an insult to the principles and values of the host country. The host country is thus entitled to respond.

European governments and non-governmental organizations frequently criticize Greece for the living conditions of illegal immigrants.
Such conditions are often appalling, yet it is profoundly hypocritical to
criticize and reprimand a country which is under the heaviest pressure in
this regard, and in practice incurs the highest cost in terms of absorbing
the flow of illegal immigrants from central and northern Europe. It
should be noted that Greece, which is on the front line, is receiving only
a negligible proportion of the related community funds. And yet, Greece
does apologize for this and puts in place new and exemplary welcome
and host centers. The truth is that the inflow of illegal immigrants is so
great that even if the government allocated huge funds it would not be
possible to ensure humane living conditions.

BALÁZS SCHANDA

IMMIGRATION AND RELIGION IN HUNGARY

Hungary has not been a country of immigration for the past century. Back in the 19th century a significant Jewish immigration, and in the 18th century an organized German immigration can be mentioned the latter partly to increase the proportion of Catholics at that time in the country. Over 5% of the population of Hungary in the late 19th had left for the United States of America. The 20th century was characterized by subsequent waves of emigration: much of the political and cultural elite of the country had to flee dictatorships in the 1940's, and later after the breakdown of the 1956 revolution. A significant number of surviving Jewry had left the country in 1956 – otherwise 20th century cross-border migration has been religion-neutral: governed by ethnic, political and economic factors. As post World War I border arrangements had cut off 1/3 of the ethnic Hungarian population of (what has been left of) Hungary, ethnic Hungarians from the neighbouring countries (especially from Romania, Serbia, and the Ukraine) continue to move to Hungary.

1. Legal provisions to facilitate or to limit immigration

Article 65 of the Constitution provides for the right of asylum:

(1) In accordance with the conditions established by law, the Republic of Hungary shall, if neither their country of origin nor another country provides protection, extend the right of asylum to foreign citizens who, in their native country or the country of their usual place of residence, are subject to persecution on the basis of race or nationality, their alliance with a specific social group, religious or political conviction, or whose fear of being subject to persecution is well founded.

(2) A majority of two-thirds of the votes of the Members of Parliament present is required to pass the law on the right to asylum.

The law on the right to asylum was passed in 2007 (Act LXXX/2007).

Hungary is a landlocked country that has had no colonies. Although the country is believed to be on the crossroads between Eastern and

Western Europe, the moderate living standard (and the language barrier) does not make the country appealing for immigrants. Policies and attitudes to immigrants cannot be described as welcoming. Demographic trends – low birth rates – make immigration inevitable, but the society is certainly not ready to integrate large numbers of immigrants who have a different cultural background. Policies towards ethnic Hungarian minorities in the neighbouring countries are twofold: on the one hand, their integration into Hungarian society raises absolutely no difficulties; on the other hand, it is regarded as of national interest that Hungarian minorities stay in their country of citizenship. Consequently, their settling in Hungary is not encouraged, but if they decide to settle in the country their rapid integration is promoted. Article 6, section (3) of the Constitution provides for their status:

(3) The Republic of Hungary bears a sense of responsibility for the fate of Hungarians living outside its borders and shall promote and foster their relations with Hungary.

It has to be noted, that in Hungary (in Hungarian) distinction is made between nationality and citizenship. As the cultural-historical concept of the nation remains dominant Hungarian citizens are not necessarily Hungarians, whereas Hungarians (living in successor states) are not necessarily Hungarian citizens. Traditional national and ethnic minorities – existing in the country for at least a century – (Armenians, Bulgarians, Croats, Germans, Gipsies, Polish, Romanians, Ruthenians, Serbs, Slovaks, Slovenes, Ukrainians) are regarded as "constituent part" of the State, having collective rights. New immigrant communities cannot enjoy the status of national minorities.

2. Resident aliens

On December 31, 2008 there were 184,568 resident aliens in Hungary (ten years earlier this figure was 148,263). 47,205 of them had immigrant status, 28,522 a domicile, 15,304 a residence permit (proportion decreasing), 30,579 an EEA residence permit (proportion increasing), 48,527 had a certificate of registration, whereas a few more had different categories for residing (for example, non-EEA citizen being a family member of resident EEA-citizens).[1] The proportion of resident aliens is

---

[1] Statistics of the Office of Immigration and Nationality www.bmbah.hu (July 5, 2009)

under 2% on average, but certainly among younger age groups – especially among men – their proportion is higher. In 2008 34,800 applications for residence permits were issued, including EU citizens moving to Hungary. Close to 40% of those settling as aliens are from Romania, 10% from the Ukraine, close to 10% from Serbia – most of them ethnic Hungarians, not "real" foreigners. 23,365 resident aliens were from Asia (over ten thousand from China), 3,557 from the Americas (2/3rd from the US), 1,913 from Africa.[2] Less than 5% of the applications for resident status are rejected.

The religious affiliation of those applying for residence cannot be collected. There are some registered religious communities that are affiliated to a particular national group of aliens (from Koreans to Anglicans). Certain denominations provide special pastoral care for migrants, e.g. in Budapest there is a Polish, a Croat, a German and an Italian Catholic personal parish, and services are offered in a number of other languages.

Immigration law has not become an issue of wide-scale public discussion so far, but theoretical immigration policies have reached the level of political debate. Centre-to-right parties were outraged by a study prepared in early 2007 on the migration strategy of the government that envisaged the integration of a million Asian immigrants. Although the government denied endorsing the paper, generally it can be stated that centre-to-left parties are more open to immigration than centre-to-right parties (and voters).

Immigrating groups do not constitute communities that would claim to live according to their own legal regime. Personal jurisdictions based on religion or on ethnicity would not be reconcilable with the Constitution.

3. Acquisition of citizenship

Naturalisation requirements are 8 years residence in the country (ethnic Hungarians can seek citizenship immediately after acquiring residence), adequate living conditions, and absence of a criminal record, and successful examination in Hungarian on constitutional and cultural issues. Refugees can seek Hungarian citizenship after 5 years of residence. Applicants under 18, and over 65, are exempt from examination, as well as those who have obtained a degree in higher education in the Hungarian language (not necessarily in Hungary).

[2] http://portal.ksh.hu/pls/ksh/docs/hun/xstadat/xstadat_eves/tabl1_06ib.html?571

There are no statistics on the religious affiliation of new citizens. One cannot speak about significant changes in the religious configuration due to naturalization, but certainly the religious diversity of the country is growing due to migration, including a rise in the Muslim population. This phenomenon, however, is still hardly visible.

The number of naturalizations has been under ten thousand per year in the last decade, for a population of about 10million. Most new citizens are ethnic Hungarians: over 60% of naturalizations are granted to Romanian citizens, further 1-10% to Serbian and Ukrainian citizens – immigrants from these countries are predominantly ethnic Hungarians belonging to the Catholic or the Reformed Church which are traditional denominations for Hungarians. The only measurable change is the emergence of the Unitarian Church in Hungary – traditionally (since the 16th century) this has been a denomination of a part of the ethnic Hungarian population in Transylvania (since 1920 Romania).

Citizenship for ethnic Hungarians in neighbouring countries has been a highly emotional topic of discussion for years (in the region a number of countries e.g. Croatia, Romania, Serbia, Slovakia provide citizenship at the demand of the applicant, without regard to his residence on an ethnic basis). Whereas the conservative side is rather in favour of the naturalization (the dual citizenship) of Hungarians without moving to Hungary, the centre-to-left/liberal side is rather fearful of granting citizenship to Hungarians cut off from the country. The right to vote and to stand for election is bound to residence in Hungary, but Hungarians in the neighbouring countries are believed to be more conservative than in Hungary itself; what could this mean if they were allowed to take part in elections? their say could be determinative. New citizens in the country at present do not constitute closed communities. Probably ethnic Hungarians rather tend to vote right, whereas others rather tend to be apolitical. No non-ethnic Hungarian new citizen or recent immigrant has made a political career so far.

4. The legal regulation of asylum

Hungary joined the Refugee Convention in 1989 applying a remarkable reservation: until 1998 the geographic scope was limited to Europe, refugees from oversees were not accepted (in 2008 43% of asylum seekers had been from oversees, in 2007 66%). Detailed legislation on asylum was passed in 2007. Recognized refugees have practically the same legal status as citizens.

In 2008 there were over 3,118 refuge seekers (of whom 2,879 arrived illegally). In 2000-2002 the number of refugee seekers had been significantly higher (over 9,000 in 2001), mainly due to Afghani, Bangladeshi and Iraqi asylum seekers.[3] Only a small portion – about 5% – of asylum seekers are granted refugee status (in 2008 160 from 3,118).[4] Usually it is not – or not only – the religious affiliation of the applicant that is a ground of application for asylum.

Humanitarian right of residence (a kind of protected status) can be provided if the application for refugee status is turned down but the applicant has a well-founded fear of returning to his country of origin. The status embraces family members too.

5. Churches and asylum

On January 14, 2009 a group of Afghani asylum seekers occupied the Saint Steven Basilica, the Catholic co-cathedral of Budapest. After a few hours they left the church without violence, and returned to the refugee camp of Debrecen (about 200 km from Budapest). Probably, the action was meant to attract media attention to the situation of asylum seekers rather than to prevent deportation. As the social relevance of the issues is not especially high, the issue of church asylum has not emerged so far. Churches do not enjoy any kind of territorial exemption (in earlier legal regimes church asylum was regarded as an instrument of criminal procedure, but not for refugees) and consequently have no legal basis for providing asylum. It is to be noted, that after the occupation of Hungary by Nazi Germany on the 19th of March, 1944, the Apostolic Nuntiature, a number of Catholic religious orders and also some Protestant ministers provided asylum for Hungarian Jews and saved lives this way.

6. Pastoral assistance to illegal immigrants

Illegal immigrants and asylum seekers have the right to stay in touch with the minister of their religion, and adequate space for worship has to be provided in facilities for asylum seekers. Refugee camps (all at former military barracks) are equipped with prayer rooms adequate for Muslims.

[3] http://portal.ksh.hu/pls/ksh/docs/hun/xstadat/xstadat_eves/tabl1_07ia.html?191
[4] http://portal.ksh.hu/pls/ksh/docs/hun/xstadat/xstadat_eves/tabl1_08i.html

There is no special pastoral assistance given to illegal immigrants. Refugee seekers do not belong to the mainstream denominations of the country. The issue does not rank as a significant social problem.

7. United family – marriage issues

Family unity is a guiding principle of the regulation of citizenship, residence permits and, also, that of granting humanitarian residence.

So far no cases have been publicised of refugee seekers living in polygamous or forced marriages.

8. Employment of Non-EU Citizens – clergy

Foreigners need a work permit (EU-citizens only need to register) in order to be employed in Hungary (residence permits are issued after an employment permit has been granted). The labour market in a given sector of the economy can be considered when employment permits are granted. The number of foreign workers in Hungary is somewhat over 50,000. The maximum figure at present as set by the government is 83,000.

Clergy usually are in the service of church and do not work on a labour contract. Ecclesiastical service is exempt from general labour regulations. Consequently, for clergy (the Hungarian terminology speaks about "ecclesiastical persons" defined by the religious community itself – embracing, definitely, a wider circle than clergy in traditional denominations) there is no need for an employment permit. Residence permits for church staff do not raise difficulties.

MAIREAD ENRIGHT

IMMIGRATION AND RELIGION IN IRELAND

1. Introduction

Historically, Ireland has been a country of emigration and emigration figures were very high until the late 1980's. Inward and outward migration
were in balance until the mid-1990s, at which point inward migration
began to grow steadily, in line with the country's rapid economic development[1]. With the economic downturn, emigration – of Irish citizens and
migrants to Ireland – has again increased; rising by 40% in 2009 at the
same time as immigration fell[2]. Although there is no 'traditional' country
of origin for migrants to Ireland, there has been a large influx of nationals
from the new EU member states since 2004. In 2007, nationals of the EU
New Member States accounted for 48 per cent of all immigrants to Ireland[3]. The policy discourse favoured by the government explicitly avoids
a 'rights-based' approach to immigration and in consequence administration of the asylum and immigration regime is heavily grounded in government discretion. In recent years, successive governments have framed
their concerns in terms of (1) a 'law and order' commitment to preserve
social order and the integrity of the state[4] (2) a 'morally freighted' acceptance of the state's obligation to offer limited protection to defined categories of deserving vulnerable migrant, with an accompanying 'mirror
image' determination to deny protection to 'undeserving' migrants who

[1] Quinn et. al. *Handbook on Immigration and Asylum in Ireland 2007* (Dublin, 2008)
6. Available at http://www.esri.ie/UserFiles/publications/20081218125059/RS005.pdf;
See also http://www.migrationinformation.org/USfocus/display.cfm?ID=740
[2] CSO, *Annual Population and Migration Estimates* (Dublin, 2009). Available at
www.cso.ie%2Freleasespublications%2Fdocuments%2Fpopulation%2Fcurrent%2Fpop
mig.pdf&ei=NDmLS-GeHJL-0gTDoKjVCw&usg=AFQjCNFVFIb8ep-Cox2GxcNNgRI
dM14sMw&sig2=v578DN8KuRdAuo5dPIXfng
[3] Quinn et. al. *Handbook on Immigration and Asylum in Ireland 2007* (Dublin, 2008)
7. Available at http://www.esri.ie/UserFiles/publications/20081218125059/RS005.pdf
[4] The courts have repeatedly confirmed that the operation of immigration controls in
the interests of the common good is one of the most important functions of government
Bode (A Minor) v. MJELR and Ors [2007] IESC 62; *Pok Sun Shun v Ireland* [1986]
ILRM 593, 599; *Osheku v. Ireland* [1986] I.R. 733, 746; *Article 26 Referral of the Illegal
Immigrants (Trafficking) Bill 1999* [2000] 2 IR 360; *FP v. Minister for Justice* [2002] 1
IR 164 and *AO and DL v. Minister for Justice, Equality and Law Reform* [2003] 1 IR 1.

attempt to bring themselves within those categories[5] and (3) a 'fiscal' project of shaping inward migration to the perceived needs of the national economy, while meeting those needs, by and large from within the EEA. The imperatives of the immigration regime captured by point (2) are often firmly subordinated to those captured in points (1) and (3).

Until quite recently, the basic legislation governing the entry and residence of non-Irish nationals in Ireland was the Aliens Act 1935 and the Aliens Order, 1946, as amended. The Regulations implementing the EU Rights of Residence Directives came into effect when Ireland joined the EEC in 1973. In recent years, however, a number of new legislative measures have been introduced -in a reactive and piecemeal fashion- to deal with immigration and asylum; the Refugee Act 1996; the Immigration Acts 1999, 2003 and 2004; the Illegal Immigrants (Trafficking) Act 2000; and the Employment Permits Acts 2003 and 2006. The Immigration, Residence and Protection Bill, 2008 was published in January 2008. With the exception of some highly skilled professionals, the vast majority of non-EEA migrants to Ireland cannot enter the country as economic migrants. Accordingly, there is a palpable division – in terms of regions of origin – between those who have come to Ireland via the asylum system and its offshoots and those who have entered the country as migrant workers. This division will become more distinct as Ireland seeks to maintain a flexible regime for desirable labour migrants at a time of competition for skilled workers, while limiting the 'perceived burden' to which the state is exposed by undocumented migrants.

The most recent development in Irish immigration legislation is the Immigration, Residence and Protection Bill, 2008 which sets out a new legislative framework for the management of inward migration to Ireland. The Bill, which is currently awaiting Report Stage in Parliament lays down a number of important principles governing the presence in the State of foreign nationals. It sets out new statutory processes for visa applications, for entry to the State, for residence in the State and for deportation. Several hundred amendments to the Bill have been proposed and it is difficult to predict its final shape. However, it may be said of the Bill that, in attempting to address issues of protection and of general immigration simultaneously, it betrays a certain lack in Irish understanding of the complex nature of international migration. The relevant elements of the reform proposals will be highlighted in the course of this chapter.

---

[5] Tormey, 'Anyone With Eyes Can See The Problem' (2007) 45(3) *International Migration* 69.

There has been no serious consideration of religious issues at the level of immigration legislation but this is not to suggest that there is no 'religion story' to be told about immigration to Ireland. Although the vast majority of Irish residents remain Christian; the greatest proportion of whom are Roman Catholic[6], immigration has brought about some some change in the country's religious configuration[7]. Members of Orthodox churches, as well as members of Apostolic and Pentecostal churches now make up a substantial proportion of Ireland's Christians and are the sixth largest religious community in the country[8]. Ireland's Orthodox Christians are largely of European origin[9], especially Russian, Ukrainian and Latvian[10]. Muslims are the third largest religious community in Ireland[11]. Most are of African and Asian origin. Nigeria, Malaysia and Pakistan are the most important countries of origin[12]. However, the 2006 census also reports that roughly 20% of Muslims resident in Ireland were born here or elsewhere in Europe[13] and almost one third are Irish nationals[14]. Orthodox Christians and Muslims saw significant growth in their numbers between the 2002 and 2006 censuses[15]. That said, their communities are in the tens of thousands; a very small fraction of the overall population[16] and they are largely concentrated in urban areas, particularly Dublin[17]. There is a greater diversity of religions in Ireland than had been the case even ten years ago, but the country is still relatively homogenous[18] in matters of faith[19].

[6] CSO, *Census 2006: Volume 13 Religion* (2007, Dublin) 17
[7] For a classification of the population by religion for the censuses 1881-2006 see CSO, *Census 2006: Volume 13 Religion* (2007, Dublin) 7 Available at http://www.cso.ie/census/census2006results/volume_13/volume_13_religion.pdf
[8] CSO, *Census 2006: Volume 13 Religion* (2007, Dublin) 17
[9] CSO, *Census 2006: Volume 13 Religion* (2007, Dublin) 107
[10] CSO, *Census 2006: Volume 13 Religion* (2007, Dublin) 109
[11] CSO, *Census 2006: Volume 13 Religion* (2007, Dublin) 23
[12] CSO, *Census 2006: Volume 13 Religion* (2007, Dublin) 109
[13] CSO, *Census 2006: Volume 13 Religion* (2007, Dublin) 107
[14] CSO, *Census 2006: Volume 13 Religion* (2007, Dublin) 108. 14 Muslims registered in the census identified as Irish-American CSO, *Census 2006: Volume 13 Religion* (2007, Dublin) 109.
[15] CSO, *Census 2006: Volume 13 Religion* (2007, Dublin) 23
[16] CSO, *Census 2006: Volume 13 Religion* (2007, Dublin) 23
[17] CSO, *Census 2006: Volume 13 Religion* (2007, Dublin) 24 and 27
[18] At a policy level, however, the government has acknowledged that many immigrants to Ireland are more actively engaged in religious practice than are Irish citizens of Irish descent. *Migration Nation* (2008, Dublin) at 44. Available at http://www.integration.ie/website/omi/omiwebv6.nsf/page/AXBN-7SQDF91044205-en/$File/Migration%20Nation.pdf
[19] One area of policy in which religious diversity is beginning to make an impact is that of education. In December 2009, the OECD proposed that the state should channel resources into multi-denominational schools in an effort to better cater to non-Catholic

2. The Protection Regime

As at January 2009, 9,730[20] recognised refugees lived in Ireland; a figure which has grown from 64 in 1996[21]. 3,866 applications for refugee status were received in 2008[22]. 4,581 cases were processed by ORAC in that year[23] and refugee status was granted in only 6.4% of these.24 In 2009, 2,689 applications were processed, of which 97 resulted in positive determinations[25]. 2009 saw the lowest annual number of applications since 1997[26]. The majority of applicants, some 60%, were male[27]. In terms of age, roughly half of all applicants were aged between 18 and 35[28]. Nigeria has been the stated country of origin of the largest number of Ireland's asylum seekers for some years[29]. The top six countries of origin for applicants for 2008 were Nigeria, Pakistan, Iraq, Georgia, China and Democratic Republic of the Congo[30].

3. Asylum

The Refugee Act 1996 as amended by the Immigration Act 1999 and the Illegal Immigrants (Trafficking) Act 2000 is the central body of statute on the processing of applications for refugee status in Ireland. The Immigration, Residency and Protection Bill is intended to transpose Directive 2003/9/EC of 27 January 2003 into Irish law. The Refugee Act gives effect to Ireland's obligations under the 1951 Geneva Convention Relating to the Status of Refugees, and the 1967

---

children and children of no religious belief. Taguma et al. *OECD Reviews of Migrant Education in Ireland* (2009, Dublin). Available at http://www.oecd.org/dataoecd/1/50/44344245.pdf. The vast majority of Irish primary schools and the majority of secondary schools are under the patronage of the Catholic church, with the majority of the balance controlled by other religious groups.

[20] http://www.unhcr.org/cgi-bin/texis/vtx/page?page=49e48e926#

[21] Ireland, 2005 UNHCR Statistical Yearbook. Available at http://www.unhcr.org/4641be5b0.html

[22] ORAC, Annual Report (Dublin, 2008) 2. Available at http://www.orac.ie/pdf/PDF-CustService/AnnualReports/2008%20Annual%20Report%20English.pdf

[23] ORAC, Annual Report (Dublin, 2008) 2.

[24] ORAC, Annual Report (Dublin, 2008) 61.

[25] Reception and Integration Agency Monthly Statistics: December 2009 (Dublin, 2009) 2. Available at http://www.ria.gov.ie/filestore/publications/RIADec(A4)2009.pdf

[26] ORAC, Annual Report (Dublin, 2008) 2.

[27] ORAC, Annual Report (Dublin, 2008) 59.

[28] ORAC, Annual Report (Dublin, 2008) 59.

[29] Quinn et. al. *Handbook on Immigration and Asylum in Ireland 2007* (Dublin, 2008) 13.

[30] ORAC, Annual Report (Dublin, 2008) 23.

New York Protocol. The Office of the Refugee Applications Commissioner (ORAC) considers applications for declaration as a refugee at first instance and applications by refugees to allow family members to enter and reside in the state. The Refugee Appeals Tribunal (RAT) considers appeals from recommendations of the ORAC. In 2008, the RAT heard some 2,091 appeals from decisions of ORAC[31]. ORAC was a respondent in 266 civil cases in 2008, most of which were judicial review cases[32]. These offices were established in 2000 and the ultimate purpose of both is to make recommendations to the Minister on the granting of asylum applications[33]. Under the Immigration Act 2003, asylum seekers from certain designated 'safe countries of origin' are presumed not to be entitled to a declaration of refugee status unless they can prove otherwise. Under the 2003 Act the Minister for Justice, Equality and Law Reform is empowered to issue prioritisation directives to the RAC and the RAT. These may require the Commissioner, the Tribunal, or both, to accord priority to a specified category of applicants whose claims are apparently unfounded claims or apparently well-founded claims, and to cases of family reunification. Under s. 13(6) of the 1996 Act a streamlined accelerated appeals regime applies to those applicants found not to be refugees at first instance whose cases display certain features considered to be indicative of abuse of the asylum process. An applicant affected by s. 13(6) loses his entitlement to an oral appeal and has ten working days, instead of the usual fifteen, to appeal a negative status determination. During the applications and appeals process, asylum seekers are housed in 'direct provision' accommodation[34]. To come within s.2 of the 1996 Act, an applicant must demonstrate a well-founded fear of persecution for a Refugee Convention reason, of which his religion may be one. Claims for asylum on the basis of religious persecution appear frequently in the case law[35].

[31] ORAC, Annual Report (Dublin, 2008) 14.
[32] ORAC, Annual Report (Dublin, 2008) 17.
[33] Quinn et. al. *Handbook on Immigration and Asylum in Ireland 2007* (Dublin, 2008) 7. Available at http://www.esri.ie/UserFiles/publications/20081218125059/RS005.pdf
[34] For a critique of the shortcomings in the direct provision system see Thornton, 'On the Limits of Rights Regimes': Reception Conditions of Asylum Seekers in the Republic of Ireland' 24(2) *Refuge* 86 and FLAC, *One Size Doesn't Fit All: A legal analysis of the direct provision and dispersal system, ten years on* (Dublin, 2010) available at
[35] See, for example, *U v. RAT* [2009] IEHC 283 (persecution of Ahmadi Muslims in Pakistan); *C v. RAT* [2007] IEHC 359 (Iranian Muslim convert to Christianity); *A.O. v. RAT* Unreported High Court, 26 May 2004 (marriage between a Nigerian Christian and a Nigerian Muslim convert to Christianity)

4. Subsidiary Protection

S.I. No. 518 of 2006 gives effect to the European Qualification Directive[36], which provides for a system of subsidiary protection. An applicant for subsidiary protection is required to show, inter alia, substantial grounds for believing that he or she, if returned to his or her country of origin, would face a real risk of suffering serious harm. Regulation 2(1) defines serious harm as consisting of (a) the death penalty or execution, (b) torture or inhuman or degrading treatment or punishment, or (c) serious and individual threat to a civilian's life or person by reason of indiscriminate violence in situations of armed conflict. There is no requirement that an applicant show a nexus to a civil or political right or ground.

5. Humanitarian Leave to Remain

A further 'humanitarian' protection option comes into play under s. 17(6) of the Immigration Act, 1999 when asylum and subsidiary protection prove not to be viable options. This section establishes the Minister's discretionary power to grant permission to remain to a person who has been refused a declaration of refugee status. In such cases, the Minister is normally empowered to make a deportation order. In determining whether or not to make the deportation order, he is required, under s. 3(6) of the Act to have regard to a number of factors including representations made by the affected party, humanitarian (including *refoulement* type) considerations, duration of residence in the state and family and domestic circumstances. If, having considered these factors, the Minister decides not to make a deportation order, the individual must be given leave to remain in the state. S. 3(6) is of particular importance where the individual has established family life within the state, as where he is now married to an EU citizen or has become the parent of an Irish-born child. A total of 1,420 people were granted humanitarian leave to remain between 1999 and mid 2007. Almost half were granted the status between 2006 and mid 2007. A person granted leave to remain does not have equivalent rights to a refugee. In particular he has no right as such to family reunification, though he may request that family members be allowed to join him in Ireland[37].

---

[36] Directive 2004/83/EC of 29 April 2004
[37] Quinn et. al. *Handbook on Immigration and Asylum in Ireland 2007* (Dublin, 2008) 7. Available at http://www.esri.ie/UserFiles/publications/20081218125059/RS005.pdf

6. Proposed Unified System

Under the 2008 Bill, the processes for determining asylum applications and applications for subsidiary protection would be merged into a unified process: the Bill specifies that decisions would be made by the Minister in the first instance, who should assess, in order, (1) whether someone is entitled to protection on the grounds that they are eligible for refugee status; (2) whether they are eligible for subsidiary protection; (3) whether the principle of *non-refoulement* under the Geneva Convention requires that they should not be returned to a country where their life may be in danger, and (4) whether there are other 'compelling reasons' they should be granted protection. All of the functions currently performed by ORAC would be divested to the Minister. Applicants for protection would be required to set out all of the grounds on which they wish to remain in the State at the outset of their claim and these would be evaluated together. As the UNHCR has noted[38], 'compelling reasons' does not explicitly include humanitarian considerations and there is some cause for concern that the new protection regime would exclude categories of person who come within the scope of the present regime. The Irish Council for Civil Liberties has also noted that 'compelling reasons' may not give an adequate account of whether a removal is likely to interfere with the family rights of the applicant[39]. The Minister's decisions would be independently reviewable by a Protection Review Tribunal, which would replace the RAT[40]. Further review would be by way of highly-restricted and unattractive judicial review proceedings[41]. Under s.4 of the new Bill a foreign national who enters the State unlawfully or whose presence is in the State is unlawful commits an offence and may be removed without notice (if necessary, following arrest and detention for this purpose). A foreign national will bear the burden of proving the legality of his or her presence in the State Immigration officers and the police would have a power of summary removal where 'it appears' that a person is unlawfully present within the state. A

---

[38] http://www.unhcr.ie/pdf/UNHCR_Comments_IRP_2008.pdf
[39] http://www.iccl.ie/iccl-submission-on-the-immigration-residence-and-protection-bill-2008-(february-2008)-.html
[40] http://www.iccl.ie/iccl-submission-on-the-immigration-residence-and-protection-bill-2008-(february-2008)-.html
[41] See http://www.legalaidboard.ie/lab/publishing.nsf/Content/The_Researcher_February_2008_Article_3. For general criticisms of restrictions on access to justice under the proposed regime see http://www.flac.ie/download/pdf/flac_submission_to_jt_oir_cte_on_irp_bill_march_2008.pdf

number of organisations have expressed concern that the Bill does not take adequate account of the situation of migrants who find themselves illegally in the State through no fault of their own[42].

7. Residency and Citizenship

Ireland is not bound by Directive 2003/109/EC, which obliges Member States to grant long-term resident status to non-EU nationals who have resided legally and continuously within the territory for an appreciable period of time. Outside of the asylum system[43], immigrants to Ireland obtain initial temporary permission to remain[44] via the work permit and green card systems[45]; whether as workers or as the family members of workers[46]. Spouses and adult dependants of work permit holders may also be entitled to work permits. The work permit system is channeled to serve the perceived interest of the Irish economy in preserving certain of its sectors to EEA nationals. Thus, some types of work – including areas such as construction and child-care – are not included within the scheme[47] and before a work permit will be granted, the employer must demonstrate that the vacancy has been extensively advertised on the FAS network and in the Irish press[48]. A work permit will not be granted where to do so would bring the total percentage of a company's workforce which was made up of non-EEA workers above 50%. In addition, the work permit

---

[42] See e.g. http://www.immigrantcouncil.ie/media/irpbilltraffickingamendments.pdf; http://www.oireachtas.ie/viewdoc.asp?fn=/documents/Committees30thDail/JJusticeEDWR/Reports_2008/submission47.doc; http://www.irishrefugeecouncil.ie/media/ Microsoft_Word_-_Submission_by_the_Irish_Refugee_Council_oin_the_Immigration_ Residence_and_Protection_Bill__2_.pdf. See especially http://www.iccl.ie/iccl-submission-on-the-immigration-residence-and-protection-bill-2008-(february-2008)-.html noting that under the summary process, individuals are denied any effective access to the justice system, may be at risk of *refoulement* and may experience radical and disproportionate interference with their rights to private and family life.

[43] The children and grandchildren of Irish nationals may apply for permission to remain 'without condition' http://www.inis.gov.ie/en/INIS/Pages/Without_Condition_Endorsement

[44] Third country nationals seek leave – with the appropriate visa – to enter the state at the border. They will ordinarily be given permission to remain in Ireland for three months or less. A third-country national who intends to remain in Ireland for longer than three months is obliged to obtain the permission of the Minister for Justice, Equality and Law Reform, via the Garda National Immigration Bureau; http://www.inis.gov.ie/en/INIS/ Pages/WP07000022

[45] A green card confers two years' residency, which is renewable year-by-year.

[46] For the catalogue of 'stamps' which correspond to various types of permission to remain in the state see http://www.inis.gov.ie/en/INIS/Pages/Stamps

[47] http://www.entemp.ie/labour/workpermits/elements/ineligible.htm lists 'ineligible jobs'.

[48] http://www.entemp.ie//labour/workpermits/labourmarketneedstest.htm

and green card schemes target workers who earn substantial salaries; €30,000 and above in the case of work permits and €60,000 and above in the case of green cards. The green card scheme is designed to target non-EEA employees in areas where high-level strategic skills shortages exist. These schemes are not designed to permit those who would do lower paid work to enter the country. Where such workers become undocumented through no fault of their own they may apply for a four month 'grace' period within which to seek new employment[49]. Applications for permission to remain in the state on the basis of working for a religious organisation are considered on a case-by-case basis[50]. In 2009, 7.962 work permits were issued to Irish companies, of which over 4,000 were new. 1,901 permits were refused. The six major countries of origin were India, The Philippines, the United States, Malaysia, China and South Africa.

Once an individual has been living in Ireland for a total of five years – otherwise than as a student, asylum seeker or undocumented migrant – they may apply for long-term residency[51]. A long-term resident may live and work in Ireland without a work permit and may take the job of their choice. Residency is renewable after five years. In the alternative, the resident may apply for citizenship or – after 8 years of legal residence in Ireland – 'permission to remain without condition as to time'. Such permission is granted at the Minister's discretion. Section 36 of the Immigration, Residence and Protection Bill makes the granting of long-term residency conditional on meeting a number of standards. The applicant must have been in the country lawfully for at least 5 out of the last 6 years. He must speak a sufficient level of English or Irish and must show that he has made reasonable efforts to integrate. He must also show that he has has during his presence in the State, been supporting himself and any dependants without recourse to certain publicly funded services. He must also be of good character. The Immigrant Council of Ireland[52] and the UNHCR have criticised these provisions on the grounds that they are not clearly defined[53].

---

[49] http://www.entemp.ie//labour/workpermits/undocumented.htm

[50] http://www.inis.gov.ie/en/INIS/Pages/Religious_and_Volunteer_Workers Members of religious orders are often prohibited from entering employment http://www.inis.gov.ie/en/INIS/Pages/Stamps

[51] Special provisions apply to workers who have become redundant by the end of the initial five year period http://www.inis.gov.ie/en/INIS/Pages/New_Provisions_for_Non-EEA_workers

[52] Bekker, 'The Irish Immigration, Residence and Protection Bill – A Critical Overview' (2008) JIANL 246

[53] http://www.unhcr.ie/pdf/UNHCR_Comments_IRP_2008.pdf

The statute governing Irish citizenship is the Irish Nationality and Citizenship Act 1956, as amended. The 1956 Act has been amended by the Irish Nationality and Citizenship Acts 1986, 1994, 2001 and 2004. Non-Irish nationals may acquire citizenship by naturalisation if they have, inter alia, one year of continuous residence along with periods amounting to four years total residence within the eight years prior to their application. The Minister may also, at his absolute discretion[54], grant an application for a certificate of naturalisation in certain categories of case, including with regard to refugees, where the applicant does not meet the conditions for naturalisation. There is no citizenship test, but proposals to develop one have been mooted by the government[55]. The applicant must be of 'good character' – as vouched by the police – and is required to make a declaration of fidelity and loyalty to the State. Under the Irish Nationality and Citizenship Act 2001, spouses of Irish citizens can naturalise by a declaration of citizenship where the marriage took place before November 30, 2002. Where the marriage took place after that date, the non-Irish national spouse may be able to naturalise at the Minister's 'absolute discretion' if s/he, inter alia, has resided for one year in Ireland and during the four years prior to application lived in Ireland for a total of two years or more[56]. The Immigrant Council of Ireland has noted that an extraordinarily high number of citizenship applications are refused each year and has criticised the citizenship regime as unpredictable and mired in the ambiguity that comes with substantial discretion[57].

It was formerly the case that Irish citizenship was acquired automatically upon birth in the island of Ireland. This position was formerly enshrined in Article 2 of the Constitution. Non-Irish parents of Irish-born children could apply for residency on the basis of their child's citizenship[58]. This possibility was confirmed in *Fajujonu*[59]. The Supreme Court held in that case that while 'parents who are not citizens

---

[54] *Pok Sun Shun vs. Ireland* [1986] ILRM 593, High Court; *Mishra vs. Minister for Justice* [1996] 1 IR 189, High Court.

[55] http://www.guardian.co.uk/education/2008/nov/14/ireland-english-teaching; http://www.kildarestreet.com/debate/?id=2009-09-22.136.5

[56] Where it is proven that the marriage was not subsisting at the time of the application, a certificate of naturalisation may be revoked; *Akram vs. Minister for Justice*,21 December 1999, High Court, unreported.

[57] http://www.immigrantcouncil.ie/press_detail.php?id=122

[58] See more fully http://rightsmonitor.org/wp-content/uploads/2008/07/immigrant_council_of_ireland-submission_to_the_un_human_rights_committee-may_2008.doc.

[59] [1990] ILRM 234

and who are aliens cannot, by reason of their having as members of their family children born in Ireland who are citizens, claim any constitutional right of a particular kind to remain in Ireland, they are entitled to assert a choice of residence on behalf of their infant children, in the interests of those infant children.' That entitlement was, of course, not absolute, but the State was obliged, in seeking to deport the parent of an Irish citizen child, to demonstrate a 'grave and substantial reason associated with the common good' for doing so. It was not possible to do so in *Fajujonu*, especially as the family had made its 'home and residence' in Ireland for a significant time. Following *Fajujonu*, applications were granted as a matter of course, but as numbers of applications grew, the state sought to limit this avenue to residency. In 2003, in *A.O. v. D.O. v. Minister for Justice*[60] the Supreme Court effectively refined *Fajunjonu*, noting that the Minister, in assessing the case against removal of the parent of an Irish citizen child from the State was 'undoubtedly entitled to take into account the policy considerations which would arise from allowing a particular applicant to remain where that would inevitably lead to similar decisions in other cases, again undermining the orderly administration of the immigration and asylum system.' This was not restriction enough for a government which sought to cut *Fajujonu* off at the root. Parental residency applications were suspended in 2003, and a year later, following a referendum to amend the constitution, the Irish Nationality and Citizenship Act 2004 was passed to eliminate this path to residency. Now the position is that a child will not automatically acquire Irish citizenship upon birth unless one of the parents was lawfully resident in Ireland for at least three out of the four years preceding the child's birth. Some 17,000 non-Irish parents of Irish-born children were subsequently granted leave to remain in Ireland under the Irish Born Child 2005 scheme[61], which was designed to clarify the position of parents whose applications had been suspended in 2003. This scheme has now run its course[62]. The law now appears to be that the Minister is required to take account – in the course of consideration of an application for leave to remain on humanitarian or other grounds– of the impact that deportation will have on the family life which exists between the Irish-born or Irish citizen child and his

---

[60] [2003] 1 IR 1
[61] See generally, Integration Ireland, *Looking Forward, Looking Back* (Dublin, 2007)
[62] In early 2010, the Immigrant Council of Ireland highlighted administrative difficulties with the renewal of parents' residence permits under the Irish Born Child Scheme; http://www.immigrantcouncil.ie/press_detail.php?id=121

relatives[63]. The 'compelling reasons' proposals in the 2008 Bill, if effective, would effectively sever the last tenuous link between a parental connection to an Irish child and a right to reside in Ireland.

8. Family Reunification[64]

EU Council Directive 2003/86/EC on the right to family reunification does not apply in Ireland. Under s.18 of the 1996 Refugee Act, Minister is obliged to grant permission to the family members of refugees to enter and reside in the State. Family members for the purposes of this Section are a refugee's spouse, his or her parents if the refugee is under 18 years of age, and any unmarried children under 18 years of age. The Minister has discretion to grant permission to certain dependent members of the family of a refugee. ORAC received 408 applications for Family Reunification in 2008, an increase of 9.4% over the 2007 figure[65]. 3,431 such applications have been received since 2001; 260 of these in the first seven months of 2009[66]. The top six applicant nationalities in the first 7 months of this year were Sudan, Somalia, Iraq, Nigeria, Zimbabwe and the Democratic Republic of Congo[67]. There is no legislation in Ireland governing the entitlements to family reunification of non-EU migrants – such as long-term residents, those who have permission to remain 'without condition as to time' or migrants who benefit from the protection regime other than as refugees – or of Irish citizens who seek to be reunited with relatives who are not EU citizens. This does not mean that family reunification does not take place in these cases. Instead, family reunification[68] is governed by an administrative scheme, connected to the visa and residency regimes. The precise terms of the reunification scheme have never been published. Section 4 of the Immigration Act, 2004 requires an immigration officer to have regard to the family relationships an applicant for reunification has with people already resident in Ireland in deciding whether to grant them permission to enter the

[63] *Bode v. Minister for Justice* [2006] IEHC 341; *Oguekwe v. Minister for Justice, Equality & Law Reform* [2008] 3 IR 795 and *Dimbo v. Minister for Justice, Equality & Law Reform* [2008] IESC 23
[64] See generally Immigrant Council of Ireland, *Family Matters* (Dublin, 2006)
[65] ORAC, Annual Report (Dublin, 2008) 14.
[66] ORAC, Monthly Statistics: July 2009 (Dublin, 2009) 7
[67] ORAC, Monthly Statistics: July 2009 (Dublin, 2009) 8
[68] Individuals in a de facto relationship with an Irish national for two or more years, or with a non EEA Irish resident fo r four or more years may apply for permission to remain; http://www.inis.gov.ie/en/INIS/Pages/WP07000278

country. Beyond that, no further statement of family reunification policy in respect of non-refugee migrants is available, with one exception: applications made by parents who gained residency under the Irish-born Child Scheme for family reunification have frequently been rejected on the basis of 'government policy'[69]. The present system is vulnerable to arbitrary decisions and inconsistencies[70] and undermines rights to private and family life enshrined in domestic and international law. The Council of Europe Commissioner for Human Rights made precisely this criticism in his 2008 Report[71]. Delay in processing applications has also proved significantly troublesome[72]. There is no appeals mechanism beyond judicial review in the High Court, which is a costly and cumbersome process. No specific family reunification provisions have been included in the 2008 Bill. Recent practice in the State has been to allow family reunification for children of a person with a protection status in the State without allowing the spouse or "the other parent of these children" to accompany them, because the couple was not formally married or their married is not considered valid in the State. Such practices would not be in line with the principle of family unity[73].

Section 123 of the 2008 Bill appears to be designed with the intention of preventing 'marriages of convenience'[74]. Section 123 (2) provides that a marriage contracted in Ireland between two people, one or both of whom is a foreign national, will be invalid in law unless they give at least three months' notice to the Minister of their intention to marry. In addition, the foreign national, or both of them, will have to be "the holder of an entry permission issued for the purpose of the intended marriage or a residence permission (other than a protection application entry permission or a non-renewable residence permission)". The effect is that asylum seekers and those on a non-renewable residence permit would not be permitted to marry in the State, even where they intend to marry

---

[69] Minister Michael McDowell, T.D., Parliamentary Debates (Official Report-Unrevised) Joint Committee on Justice, Equality, Defence and Women's Rights on Wednesday, 14 December 2005 (Vol. No. 106).

[70] For further detail see http://www.immigrantcouncil.ie/images/7509_familymatters. pdf

[71] https://wcd.coe.int/com.instranet.InstraServlet?Index=no&command=com. instranet.CmdBlobGet&InstranetImage=879058&SecMode=1&DocId=1272888&Usage=2

[72] T (PO) v Minister for Justice [2008] IEHC 361

[73] http://www.unhcr.ie/pdf/UNHCR_Comments_IRP_2008.pdf

[74] The Garda National Immigration Bureau has also begun to devote significant resources to preventing 'sham marriages'. See e.g. http://www.irishtimes.com/newspaper/ireland/2010/0126/1224263119350.html

an Irish or EU citizen. The Minister could refuse permission under s. 123(4) where the marriage would [a]dversely affect the implementation of an earlier decision under the Act, [c]reate a factor bearing on a decision yet to be taken under the legislation relating to one or both of those parties, not be in the interests of public security, public policy or public order or affect the implementation of a decision under the Irish Nationality and Citizenship Acts 1956 to 2004 or the European Communities (Free Movement of Persons (No2) Regulations 2006 (S.I. No. 656 of 2006).' The Bill gives the Minister general discretion not to apply the requirement to whomsoever he chooses and does so in extremely ambiguous terms[75]. Section 123(7) seeks to impose criminal sanctions upon anyone who solemnises, facilitates or is a party to a form of marriage which requires the Minister's permission where that permission has not been sought. These powers are held in addition to those which the Bill would confer upon the Minister to refuse or withdraw a residence permit in circumstances where a marriage has been contracted for the purposes of circumventing immigration restrictions. The Immigrant Council of Ireland has argued that s. 123 represents a disproportionate infringement on the right to marry, and that, in addition '[t]he Government runs the risk of criminalising ministers of religion who consider the right to marry members of their congregation as essential to their religious beliefs and, in addition to infringing the fundamental right to marry, this constitutes a potential infringement of the right to freedom of religion as protected under Article 9 of the European Convention on Human Rights and Fundamental Freedoms and Article 44 of the Irish Constitution'[76]. This provision will likely not survive constitutional challenge – in all probability it infringes the constitutionally protected right to marry, rights of religious freedom and the constitutional equality guarantee – but its existence indicates the approach of the Irish government to accommodation of family and religious life within the immigration system: both appear to be viewed with a certain suspicion, as chinks in the armour of immigration law[77].

9. Religious and Cultural Practices in Marriage

As regards specifically religious problems, there are acknowledged difficulties with the recognition of African customary and traditional

[75] http://www.immigrantcouncil.ie/images/8470_091008_ACJRDpaper.pdf
[76] http://www.immigrantcouncil.ie/images/8470_091008_ACJRDpaper.pdf
[77] http://www.immigrantcouncil.ie/images/8470_091008_ACJRDpaper.pdf

marriages and potentially polygamous marriages for the purposes of family reunification in Ireland. It will often be necessary for the purposes of family reunification to seek a declaration that a marriage is valid at Irish law under s. 29 of the Family Law Act, 1995[78].The issue of recognition of Muslim marriages for immigration purposes (though not for the purposes of s.29) recently came before the High Court in *R.M.R. and B.H. v. MJELR*[79]; a judicial review of the Minister for Justice's refusal of a travel visa to the applicant's wife. The applicant had been granted leave to remain in Ireland in 2007. During a brief visit home to Sri Lanka, a marriage was arranged for him and he and his wife were wed in a Muslim ceremony. He returned to Ireland and his wife applied for a long-stay visa to join him there. The visa was refused because the couple could not demonstrate that they had been in a relationship with one another prior to their wedding. In the High Court, Clarke J. held that that, in examining the bona fides of a marriage, the Minister was entitled to examine whether there was evidence of a pre-marital relationship, courtship or intention to marry between the parties.

It appears so far that a resident of Ireland will not be permitted to bring more than one spouse into the country for the purposes of family reunification and, as such, the immigration system is not a conduit for polygamous marriages[80]. In June 2004, it was reported that the Department of Justice was requiring male Muslims who were married to Irish citizens to swear a special affidavit on their intention of future marriages, before their own applications for citizenship would be processed[81]. The Civil

---

[78] See "Immigration and Residence in Ireland:Outline policy proposals for an Immigration and Residence Bill: A discussion document." Dublin, 2005, 87. The UNHCR Representative for Ireland advocates a liberal approach to recognition of customary marriage; Manuel Jordão.Statement Cork:2007), 7 For a critical analysis of states' reluctance to recognise polygamous marriages and its relationship to a 'control' impulse in immigration law see Staver, Anne. *Family Reunification: A Right for Forced Migrants?*. Refugee Studies Centre Working Papers Series. Oxford, 2008 17-19. In February 2010, the *Sunday Times* reported that a Lebanese citizen of Ireland was about to seek recognition of his marriage under s. 29. The application arose from the refusal of a visa to one of the man's two wives. He had been married to both in Lebanon, had lived with both there and had children with both; http://www.timesonline.co.uk/tol/news/world/ireland/article7018015.ece

[79] [2009] IEHC 279

[80] In 2003, the Irish Independent reported that the Minister for Justice had refused permission to Hussein Ali Hammoud, a Lebanese refugee, to bring his second wife and her children to Ireland. "Lebanese man disputes refusal to allow his two wives live here." *Irish Independent*, 2003.

[81] Harding, Thomas. "Irish outlaw Muslim second wives." *Daily Telegraph*. London, 2004. The Irish Council for Civil Liberties criticized the requirement as based in unjustified religious discrimination. Irish Council for Civil Liberties, Press Release, June 23 2004 http://tinyurl.com/iccl2004

Registration Act, 2004 lists a number of impediments to marriage – facts
the presence of which will deprive a person of legal capacity to marry.
Where such an impediment exists, the marriage may not be solemnised[82]. A marriage may not be solemnised where one or both of the
parties is already married[83] and a marriage may not be solemnised unless
both spouses are present[84]. The Act therefore indicates a firm public
policy against the recognition of polygamous and proxy marriages. In
this regard, it is consistent with the relevant body of common law. lyga-
mous marriage does not fit Irish law's conception of marriage – drawn
from the old case of *Hyde v. Hyde*[85] – as 'the voluntary union of one
man and one woman to the exclusion of all others for life'. Irish law's
reliance on this conception means, first, that a marriage conducted in
this jurisdiction is automatically invalid if either the husband or the wife
is validly married to someone else at the time of the ceremony. The
monogamous conception of marriage also generates a public policy
ground for the non-recognition of polygamous marriages entered into
abroad. In other words, marriages which take place abroad under systems which permit polygamous marriage may not be recognized at Irish
law because they conflict with Irish public policy or affront 'the accepted
morality of the domestic forum.'[86] Ní Shúilleabháin identifies[87] such a
public policy objection to the recognition of foreign polygamous marriages in *Conlon v. Mohamed*[88]. In that case, Finlay C.J. argued that 'It
has not been contested that a polygamous marriage cannot be recognised
in our law as a valid marriage'[89]. Ní Shúilleabháin goes on to argue that,
since, in *Conlon*, the couple's marriage was in fact monogamous, the
court's objection seems to have been to the recognition of marriages
which were concluded subject to rules which merely permitted polygamous marriage. Irish courts may, therefore, refuse to recognise potentially polygamous marriages even where the husband has not taken a
second wife.

[82] S. 58(7)
[83] S. 2(2)(b)
[84] S. 51(2) (a)
[85] *Hyde v Hyde* (1866) L.R. 1 P. & D. 130 at 133 ; *approved by Haugh J. in Griffith
v Griffith* [1944] I.R. 35 at 40
[86] This ground for non-recognition was first stated in *Buchanan v McVey* [1954] I.R.
89 at 106
[87] Maire Ni Shuilleabhain."Accommodating Cultural Diversity Under Irish Family
Law"(2002)9Dublin University Law Journal 175
[88] [1989] I.L.R.M. 523
[89] [1989] I.L.R.M. 523, 525

Although Ireland has not specifically legislated for the issue of forced marriage, Irish law retains a broad nullity jurisdiction, which may be of some utility where the consent of parties to a marriage is defective. The Irish law of nullity sets a very strict consent requirement at the threshold for entry into marriage. In *N (otherwise K) v K* Finlay C.J. ruled that consent to marriage must be nothing less than 'a fully free exercise of the independent will of the parties'. Ní Shúilleabháin suggests[90] that this consent requirement is so stringent as to catch not merely, forced marriages but also those which have been arranged by third parties to the marriage, such as parents. She bases this argument on two points. First, the test employed by Finlay C.J. requires the courts to exercise particular caution in examining marriages which have apparently taken place at the urging of parents. In *N (otherwise K) v K*, the then Chief Justice stated that '[i]f...the apparent decision to marry has been caused to such an extent by external pressure or influence, whether falsely or honestly applied, as to lose the character of a fully free act of that person's will, no valid marriage has occurred'[91]. In that case, the pregnant bride, aged 19, married the father of her child at her parents' insistence. She would not have married him but for the pregnancy. The court placed great weight on her 'quiet' and 'unassertive' nature, on her habitual obedience to her parents and on her trust in the correctness of their determination that she should get married. Second, the courts have developed an 'informed consent' ground for nullity, which evidently applies even where no question of improper pressure arises. This ground will be relevant to arranged marriages where the spouses have had limited contact with, or knowledge about, one another before the marriage ceremony. The test is not whether each spouse knew every detail of the other's life and relationships[92] before the marriage: spouses may keep some secrets from one another. Rather, the marriage will be void where one spouse, at the point of marriage, lacked adequate knowledge of some 'condition, disposition or proclivity'[93] on the part of the other. Thus if one spouse was not aware of the other's past mental illness[94] or physical disfigurement[95] at the point of wedding, the marriage is void.

---

[90] Maire Ni Shuilleabhain."Accommodating Cultural Diversity Under Irish Family Law"(2002)9Dublin University Law Journal 175

[91] [1985] I.R. 733, 742.

[92] *PF v G O'M* [2001] 3 I.R. 1, 23

[93] *PF v G O'M* [2001] 3 I.R. 1, 23

[94] *M O'M v B O'C* [1996] 1 I.R. 208

[95] *BJM v CM* Unreported, High Court, July 31, 1996.

10. Involvement of Religious Organisations in Immigration Controversies.

In general, leaders within the Catholic church have taken a firm stand against the government's immigration policy[96]. For instance, at the March 2008 General Meeting of the (Catholic) Irish Bishops' Conference, the bishops issued a statement criticising the Immigration, Residence and Protection Bill, 2008.[97] Catholic organisations, such as the Crosscare Migrant Service have been important advocates for reform of the asylum regime[98]. There is no legal basis upon which churches might 'give asylum' and incidents of civil disobedience by church members are not widely reported. However, a well-known incident took place in 2006[99], when 41 Afghan asylum seekers, based in Kerry, Cork, Mayo, Limerick, Galway and Dublin entered St Patrick's Cathedral (Church of Ireland) in Dublin, refused to leave and began a hunger strike. Some younger members of the group threatened suicide if they were made to leave the cathedral. The men were protesting delays in processing their asylum applications and poor living conditions at direct provision accommodation centres and hoped to use their protest to obtain certain commitments from the Ministry for Justice, Equality and Law Reform. The Church of Ireland authorities allowed the men to remain in the cathedral for two weeks and negotiated with police and with the government on their behalf. The government at the time took the view that the men were attempting to illegitimately bypass the asylum system. 31 of the men were subsequently charged with public order offences under the Forcible Entry and Occupation Act (1971).

Religious organisations have also been active in the provision of pastoral care to migrants and asylum seekers. By and large, asylum seekers are reliant on the outreach efforts of voluntary bodies for the provision of support services. Pastoral services are no different and appear to be

---

[96] See e.g. CORI (Congregation of Religious in Ireland) http://www.cori.ie/justice2/Specific_Policy_Issues/38-migrationandinterculturalissues *cf* Fintan O'Toole's critique of the Catholic church's interest in multiculturalism as driven by a need to retain power in this sector of society as its power in education and health wanes and appears threatened; http://www.irishtimes.com/newspaper/opinion/2009/1222/1224261109443.html.

[97] See also Lentin and McVeigh, *After Optimism: Ireland, Racism and Globalisation* (Dublin, 2007) 85 on the objections of the Methodist Church to the citizenship referendum. Available at http://www.tara.tcd.ie/bitstream/2262/25156/1/after%2Boptimism.pdf

[98] See e.g. http://www.migrantproject.ie/images/crosscare_migrant_response_bill_2008.pdf

[99] http://news.bbc.co.uk/1/hi/4997332.stm

provided on an *ad hoc* basis without government funding[100]. The Reception and Integration Agency, where it administers funds for integration-related activities and projects – does not fund religious activities. The Irish Episcopal Council for Immigrants co-ordinates the provision of Catholic pastoral services to immigrant communities throughout Ireland[101]. Men and women detained under immigration provisions at Cloverhill Prison receive chaplaincy visits from the Jesuit Refugee Service Europe[102] while local Muslim leaders attend to the religious needs of Muslim prisoners[103]. Spaces for prayer are provided at direct provision centres, evidently on an ad-hoc basis, though in the early years of direct provision in was very difficult for asylum seekers based in the country-side to be part of a meaningful religious community[104]. Very often, organisations providing pastoral care also provide services with no direct religious purpose, such as English language classes. A particularly interesting example is the Spiritan Fathers' organisation SPIRASI, which runs programmes for asylum-seekers who are survivors of torture, and prepares medico-legal reports for use in asylum applications. It is funded in this regard by the European Refugee fund, via the Department of Justice, Equality and Law Reform, and by the Eastern Health Board.

11. Conclusion

In general, Irish immigration policy has had little to say to religion. Religion has been important at the level of civil society engagement with new migrant communities and with groups of asylum seekers, but if anything, religious input has been so visible because it exists in spite of rather than alongside state immigration policy. As it is, religiously-inflected family law issues have appeared infrequently in the reported cases to date. Moreover, our legislature has not been proactive in responding to issues, such as polygamous and forced marriage which have sparked law reform in other European jurisdictions. It is difficult to

---

[100] It should be noted, however, that at the level of migrant integration, the Department of Integration has acknowledged the role of 'faith-based groups' in facilitating integration and has committed to work with and fund them. See e.g. *Migration Nation* (2008, Dublin) at pp. 44-45. Available at http://www.integration.ie/website/omi/omiwebv6.nsf/page/AXBN-7SQDF91044205-en/$File/Migration%20Nation.pdf

[101] http://www.catholicbishops.ie/migrants/1575

[102] http://www.jrseurope.org/countries/ireland.htm

[103] http://www.irishprisons.ie/care_and_rehabilitation-chaplaincy.htm

[104] http://www.drogheda-independent.ie/news/mosney-facility-to-house-asylum-seekers-until-2010-596347.html

say what shape the 'private' family-driven side of minority religious engagement with Irish law may take in the future. What emerges very clearly is the stratification of the Irish immigration regime as between one category of non-EEA migrants, who come to Ireland via the work permit regime enjoy a great degree of freedom, and their much poor counterparts who come to Ireland via the asylum system, or as 'illegal' workers, and enjoy a very precarious status – if they enjoy any at all – under Irish law. The construct of family relationships has been an important point at which these more vulnerable migrants could gain purchase on Irish law. Of course, it has been ruthlessly scaled back as its utility has become clear. In speculating about the future shape of religiously-inflected family law issues in Ireland, we might wonder whether these will take different guises as between the communities of affluent 'work permit' migrants and their 'outlawed' counterparts. One question is whether the transnational family arrangements of secure economic migrants will reflect a certain desired cosmopolitanism while less secure migrants aim to use religious law strategically as a shield for private and family life against the worst excesses of state regulation. A second is whether the state's current tendency towards strong discretion will prevail in any engagement with religious law, or whether Ireland will in its turn adopt the tactic of selective hyper-regulation of minority religious practice familiar from other jurisdictions. So far, religious input into the public discourse around immigration has been led by the majority Christian churches. As Ireland's minority religious communities mature and begin to become more vocal the frame of an Irish approach to religious difference in immigration will appear in sharper outline.

ROBERTO MAZZOLA

LA RELIGION FACE À L'IMMIGRATION DANS LE SYSTÈME JURIDIQUE ITALIEN

Le phénomène de l'immigration présente multiples aspects, dont beaucoup sont aussi de nature religieuse. En particulier l'analyse qui suivra aura comme but de mettre à jour les principaux problèmes que les dynamiques de l'immigration posent au point de vue juridique dans le système normatif italien. Nous nous attacherons aux plus importantes questions relatives à la liberté religieuse par rapport aux trois principales phases du phénomène de l'immigration: la phase d'entrée, la phase de séjour et, enfin, la phase de retour du sujet immigré.

1. Phase d'entrée

C'est entre la fin des années 60 et le début des années 80 que l'Italie a commencé à être concernée par le phénomène de l'immigration[1]. Les zones géographiques de provenance des premiers flux étaient principalement au nombre de trois: l'Afrique du Nord (Maroc et Tunisie); les anciennes colonies italiennes (l'Erythrée); et les pays en voie de développement où se trouvait un nombre important de missions catholiques (Cap Vert et Philippines). Dans ces deux derniers cas, le flux migratoire, favorisé par l'histoire coloniale italienne et par la présence d'institutions catholiques, a notamment permis à des personnes de demander un «visa d'entrée» ou un «permis de séjour» pour des motifs religieux[2].

Ce phénomène est réglementé par l'art. 4 du D.L. du 25 juillet 1998, n.286 contenant le T.U sur l'immigration et l'application des normes promulguées dans le D.P.R. du 31 août 1999, n. 394 modifié par la suite par le D.P.R du 18 octobre 2004, n.334 et par le Décret Ministériel Affaires Etrangères du 12 juillet 2000. Cette réglementation prévoit que:

---

[1] Cf. I. Ponzo, *Introduzione*, in *Conoscere l'Immigrazione. Una cassetta degli attrezzi*, I. Ponzo (dir.), Carocci, Rome, 2009, p. 13 ss.

[2] *Ibid.* Cf. aussi G. Rivetti, *Migrazione e fenomeno religioso: problemi (opportunità) e prospettive*, in *La coesistenza religiosa: nuova sfida per lo Stato laico*, G.B. Varnier (dir.), Rubettino, Soveria Mannelli (Cosence), 2008, p. 109 ss.

a) la demande et la délivrance du permis de séjour pour des motifs religieux peut être présentée par l'intéressé ou par la personne qui préside l'Institut ou la Communauté religieuse dans laquelle l'étranger doit séjourner; b) la durée du permis de séjour peut être brève, s'il s'agit d'un visa de court séjour (1-90 jours) ou de longue durée s'il est supérieur à 90 jours: c) le permis est renouvelable et permet l'inscription gratuite au *Service Sanitaire National*. Il est possible, en outre, selon ce qu'a établi le Tribunal Administratif Régional du Latium, dans son arrêt du 6 février 2009, n. 1206[3], de transformer le permis de séjour pour des raisons de religion en permis de séjour pour des motifs de travail. Ce phénomène est particulièrement répandu parmi les sœurs-infirmières qui abandonnent leur ordre religieux pour poursuivre leur activité d'assistantes médicales dans des structures hospitalières publiques ou privées. Le système juridique italien permet, en outre, aux étudiants étrangers possédant un permis de séjour pour études de pouvoir le transformer en permis pour causes religieuses. Ceci est valable pour les étudiants qui à la fin de leurs études religieuses sont appelés à une activité religieuse en Italie. Il est en outre possible que le permis de séjour pour des raisons de religion puisse être transformé en carte de séjour.

Toutefois l'Italie a aussi connu, à partir des années 90, une immigration en provenance d'Afrique du Nord[4], favorisée, non seulement par la proximité géographique et la facilité d'accès, mais aussi par la fermeture des frontières des principaux pays importateurs de main-d'œuvre comme la France et l'Allemagne. Cette phase migratoire présente des aspects nouveaux et intéressants du point de vue du rapport entre immigration et religion. En premier lieu, le fait qu'il s'agisse d'une immigration constituée principalement d'hommes jeunes, seuls et de religion islamique a créé une série de problèmes pour leur regroupement familial. Il s'agissait de réglementer cette institution en évitant les regroupements pouvant donner naissance à des modèles familiaux contraires à l'ordre public. L'article 29 du D.L du 25 juillet 1998, n. 286, modifié par le décret du 8 janvier 2007, n.5 exécutant la directive 2003/86/CE sur le regroupement familial et par le D.L successif du 3 octobre 2008, n.160 a donc interdit au bénéficiaire d'un permis de séjour déjà marié en Italie

---

[3] Arrêt TAR Latium, 6 février 2009, n. 1206, in <www.immigrazione.biz/sentenza. php?id=182> (visité le 7 mai 2009)

[4] Cf. I. Ponzo, *Introduzione*, in *Conoscere l'Immigrazione. Una cassetta degli attrezzi*, cit., p. 14. Cf. aussi: T. Caponio, *Le politiche per gli immigrati*, in *Conoscere l'Immigrazione. Una cassetta degli attrezzi*, cit., p. 23; *Città italiane e immigrazione. Discorso pubblico e politiche a Milano, Bologna e Napoli*, il Mulino, Bologne, 2006, cap. II, pp. 59 ss.

le regroupement familial avec un autre conjoint résidant à l'étranger. Cette réglementation a été confirmée par les organes compétents du Ministère de l'Intérieur à l'occasion de la séance de «Question Time» du 21 février 2007 à la Chambre qui portait sur le regroupement familial et au cours de laquelle le Ministre de l'Intérieur a répondu aux questions des députés. À cette occasion on a rappelé l'incompatibilité entre la polygamie et les principes de l'ordre public et des bonnes mœurs en vigueur dans le droit italien, conformément avec ce qu'a établi le Tribunal Administratif Régional de l'Emilie Romagne[5], qui a reconnu l'institution du mariage polygamique contraire à la dignité de la femme.

La recomposition des noyaux familiaux entre immigrés s'est effectuée aussi à travers un autre concept juridique de tradition islamique: la *kafala*[6]. À cet égard, la procédure administrative des Consulats italiens et la Juridiction de fond en la matière sont en désaccord. Les premiers tendent à refuser l'entrée en Italie aux mineurs recueillis avec la *kafala* par des étrangers résidant dans notre pays. Cette position se base sur une interprétation restrictive de l'article 29 alinéa 2 du T.U. sur l'immigration fondée sur la conviction qu'on ne pourrait pas appliquer les normes en matière d'adoption et de placement en famille d'accueil au mineur accueilli par *kafala*.

La position de la jurisprudence de fond et surtout de légitimité est différente. La Section I de la Cour de Cassation, avec une sentence du 20 mars 2008, n. 7472[7], a en effet confirmé qu'entre *kafala* islamique, telle qu'elle est réglementée au Maroc, et placement en famille d'accueil national, ce sont les affinités qui prévalent. D'où la conviction que la *kafala* peut faire fonction de condition au regroupement familial. Dans le sillage de cette sentence, le Tribunal de Rovereto a donc reconnu, avec un arrêté du 21 mai 2009[8], l'aptitude à l'accueil consensuel en famille d'un mineur à travers l'application de cette institution.

Avec les flux des années 90, arrivent en Italie des immigrés souvent victimes de discrimination religieuse, ayant besoin de protection et demandant des services juridiques spécifiques comme l'asile politique, le statut de réfugié ou de simples permis de séjour. En ce qui concerne

[5] Cf. C. Campiglio, *Il diritto di famiglia islamico nella prassi italiana*, in *Riv. dir. inter. priv. proc.*, n. 1 (2008), pp. 43-76.

[6] Cf. R. Aluffi Beck-Peccoz, *Introduzione*, in *Dossier Mondo Islamico 4. Le leggi del diritto di famiglia negli stati arabi del Nord-Africa*, R. Aluffi Beck-Peccoz (dir.), Ed. de la Fondation Giovanni Agnelli, Turin, 1997, pp. 7; 21.

[7] Arrêt Cour de Cassation, 20 mars 2008, n. 7472, in <www.meltingpot.org> (visité le 5 avril 2009)

[8] Arrêt Tribunal du Rovereto, 21 mai 2009, in <www.asgi.it> (visité le 7 avril 2009)

les demandes d'asile politique, la Cour de Cassation dans l'arrêt du 18 juin 2004, n. 11441[9] a reconnu comme norme immédiatement appicable l'article 10 alinéa 3 Const. qui prévoit que l'étranger, privé dans son pays d'origine de ses droits et de ses libertés, ait le droit de demander asile sur le territoire de la République italienne, selon les conditions prévues par la loi. Une orientation jurisprudentielle confirmée par la sentence du Tribunal de Venise du 6 septembre 2007, n.1958[10]. Il en va de même en matière de réfugiés politiques. Dans ce cas, il y a aussi opposition entre pouvoir exécutif, en particulier les Commissions territoriales et pouvoir judiciaire. En particulier les Sections Unies de la Cour de Cassation,17 décembre 1999, n. 907, qui se réfèrent constamment à la Convention de Genève afférant au statut de réfugié, ont reconnu à l'étranger persécuté pour des raisons de religion, le statut de réfugié politique, entendant par cette expression, tout étranger qui «par crainte fondée d'être persécuté pour des raisons de race, de religion, de nationalité, d'appartenance à un groupe social ou d'opinion politique déterminé, se trouve hors du territoire du pays dont il a la nationalité et ne peut pas, ou bien à cause de cette crainte, ne veut pas user de la protection de ce pays»[11]. C'est dans ce sens qu'il faut lire l'arrêt du tribunal de Venise, de 12 octobre 2007, n. 22550. Enfin il faut prêter attention à l'article 4 bis du décret de loi 773-b du 2009[12]. Cette norme subordonne la délivrance du permis de séjour à un "Accord d'intégration". Le second alinéa de cette norme prévoit, en effet, que "Dans les cent quatre-vingts jours suivant l'entrée en vigueur du présent article, (…) (soient) établis les critères et les modalités de souscription, de la part de l'étranger, simultanément avec la présentation de la demande de délivrance de permis de séjour conformément à l'article 5, d'un Accord d'intégration, articulé en crédits, avec l'engagement à souscrire des objectifs spécifiques d'intégration, qu'il devra obtenir pendant la période de validité du permis de séjour ». Il faudra attendre le règlement exécutif pour comprendre ce que seront réellement les exigences que l'on requièrt des étrangers pour qu'ils puissent être considérés comme intégrés.

---

[9] Arrêt Cour de Cassation, 20 mars 2008, n. 7472, in <www.meltingpot.org.> (visité le 10 avril 2009)

[10] Arrêt Tribunal de Venise, 6 septembre 2007, n. 1958, in <www.asgi.it> (visité le 7 avril 2009)

[11] Arrêt S.U. de la Cour de Cassation, 17 décembre 1994, n. 907, in <www. alphaice. com/giurisprudenza> (visité le 3 mai 2008)

[12] d.l. 773-b 2009, in <www.giuristidemocratici.it> (visité le 3 mai 2009)

2. Phase de séjour

L'augmentation des regroupements familiaux a provoqué un enracinement croissant sur le territoire d'immigrés dont l'objectif est de s'établir en Italie pour une période de moyen à long terme[13]. La nature structurelle de l'immigration peut avoir des conséquences directes et indirectes sur le plan de la liberté religieuse et de la liberté de conscience. À cet égard, il faut en premier lieu vérifier si l'acquisition de la nationalité de la part des immigrés désormais enracinés sur le territoire est subordonnée à des exigences ethniques, culturelles et religieuses particulières. La L. du 5 février 1992, n. 91 qui règlemente l'accès à la nationalité ne demande aucunement à l'étranger, de remplir des conditions de nature culturelle ou religieuse. En Italie, le régime de nationalité se fonde en effet sur d'autres règles comme celle de la complète égalité entre homme et femme, la nationalité transmissible par «*iure sanguinis*»; l'acquisition, uniquement dans certains cas précis, de la nationalité par «*iure soli*»; la possibilité de conserver la double nationalité; la manifestation expresse de la volonté d'acquisition ou de perte de la nationalité. Toutefois quelque chose est en train de changer quant aux exigences de nature culturelle, requises pour l'acquisition de la nationalité italienne. Le Texte Unique élaboré par un Comité restreint au sein de la 1ère Commission Affaires constitutionnelles de la Chambre, apportant les «Modifications à la loi du 5 février 1992, n. 91, en matière de nationalité» indique dans l'article 3 les nouvelles conditions requises pour qu'un étranger puisse en faire la demande. Parmi ces exigences, l'obligation de «connaître de manière convenable la langue et la culture italienne». Dans un discours tenu au Quirinal à l'occasion de la rencontre avec une délégation de «Nuovi Cittadini» *Nouveaux Citoyen,* le Ministre de l'Intérieur a en effet déclaré que «le respect de nos valeurs fondamentales et la connaissance essentielle de notre langue et de notre histoire doivent être évalués avec sérénité et équilibre afin que le bénéfice de la nationalité ne soit pas accordé indistinctement à tous à travers des évaluations superficielles»[14]. La permanence sur le territoire des communautés immigrées fait surgir en outre des problèmes dans le domaine de l'éducation: la population scolaire en Italie est toujours plus diversifiée, même du point de vue

---

[13] Cf. G. Zincone, *Introduzione. Il passaggio al primo piano*, in *Immigrazione: segnali di integrazione. Sanità, scuola e casa*, G. Zincone (dir.), il Mulino, Bologne, 2009, p. 7 ss.

[14] On peut lire les principaux passages du discours de Ministre par l'Intérieure pendant la visite au Palais du Quirinal in <www.immigrazioneoggi.it/daily_news > (visité le 12 avril 2009)

religieux[15]. Les chiffres fournis par la Caritas/Migrantes[16] dans le Dossier statistique 2007, indiquent que sur 498.735 élèves étrangers inscrits pour l'année scolaire 2006/2007: 236.000 sont chrétiens, 185.000 musulmans, 16.000 hindouistes ou bouddhistes, 14.000 sont protestants; 6.000 appartiennent à des religions animistes africaines et enfin 1.000 sont juifs. C'est pourquoi la circulaire ministérielle du 26 juillet 1990, n. 205 parle de la nécessité d'une "éducation inter-culturelle" dont l'objectif est, non seulement l'acceptation et le respect de l'autre mais aussi la reconnaissance de la diversité identitaire et culturelle, «dans la recherche quotidienne de dialogue, de compréhension et de collaboration, dans une perspective d'enrichissement réciproque»[17]. En particulier, c'est la nécessité d'insister sur une plus grande connaissance des diversités religieuses qui ressort, en encourageant le dialogue et en le canalisant dans le respect des valeurs constitutionnelles de la société. La législation régionale mérite attention. La L. rég. des Marches du 26 mai 2009, n. 13, par exemple, dans l'article 10 alinéa 3, prévoit que les organismes locaux et les institutions scolaires, dans le respect de la réglementation étatique en vigueur, concourent à la réalisation de projets en vue de l'éducation interculturelle (et) et permettant de résoudre des difficultés linguistiques et formatives.

Dans les années quatre-vingt-dix, le rôle toujours plus actif que jouent les confessions religieuses dans les politiques pour les immigrés et pour les migrants apparaît comme un autre aspect lié au phénomène de l'immigration. Dans ce domaine, les typologies d'interventions sont de diverses natures. Mises à part quelques actions isolées de moindre importance destinées aux étrangers de religion non chrétienne, si on limite l'analyse à la seule confession catholique, il ressort que les actions efficaces sur le plan de l'intégration ont été menées à la fois par la Conférence épiscopale italienne et par chacun des Diocèses. Le Conseil permanent de la *CEI*, a, par exemple, maintes fois souhaité la création d'aumôneries spécifiques pour les immigrés dans les Diocèses où le pourcentage d'immigrés de confession catholique est le plus élevé. Un phénomène présent, non seulement dans certaines villes italiennes, mais

---

[15] Cf. A. Luciano, M. Demartini, R. Ricucci, *L'istruzione dopo la scuola dell'obbligo. Quali percorsi per gli alunni stranieri?* in *Immigrazione: segnali di integrazione. Sanità, scuola e casa*, cit., p. 113 ss.

[16] On peut voir le projet présenté par l'association Caritas/Migrantes dans le Rapport 2007, in <www.giuristixcattolici.it> (visité le 4 juin 2009)

[17] Le texte de la circulaire ministérielle on peut le lire sur le site: <www.edscuola.it> (visité le 12 avril 2009)

aussi dans des centres mineurs où l'on trouve une présence significative d'immigrés catholiques. Dans les Pouilles, par exemple, il y a des petites villes où vivent des centaines de Philippins ou de Sri Lankais catholiques auxquels il faut assurer une assistance religieuse particulière.

Dans d'autres cas, les diocèses interviennent, en collaboration avec les organismes locaux dans l'activité de médiation entre communautés immigrées et citoyens italiens. Un exemple: l'activité menée en collaboration avec la Mairie de Turin par le Centre de Médiation Familiale du Centre Peirone du Diocèse de Turin[18]. Une activité destinée aux couples mixtes et aux familles immigrées islamiques ou, encore, le Centre de consultation pour les familles interethniques du Diocèse de Milan en activité, depuis 1988, dans le cadre du *Centro Ambrosiano di Documentazione per le Religioni*[19]. Les objectifs poursuivis par ces centres concernent: a) la formation et le soutien des couples chrétiens-islamiques; b) l'écoute des couples musulmans afin de leur offrir un soutien en cas de difficultés de couple, avec une attention toute particulière à la tutelle de la femme; c) favoriser les parcours d'intégration familiale et sociale.

La *CEI*, enfin, a pris position de manière fort critique, et à maintes reprises, en vertu du peu de sensibilité dont fait preuve la réglementation italienne sur l'immigration envers les droits humains[20].

3. Phase de retour

Au phénomène d'entrée correspond son opposé: le retour définitif, ou seulement espéré, des immigrés dans leur pays d'origine. Dans ce dernier cas, le désir de retour ralentit le processus d'intégration, en favorisant le maintien de coutumes du pays d'origine, surtout au sein du milieu familial. Dans certains cas, la référence à ces traditions a été invoquée comme justification pour des actions pénales d'importance. Sur ce point, la jurisprudence italienne a pris une position précise. La Cour de Cassation, dans sa sentence du 8 janvier 2003, n. 55[21], a en effet été très ferme

---

[18] Cf. B. Ghiringhelli-A. Negri, *I matrimoni cristiano-islamici in Italia. Gli interrogativi il diritto la pastorale*, Centro editoriale dehoniano, Bologne, 2008. Cf. en particulier le chapitre n. VIII: « *L'esperienza di accompagnamento nelle Arcidiodeci di Milano e Torino* » à propos de l'expérience des mariages mixtes entre chrétiens et musulmans, p. 133.

[19] *Ibid.*, p. 125.

[20] Cf. en particulier le Rapport de l'Assemblée général de la CEI: « *Immigrazione: ospitalità e legalità all'Assemblea Generale della CEI* », in <www.chiesacattolica.it> (visité le 9 avril 2009)

[21] Arrêt Cour de Cassation, 8 janvier 2003, n. 55, in <http://abcdiritto.it/cassazione-sez-vi-penale 8 gennaio-2003-n.55 > (visité le 12 mai 2009)

lorsqu'elle a retenu les chefs d'accusation du délit de mauvais traitements en famille, ex art. 572 c.p., dans le cas d'un mari qui, alléguant comme justification les us et coutumes de sa culture et de sa religion islamique, a soumis sa femme à la réitération d'actes vexatoires lui causant souffrance, humiliation et prévarication. Dans le cas où, au contraire, le retour est effectif, il faut distinguer entre des séjours de brève durée et un abandon définitif du pays d'immigration. Dans le premier cas, le retour dans le pays d'origine est souvent utilisé pour pratiquer des actes qui seraient interdits dans le pays d'immigration, comme en témoigne la sentence de condamnation prononcée en 1999 par le Tribunal de Milan pour lésions graves ex art.582, 583, 585, et 577, n. 1 c.p., contre un père égyptien responsable d'avoir soumis à infibulation sa fille pendant leur séjour chez des parents en Égypte. La fréquence de ce phénomène a poussé le législateur italien à introduire une disposition spéciale dans l'art. 6 de la L. du 9 janvier 2006, n. 7. Cette dernière, en modifiant le code pénal, par l'introduction du délit de mutilation génitale ex art. 583 bis prévoit, au dernier alinéa, que la norme soit appliquée «quand le fait est commis à l'étranger aussi bien par un citoyen italien que par un étranger résidant en Italie, ou bien au préjudice d'un citoyen italien ou d'un étranger résidant en Italie».

Le retour dans le pays d'origine peut au contraire être définitif, soit quand l'immigré décide volontairement de retourner dans son pays d'origine, soit s'il y est contraint par des mesures d'expulsion administrative[22], comme cela s'est produit en Italie pour certains imams[23]. Le régime juridique en matière d'expulsions, contenu dans les art. 13, 15, 16, et 19 du D.L. du 27 juillet 1998, n. 286, tel qu'il est rapporté par la L. 189/2002, peut être ainsi synthétisé: l'étranger peut être expulsé au moyen d'un acte «d'expulsion administrative» par le Ministère de l'Intérieur ex art. 13, ou bien par un acte d'expulsion administrative ordonnée par le Préfet ou par le *Questore*. Ce type d'expulsion peut revêtir quatre formes différentes: i) décret d'expulsion exécuté immédiatement par le Préfet; ii) mesures d'accompagnement immédiat à la frontière établies par le *Questore*; iii) mesures de rétention de sûreté dans un *CPT* (Centre de permanence temporaire), aujourd'hui *CIE* (Centre d'identification et d'expulsion) conformément à l'art. 9 du décret de loi du 23 mai

---

[22] Cf. Cour. Cass. Civ. I, 10 avril 2003, n. 5661 et encore l'arrêt du Tribunal de Turin, 28 juillet 2003, in *Diritto Immigrazione e Cittadinanza*, n. 1 (2004), pp. 130-136.

[23] Arrêt Tribunal de Turin, 11 novembre 2004, n. 15336, in <www.olir.it > (visité le 6 janvier 2009)

2008, n.92, contenant les «Mesures d'urgence en matière de sûreté publique» dans le cas où le rapatriement immédiat ne serait pas possible; iv) mesures d'intimation du *Questore* à l'étranger de quitter l'Italie dans les cinq jours qui suivent dans le cas où ni le rapatriement immédiat ni la rétention dans les *CEI* ne seraient possibles. L'expulsion peut ensuite avoir lieu comme mesure de sécurité (art. 15), ou comme sanction alternative à la détention (art.16). Le T.U. de loi de 1998 établit, en outre, à l'art.19, les limites auxquelles doit se soumettre l'autorité dans l'exécution des expulsions. L'expulsion n'est pas autorisée en réalité, exceptée celle du Ministère de l'Intérieur si elle appliquée comme mesure d'urgence, pour des mineurs de moins de 18 ans, excepté si ceux-ci veulent suivre, comme de droit, l'un de leurs parents ou un membre de leur famille d'accueil si ceux-ci sont expulsés, pour des étrangers possédant une carte de séjour, pour des étrangers cohabitant avec des parents jusqu'au 4ème degré de parenté et avec leur conjoint, pour les femmes enceintes ou pendant les mois qui suivent la naissance d'un enfant dont elles doivent prendre soin.

Il n'est jamais possible, au contraire, d'expulser des personnes pouvant être persécutées, entre autres, pour des raisons de religion (art.19) et des personnes qui, de retour dans leur pays, peuvent être envoyées dans un autre pays que le leur, où elles risquent d'être persécutées aussi pour raisons de religion, comme en témoigne l'annulation du décret d'expulsion du préfet de la *Provincia* de Bologne de la part du juge de paix avec le décret du 27 juillet 2007. La réglementation a été soumise à un jugement sévère de la part de la Cour constitutionnelle. Avec deux sentences successives, la 222[24] et la 223 de 2004[25], le juge constitutionnel a en effet dénoncé la réforme qui confierait les mesures d'expulsion exclusivement à l'autorité de sûreté publique, sans procédure contradictoire et sans contrôle de la part de l'autorité judiciaire. Les vides provoqués par les sentences du juge constitutionnel ont été en partie comblés par la L. du 12 novembre 2004, n. 271, qui a prévu que les mesures d'accompagnement à la frontière soient soumises à la confirmation du juge de paix dans les 48 heures et ne soient pas exécutées tant que cette confirmation n'a pas été prononcée, perdant tout effet si celle-ci est refusée ou bien si le juge ne statue pas dans les 48 heures qui suivent. C'est là une timide tentative pour ramener dans le cadre des garanties constitutionnelles les mesures d'expulsion des étrangers hors du territoire italien.

---

[24] Cour. const., 8-15 juillet 2004, n. 222, in *G.U.* 21 juillet 2004
[25] Cour const, 8.-15 juillet 2004, n. 223, in *G.U.* 21 juillet 2004

RINGOLDS BALODIS

IMMIGRATION AND RELIGION IN LATVIA

1. Immigration, emigration and the main problem-questions in connection with it within the framework of the given subject

Emigration. Modern Latvia is not a country to which people immigrate but rather a country from which they emigrate. On the state level there are concerns about the increasing outflow of population to the more advanced countries of the EU. The main reason for this is economical. Emigration has increased due to the economic crisis which started in 2008. Although citizens of Latvia have been leaving the country and going to Germany, Norway, Sweden, Great Britain etc. since the end of the 1990s many have chosen **Ireland** as their final destination. Most of them are guest workers; however, some of them stay abroad permanently. Regarding emigration, the first big wave of emigration in the 20th century was seen in the departure of the Baltic Germans from Latvia in 1939. The second wave of emigration took place in 1944 when many inhabitants of Latvia who had experienced the "Terrible Year"[1] emigrated to the West as the Soviet army was approaching the territory of Latvia.

Immigration. Unlike other member countries of the European Union, immigration in Estonia, Lithuania and Latvia is connected with the **theme of occupation**. All these mentioned Baltic States lost their statehood in 1940, experienced the German occupation (1941 – 1944) and after World War II were *"set free"* and were constrained to the status of socialistic republics of the Soviet Union. Latvia, as well as the other Baltic states, had the status of a colony, without any rights. Migration was both organized and spontaneous. On the one hand, there was organized recruitment of workers; on the other hand, officials of the party and the managerial staff, as well as technical specialists, were appointed and sent to work in Latvia. There was also a spontaneous inflow[2] of

---

[1] The first Soviet occupation was from 1940-1941; the second from 1945-1990
[2] Bleiere D., Butulis I., Stranga A., Zunda A. History of Latvia 20th century – Rīga. Jumava. 2005. 328.lpp.

workers. From 1945 – 1990 hundreds of thousands of Russian-speaking immigrants came to Latvia and most of them stayed permanently. After the restoration of independence in 1991, these people became non-citizens. It may be said with assurance, that the uncontrolled and permanent settling of the inhabitants of the USSR in Latvia in the middle of the last century has caused **the biggest wave of immigration**. These hundreds and thousands of migrants were either sent to Latvia as a work force in the factories built during the years of occupation, or they chose Latvia as their place of residence after serving in the USSR military. Some historians in compliance with the UN definition of 1948 regard this action as genocide because it involved forcible change of the inhabitants of the occupied country. Since Latvia is one of the poorest member countries of the EU, it is not a destination for illegal immigrants and, therefore the matter of about providing help for this group of inhabitants does not arise.

In connection with the religious dimension regarding immigration we should stress the growth of the number of the Orthodox believers and the rise of Islam. Orthodox believers now form the third biggest religious confession. According to its own data, it consists of approximately 350,000 members. There are 1 to 2 thousand Muslim believers.[3] Traditionally, Orthodox believers are Russians, Byelorussians and Ukrainians who, by staying permanently in Latvia after the Soviet regime, also increased the number of believers of the Orthodox Church of Latvia. The community of Islam-believers was formed by Tatars whose traditional religion is Islam. Recently, other Muslim believers have arrived from Saudi Arabia and other Muslim countries.

2. Non-citizens, Conditions of citizenship and procedures of naturalization

Former USSR republics have chosen different means of determining citizenship. The total number of citizens was determined based on territorial origin, and permanent residence in the particular territory before the restoration of independence. In some former USSR republics registration of residence in the place of residence was sufficient for an automatic

---

[3] Balodis R. Staat und Kirche in Lettland/Gerhard Robbers (Hrsg.) Staat und Kirche in der Europäischen Union/ Zweite Auflage Nomos Verlagsgesellschaft, Baden – Baden 2005. s. 281-282

acquisition of citizenship of the new country. In others, the main criterion for determining citizenship was the number of known years of permanent residence.[4] The concept of citizenship is entwined with statehood in that it is an enduring legal connection of a person and a country; therefore, questions regarding who can be a citizen are often subject to serious issues. There have also been a lot of arguments regarding citizenship in Latvia. The specifics of Latvia regarding citizenship are connected to the continuity[5] of Latvia subject to international laws which enable the lawmakers of Latvia to define the total number of citizens of Latvia and create a legal base for persons of a given group not to be automatically given the status of a citizen.[6] Specific to Latvia is the formation of a non-citizen body[7]; these non-citizens have also received appropriate passports.[8] While working on the Citizenship Law, the lawmakers of Latvia had to face two different tasks: firstly, based on the doctrine of the continuity of a state, **to define the range of the citizens of the country, which had restored independence**, and, secondly to define the status of those persons, who have lived in the country after the restoration of independence. Thirdly, the lawmakers also had to define a clear path in the Citizenship Law on how this numerous range of persons would gain citizenship of Latvia in the near future. This last task was the hardest and perhaps that is why the Citizenship Law of Latvia has such a long prehistory. Unlike the other Baltic countries, (for example, Estonia, where naturalization was scheduled immediately) citizenship in Latvia was restored, based on

---

[4] Ziemele I. Citizenship and human rights in the context of exploration of the countries// Likums un Tiesības, 2002, Nr. 8, 234. lpp.

[5] The legal base of continuity of Latvia is approved in the Declaration of May 4, 1990 of the Supreme Council regarding the restoration of independence of the Republic of Latvia; it regulates both the legal status of Latvia for the purpose of international rights, and the main legal questions of the state.

[6] Paragraph 12 in the conclusion part of the Satversmes court judgement of March 7, 2005 case Nr. 2004-15-0106

[7] When the Non-citizen Law was passed a new category of persons unknown to international rights was created – non-citizens of Latvia. Granting the status of a non-citizen to a specific group of persons was a result of complicated political compromise. Latvia complied with the international human rights standards that forbid the increase of number of stateless persons. Non-citizens of Latvia are considered neither citizens nor foreigners nor stateless persons. They are considered to be persons with "special legal status". The status of a non-citizen should not be and is not a variety of the citizenship of Latvia. Naturalization limitations for non-citizens have been removed since 1998; they have rights to naturalize, gain the citizenship of Latvia and enjoy the rights of a Latvian citizen. *(Paragraphs 14-17 in the conclusion part of the Satversmes court judgement of March 7, 2005 case Nr. 2004-15-0106)*

[8] Balodis R. Latvia/ Encyclopedia of World Constitutions Volume II Ed. G.Robbers – U.S. Facts on File, 2007 p.517

the **Law on Citizenship**[9] of the first independence, but the question regarding non-citizens was postponed indefinitely for the matter of naturalization to be regulated in the future with further laws and regulations. The Parliament of Latvia considered the legal provisions of the Convention of the Saeima as their primary task – determination of a range of those persons (citizens) who would be entitled to elect the 5th Saeima[10]. In 1991, a decision was made[11], which **actually did not define citizenship anew, but renewed it**. It is indicated in their decision: although the Republic of Latvia was occupied on the June 17, 1940 and the country lost its sovereign power, the body of its citizens, in accordance with the "Law on Citizenship" of August 23, 1919 of the Republic of Latvia, continues to exist. This decision provided both the means of determining the citizen body of the Republic of Latvia, and the basic regulations of naturalization. **The body of citizens of Latvia included persons who were the citizens of the Republic of Latvia before the time of the occupation (June 17, 1940) as well as their descendants who were living in Latvia at the moment of the making of the decision.**[12] Thereby, Latvia did not grant citizenship to persons who already had it before the occupation of Latvia but it renewed the rights of these persons *de facto*.[13] Persons who were not citizens of Latvia and had arrived to Latvia during the occupation were given rights to acquire the citizenship of Latvia

---

[9] **Law on Citizenship**: Tautas padomes likums. Likumu un Valdības Rīkojumu Krājums, 1919, 10.burtnīca

[10] The reason for this was that although Latvia was restored as a state, the lawmaker of Latvia was still the Supreme Council elected undemocratically. The idea of Saeima as the only one to pass the Citizenship Law was met with approval. It was based on findings that the Supreme Council cannot be a fully legitimate lawmaker, it is considered a reminant of the soviet times. On the other hand there was an opinion that the elections of Saeima can only be organized after the pull-out of the Russian army, international admission of the occupation and the removal of consequences of occupation. Although the mentioned opinion is reasoned we have to conclude that doing so would delay the process of international admission, pull-out of the Russian army, convocation of the constitutional parliament and the formation of a legitimate government for an uncertain period of time.

[11] **Regarding the renewal of citizen rights of the Republic of Latvia and basic regulations of naturalization**: Decision of the Supreme Council of the Republic of Latvia. Speaker of the Government and the Supreme Council, 1991, Nr.43

[12] July 1, 1992 was the deadline for registration; it was prolonged later. The circle of these persons was later extended with those persons (and their descendants) who live abroad but were citizens of Latvia on June 17, 1940. Although Latvia does not apply in practice double-citizenship institute, it created a situation where some persons had two citizenships. In addition we should mark out that on this basis approximately 40 000 persons of Latvian nationality who themselves or their parents had moved to Latvia after the USSR occupation did not gain citizenship.

[13] Ziemele I. International rights and human rights in Latvia: abstraction or reality. Rīga: Tiesu namu aģentūra, 2005, 103. lpp.

through naturalization.[14] In 1994, the Saeima passed the Citizenship Law[15] defining the citizens of the Republic of Latvia as "those persons who were citizens on June 17, 1940." The descendants of the mentioned persons, Latvians and Livs, if their permanent place of residence is Latvia, are recognized as citizens. In addition, as well as persons who have naturalized are also recognized as citizens. **As for the others, the Citizenship Law prescribed gradual naturalization**. Quotas (windows) were defined for this purpose which before the promulgation of the law were considerably limited. After international criticism, on June 22, 1998 a new Citizenship Law[16] was passed which removed the "window" system by defining that children of non-citizens who were born after August 21, 1991 were recognized as citizens if their permanent place of residence was the Republic of Latvia. There was resistance in connection with this law that resulted in a referendum. 53% of electors took part in the referendum and most of them supported the new Citizenship Law.

Naturalization is a process of granting citizenship to a person. Naturalization began on February 1, 1995. A Naturalization Board was formed to this end. In accordance with the laws and regulations of Latvia, especially those prescribed in the Citizenship Law, naturalization is a process by which the applicant for citizenship, after performing certain criteria, gains the citizenship of Latvia. Naturalization begins, at the moment when a person of his own free will makes an application to the Naturalization Board. Because of this nature, it is of an individual nature. Applicants have to pass a **test of basic knowledge** of the Satversme (the Constitution) of the Republic of Latvia, and the history of Latvia about which they have to answer questions (for example, in which event the national anthem was first played, when the country's independence was proclaimed, who the president of Latvia is, which religious confession is the biggest in Latvia etc.) Applications regarding the acquisition of citizenship of Latvia have been accepted by the Naturalization Board through naturalization since 1995. Up to 2009, 128 159 naturalization applications had been received regarding 141 255 persons, although 740 000 permanent residents could actually apply for naturalization most of whom

---

[14] Paragraph 13 in the conclusion part of the Satversmes court judgement of March 7, 2005 case Nr. 2004-15-0106
[15] **Citizenship Law:** LR likums. *Latvijas Vēstnesis*, 1994. 11.augusts, nr.93
[16] 7 858 applications regarding granting of a citizenship of Latvia to a child of a non-citizen or a stateless person, born in Latvia after August 21, 1991, have been received until 2009. 42 of them have been rejected.

had arrived during the occupation of the USSR. Under the order of the
Cabinet of Ministers, 131 118 persons, including 13 745 under-aged children who have naturalized with their parents, have been given the citizenship of Latvia. Applications regarding recognition of citizenship of
children of stateless persons, or non-citizens born in Latvia after August
21, 1991 have been accepted since 1999 by the Naturalization Board.

3. Asylum seekers and illegal immigration

Registration of citizens of Latvia, non-citizens of Latvia as well as persons who have received residences permit, registration certificates or
permanent residence certificates are managed by the Office of Citizenship and Migration Affairs of the Ministry of the Interior of the Republic
of Latvia, which also summarizes statistical data regarding illegal immigrants and asylum seekers.

In Latvia the procedure of asylum-seeking started in 1998. Since
1998, 254 persons have requested asylum. 17 persons have been given
refugee status. The number of asylum seekers has a tendency to increase.
In 2007 asylum in Latvia was requested by 34 persons, in 2008, there
were 51 requests.[17] Asylum seekers (legal regulation) and religion (special laws).

None of the Churches are referred to in the paragraphs of the fore-
mentioned laws favouring the staying of asylum seekers in Latvia. Religious dimensions for family unification have not been observed.

Polygamous or marriages contracted by force have not been observed
and therefore do not...

From the seven special laws concerning churches, and the cooperation of the state and churches, **the process of granting of asylum is
defined** in five of them: in the 12th paragraph in the respective laws for
Lutherans, Seventh Day Adventists and Baptists; in the 11th paragraph
in the respective law of Hebrews, and in the 13th paragraph in the
respective law of Orthodox-believers. Old-believers and Methodists did
not want such legal regulation in their laws, and in the agreement with
the St.Chair this matter is not dealt with. It is prescribed in these special
laws that an asylum seeker who is afraid of being pursued because of
his religious beliefs, has the right of having a representative from the
Church present during negotiations in the process of acquiring asylum.

---

[17] Home page of the Office of Citizenship and Migration Affairs http://www.pmlp.
gov.lv/lv/statistika/patveruma.html

If necessary, government institutions can request a judgement from the Church regarding the possible pursuance of the asylum seeker because of his religious beliefs.

The number of foreigners who have illegally crossed the state border into Latvia has doubled; in the five months of 2009, the State Border guards arrested 56 residents of the third-world countries for illegal crossing of the state border, which is twice as much as in the whole year of 2008. 34% of the illegal border crossers are residents of Moldova; the rest are mainly the residents of Congo, Togo, Gana, Syria, Cote d'Ivoire, Egypt, Republic of China and Byelorussia. Residents of the third-world countries arrested at the border control checkpoints used fake residence permits, visas and travelling documents of the Schengen zone countries to illegally cross the state border.

4. Chaplaincy

According to Article 1(8) of the Law on Religious Organisations, chaplains are the spiritual personnel who perform duties at penal institutions, units of the National Armed Forces and elsewhere, where ordinary pastoral care is not available. In accordance with Article 14(5) of the Law on Religious Organisations, chaplains in Latvia function according to the Regulations of the Council of Ministers on the Chaplain Service. The Council of Ministers issued the Chaplain Service Regulations on 2 July 2002. Chaplains' activity is financed and given material and technical support by the appropriate state or self-governmental institution within its regular budget, or by the relevant religious organisation. The Regulations govern the work of the chaplaincy service in the Republic of Latvia and provide that in Latvia Chaplains of custody institutions, National Armed Forces Chaplains, Chaplains of institutions of medical and social services and Chaplains of airports, sea-ports and land transport terminals exist.

Andrius Sprindziunas

IMMIGRATION AND RELIGION IN LITHUANIA

1. The legal provisions concerning immigration in Lithuania

Immigration to the Republic of Lithuania is generally regulated by the following national legal acts:

- Law of Legal Status of Aliens
- Law of Citizenship
- Readmission treaties, which are signed between Lithuania and other foreign countries
- Passport Law
- Law of Passport Law Realisation
- Law on Identity Cards
- Law on Identity Cards Law Realisation

as well as the 1951 Convention Relating to the Status of Refugees and other international legal acts, ratified by Lithuanian legislators.

Lithuania is not a popular country of immigration – probably for several reasons, such as relatively low average earnings compared with European standards, the relatively cold climate, the difficulty of learning the language, moderate economical development and maybe – dominant Roman Catholic church, encompassing almost 80% of local residents.

With quite moderate immigration, Lithuania has encountered a rise in racial and xenophobic tendencies during past years, according to the recent data from the national Human Rights Monitoring Institute. It must be mentioned, that many racial misdemeanors in Lithuania have attracted special interest in the national mass-media and have induced public discussion; over recent years the main focus of national legal discussions on the issues of emigration were not just about single examples of xenophobia but rather a question of so-called double citizenship, as it related to the right of Lithuanian emigrants to preserve the citizenship of the Republic of Lithuania as well as citizenship of other foreign countries like the USA, Ireland, Spain, Russia or others, with large numbers of Lithuanian immigrants. The matter of double citizenship was recently explained by The Constitutional Court of the

Republic of Lithuania, concluding that double citizenship in the Republic of Lithuania is affordable only in rare separate cases, and thereafter the problem has been raised repeatedly again, with various suggestions for legislators, including a proposal to solve it by a general national referendum.

Lithuania had no colonies, but with its number of residents of approximately 3 million it has been under constant political and demographic pressure from much larger neighbor countries, firstly Poland and Russia. To describe the situation briefly, it might be said that people of Russian nationality tend to naturalise, while Polish people, living in compact territories, tend towards a kind of ethnic autonomy within the Republic of Lithuania, fighting for right to use the Polish alphabet and language in public life and official documents. The vast majority of Polish people in Lithuania are Roman Catholics, while most Russians are Orthodox, unreformed Orthodox or indifferent. It's quite interesting to mention that the Vilnius District Municipality (with the heads of Polish nationality, elected by the compact Polish community of the district) in June 2009 announced an Act of Enthronement of the Lord Jesus Christ, by this conveying control of the district to Jesus Christ and inviting other municipalities to join their initiative. No other municipalities followed the step and national public opinion was one of confusion rather than of approval. In the context of the light national separatism of the Vilnius District Municipality, the Act of Enthronement of the Lord Jesus Christ could be interpreted as unconscious resistance towards the administration of the Lithuanian Republic.

Therefore, no significant increasing tendencies of immigration to Lithuania from Poland, or Russia or other foreign countries were registered during the last decade.

2. The statistical data about immigration issues in Lithuania.

The Migration Department of the Republic of Lithuania presents basic statistical data of the number of applications for permanent or temporary residence in the Republic of Lithuania, as well as the number of permits granted or refused in its official annual reports over decades. These reports are available on the internet, along with a broad suite of legal information to facilitate interested people in questions of migration, citizenship, declaration/registration of place of residence, visas, granting asylum and refugee status and legal status of foreigners in the Republic of Lithuania. The Migration Department, in general, works to meet European Union standards in its policy and control of migration processes.

The official site of the Migration Department of the Republic of Lithuania is www.migracija.lt it contains a large amount of detailed statistical information about issues of migration and this can be demonstrated within this paper by just a few tables:

1.5. Number of aliens residing in the Republic of Lithuania as of the beginning of 2009 (thous.)

	2005	2006	2007	2008	2009
Population[1], including:	3 425,3	3 403,3	3 384,9	3 366,2	3 350,1
Aliens[2]	32,6	35,3	33,1	33,4	32,9
Share of aliens in total national population, %	0,95	1,04	0,98	0,99	0,98

Sources: [1] Department of Statistics under the Government of the Republic of Lithuania.

[2] 2005–2006, 2009 – data of Personalization of Identity Documents Centre under the Ministry of the Interior, 2007–2008 – data of Migration Services.

1.6. Number of aliens residing in the Republic of Lithuania, by nationality

Nationality	2005	2009
European States, including:	**22 605**	**25 500**
- EU Member States, including:	**1 965**	**2 261**
- Latvia	355	374
- Poland	491	479
- Germany	314	406
- EFTA Member States	100	115
- Other European States, including	**20 540**	**23 124**
- Armenia	284	293
- Belarus	3 025	5 956
- Georgia	...	217
- Russia	14 493	12 627
- Ukraine	2 155	3 052
North America States, including:	**420**	**527**
- the USA	389	473
Central and South America States	**52**	**82**
Australia and Oceania	**20**	**23**
Asian States, including:	**1 555**	**1 803**
- Israel	326	400
- Kazakhstan	288	256
- China	253	436
- Lebanon	195	139
African States	**47**	**123**
Stateless persons	**7 914**	**4 844**
Total:	**32 613**	**32 902**

Note. At the beginning of 2009 nationals of 118 states were residing in the Republic of Lithuania.

Source. Residents' Register Service under the Ministry of the Interior.

So, according to official data sources, the vast number of aliens in the Republic of Lithuania during recent years was around 33 thousand people, and they comprised approximately 1% of the total population. Also, information about asylum applications and decisions are available on the same internet source (www.migracija.lt):

INFORMATION ABOUT ASYLUM APPLICATIONS AND DECISIONS, MADE IN 2008

Citizenship	Number of applications pending at the beginning of the year	Number of asylum applications				Decisions						Number applications pending at the end of the year
		First applications	Second applications	Returned according to the Dublin II	Total	With status		Rejected	Terminated cases	Expelled according to the Dublin II	Total	
						Geneva Convention status granted	Subsidiary protection					
Afghanistan	2	1	15		16		15				15	3
Algeria		1			1							1
Angola		1			1			1			1	
Armenia		1	1		2			2			2	
Belarus	2	10	3	2	15	2	2	6	3		13	4
Ethiopia	1		3		3	1 (2*)	3				4 (2*)	
Georgia	1	7		2	9			4	4		8	1***
India	3							3			3	
Iran		1			1			1			1	
Iraq	2	1	3		4		5				5	1
Israel	1							1			1	
Cameroon		3	3		6		5			1	6	
China	1	2			2			2			2	1
Kyrgyzstan		1		1	2				2		2	
Congo		3	1		4		1	3			4	
Cuba	3	8			8		3	3	1		7	4
Nepal			2		2			1			1	1
Nigeria		1		1	2				1		1	1
Pakistan	2	6	1		7			3	1		4	5
Russia	37	137	275	3	415	6	301(1**)	12	10	18	347	106**
Serbia			1		1							1
Syria	1	5	1		6		1			5	6	1
Somalia		1			1		1				1	
Sri Lanka		6	1		7							7
Tadzhikistan		1	1		2	1		1			2	
Turkey		3			3				3		3	
Ukraine	1	3			3			3	1		4	
Uzbekistan		6	6		12	2	6	2	1		11	1
Viet Nam	1	1			1		1	1			2	
Zimbabwe	1	1	1		2		2				2	1
Stateless	2		2		2				1		4	
Total	**61**	**210**	**318**	**12**	**540**	**12 (2*)**	**349(1**)**	**49**	**28**	**24**	**462**	**139**

* 2 Ethiopian nationals, who had subsidiary protection status, later were granted the refugee status due to the fact that the refugee status had been granted to their daughter;
** 1 Russian Federation citizen was granted subsidiary protection after the court's decision to return his case to the Migration Department for review;
*** During the investigation, 1 national of Georgia appeared to be a national of the Russian Federation, therefore, the last decision was on him as on the citizen of the Russian Federation.

According to the general principles of the law of the Republic of Lithuania, international treaties and particular laws on the legal status of aliens and asylum, religion, race and ethnicity alike, can not be subject to any kind of discrimination. Until now, legal suits concerned with deprivation of visas, citizenship or asylum status in Lithuania on the grounds of religion were not registered with the Lituanian courts nor the European Court of Human Rights.

3. Legal requirements upon the acquisition of citizenship of the Republic of Lithuania

The Lithuanian law sets out 6 preconditions for applicants of citizenship of the Republic of Lithuania (see Apendix 1). Among them are a test in the Lithuanian language (with exception for persons above 65, disabled persons, etc.) and an examination in the basic provisions of the Constitution of the Republic of Lithuania. To receive citizenship, applicant must take the oath to the Republic of Lithuania. Among basic preconditions, the duration of residence in the country and legal source of support are listed.

During the last decades no significant demographic or religious changes have happened in Lithuania.

4. The right of asylum in Lithuania

The right of asylum in the Republic of Lithuania is respected and recognized as one of birthright. Therefore, Lithuanian law determines three kinds of asylum in Lithuania:

1. Refugee status
2. Subsidiary protection
3. Temporary protection

Again, personal religion is in no way a ground for rejection of an application for asylum in Lithuania.

5. On the question of churches or religious communities giving asylum

According to the registry of the Ministry of Justice of the Republic of Lithuania, religious communities have never taken up the official order and process of giving asylum in the Republic of Lithuania since the re-establishment of the independant state in 1991.

6. Pastoral assistance of illegal immigrants

Pastoral assistance is available in all state institutions, including prisons, and centers for illegal immigrants and refugees. Of course, pastoral assistance can be provided if requested by anyone, including detainees. Most prisons in Lithuania have their ordained Catholic, Orthodox and Protestant chaplains while centers for immigrants are usually under the care of parish priests who are, of course, not paid by the state. In general, all religious communities in Lithuania recognized by the state may negotiate with state officials to facilitate pastoral service for specific groups of people such as illegal immigrants. There is no common rule, the pastoral service provided by any religion recognized by the state might be supported by their local communities, state institutions or other funds.

7. With regard to the principle of the united family on immigration law and practice

According to the law of citizenship, contracting a marriage with a citizen of the Republic of Lithuania is a good reason for applying to receive citizenship for an alien who meets the particular legal preconditions (see Apendix 1). Again, religion is not considered an issue.

Lithuanian civil law recognizes only monogamous marriage and until now does not allow exceptions. Besides, Islam is in the official list of the nine traditional religions recognized by the state in Lithuania, but local Muslims and other religious communities do not practice polygamous marriages.

In general, foreign marriage certificates if valid in the first country, should also be recognized as valid in Lithuania as well.

A complaint of forced marriage would entail an investigation of the case and would be treated as a crime according to the laws of the Republic of Lithuania.

8. Exceptions to the employment of non-EU citizens as clergy and pastors

According to articles of the section five of The Law on the Legal Status of Aliens in the Republic of Lithuania, concerning alien's work in the Republic of Lithuania, many exceptions exist to permit foreigners to work in Lithuania despite typical EU quota and restrictions. Specific employment of clergy and pastors from various foreign countries might be regulated by specific treaties between religious communities and the Government of the Republic of Lithuania, as has happened in the case of the Concordat between the Roman Catholic Holy See and the Republic of Lithuania.

Appendix 1

GRANTING CITIZENSHMIP (NATURALISATION)

Conditions for granting citizenship

Granting citizenship of the Republic of Lithuania upon contracting a marriage

Conditions for granting citizenship

According to Article 12 of the Law on Citizenship of the Republic of Lithuania (which was adopted on 17 September 2002 and came into force on 1 of January 2003. On 15 July 2008 the Law on Citizenship of the Republic of Lithuania was amended and set forth as a new version, which came into force on 22 July 2008) (hereinafter – the Law on Citizenship) citizenship of the Republic of Lithuania may be granted to a person if he meets the following conditions:

1. has passed the examination in the state language*;
2. at the time of submission of the application has a document certifying his right to habitually reside in the territory of the Republic of Lithuania;
3. has been residing in the territory of the Republic of Lithuania for the last ten years;
4. has a legal source of support;
5. has passed the examination in the basic provisions of the Constitution of the Republic of Lithuania1;
6. is a stateless person or is a citizen of a state under the laws of which he shall lose citizenship of the said state upon acquiring citizenship of the Republic of Lithuania or notifies in writing of his will to renounce citizenship of another state held by him after he is granted citizenship of the Republic of Lithuania**.

Oath of allegiance to the Republic of Lithuania

The citizenship of the Republic of Lithuania shall be granted by the President of the Republic. Upon granting citizenship of the Republic of Lithuania the rights and obligations of the citizen of the Republic of Lithuania shall arise only after the person takes the oath to the Republic of Lithuania. The person must swear an oath of allegiance to the Republic of Lithuania **within 1 year** from the day of entry into force of the Decree of the President of the Republic, whereby the person is granted citizenship of the Republic of Lithuania.

Reasons on the ground whereof citizenship of the Republic of Lithuania shall not be granted

Citizenship of the Republic of Lithuania shall not be granted to persons who:

1. have prepared, attempted to commit or committed international crimes such as: aggression, acts of genocide, crimes against humanity, war crimes;
2. have prepared, attempted to commit or committed criminal acts against the State of Lithuania;
3. before coming to reside in the Republic of Lithuania have been imposed in another state a custodial sentence for a premeditated crime for which the laws of the Republic of Lithuania also prescribe criminal liability or have been convicted in Lithuania for a premeditated crime punishable by a custodial sentence;
4. according to the procedure established by laws have no right to be issued a document certifying the right to habitually reside in the Republic of Lithuania.

Where to apply and what documents shall be submitted?

The applications for granting citizenship of the Republic of Lithuania shall be submitted to the President of the Republic of Lithuania via the migration service.

The following documents shall accompany the application to grant citizenship of the Republic of Lithuania under Article 12 of the Law on Citizenship:

- a copy of the person's identity card;
- a copy of the birth certificate;
- a document entitling to habitually reside in the Republic of Lithuania at the moment of submission of the application;
- a document providing evidence that the person has been living in the territory of the Republic of Lithuania over the last 10 years;
- a document evidencing that the person has a legal source of support;
- a document evidencing that the person has passed the examination in the state language and basic principles of the Constitution of the Republic of Lithuania.
- If a person hold a citizenship of another state he shall submit a written application for the renunciation of the citizenship of another state held when he is granted citizenship of the Republic of Lithuania.

How the documents shall be processed?

Documents issued by the foreign states must be legalized or approved by the „Appostile" according to the conditions laid down by law.

Documents issued abroad must be translated into Lithuanian language. Translations must be certified according to the conditions laid down by law.

Copies of the documents must be certified according to the conditions laid down by law.

Granting citizenship of the Republic of Lithuania upon contracting a marriage

According to the paragraph 1 of Article 14 of the Law on Citizenship, a person, *who contracted a marriage with a citizen of the Republic of Lithuania and has maintained his marital status for the last 7 years while residing in the territory of the Republic of Lithuania,* shall be granted citizenship of the Republic of Lithuania provided that there are no reasons on the ground whereof citizenship of the Republic of Lithuania shall not be granted and provided that the person meets the conditions established in subparagraphs 1, 2, 5 and 6 of paragraph 1 of Article 12 of the Law on Citizenship, that is:

- has passed the examination in the state language*;
- at the time of submission of the application has a document certifying his right to habitually reside in the territory of the Republic of Lithuania;
- has passed the examination in the basic provisions of the Constitution of the Republic of Lithuania*;
- is a stateless person or is a citizen of a state under the laws of which he shall lose citizenship of the said state upon acquiring citizenship of the Republic of Lithuania or notifies in writing of his will to renounce citizenship of another state held by him after he is granted citizenship of the Republic of Lithuania**.

Upon granting citizenship of the Republic of Lithuania the rights and obligations of the citizen of the Republic of Lithuania shall arise only after the person takes the oath to the Republic of Lithuania. The applications for granting citizenship of the Republic of Lithuania shall be submitted to the President of the Republic of Lithuania *via the migration service.*

Where to apply and what documents shall be submitted?

The following documents shall accompany the application to grant citizenship of the Republic of Lithuania under the paragraph **1** of Article **14** of the Law on Citizenship:

- a copy of the person's identity card;
- a copy of the birth certificate;
- a copy of the marriage certificate;
- a copy of the document certifying the Republic of Lithuania citizenship of the spouse;
- document certifying the right of residence in the Republic of Lithuania at the moment of submission of this application;
- a document certifying that the person has been living in the territory of the Republic of Lithuania for the period referred to in paragraph 1 of Article 14 of the Law on Citizenship;

- a document evidencing that the person has passed the examinations in the state language and basic principles of the Constitution of the Republic of Lithuania;
- If a person hold a citizenship of another state he shall submit a written application for the renunciation of the citizenship of another state held when he is granted citizenship of the Republic of Lithuania.

All documents must be processed according to the conditions laid down by law.

* * *

According to the paragraph **2** of Article **14** of the Law on Citizenship, *persons who contracted marriage with citizens of the Republic of Lithuania: deportees, political prisoners or their children born in exile* shall be granted citizenship of the Republic of Lithuania if, after contracting marriage, they move to the Republic of Lithuania for habitual residence *and provided that they have resided for the last five years in the Republic of Lithuania together with their spouse* who is a citizen of the Republic of Lithuania and meet the conditions established in subparagraphs 2, 5 and 6 of paragraph 1 of Article 12 of the Law on Citizenship, that is:

- at the time of submission of the application has a document certifying his right to habitually reside in the territory of the Republic of Lithuania;
- has passed the examination in the basic provisions of the Constitution of the Republic of Lithuania*;
- is a stateless person or is a citizen of a state under the laws of which he shall lose citizenship of the said state upon acquiring citizenship of the Republic of Lithuania or notifies in writing of his will to renounce citizenship of another state held by him after he is granted citizenship of the Republic of Lithuania**.

Upon granting citizenship of the Republic of Lithuania the rights and obligations of the citizen of the Republic of Lithuania shall arise only after the person takes the oath to the Republic of Lithuania. The applications for granting citizenship of the Republic of Lithuania shall be submitted to the President of the Republic of Lithuania *via the migration service*.

Where to apply and what documents shall be submitted?

The following documents shall accompany the application to grant citizenship of the Republic of Lithuania under the paragraph **2** of Article **14** of the Law on Citizenship:

- a copy of the person's identity card;
- a copy of the birth certificate;
- a copy of the marriage certificate;
- a copy of the document certifying the Republic of Lithuania citizenship of the spouse;

- document certifying the right of residence in the Republic of Lithuania at the moment of submission of this application;
- a document certifying that the person has been living in the territory of the Republic of Lithuania for the period referred to in paragraph 2 of Article 14 of the Law on Citizenship;
- a document evidencing that the person has passed the examination in the basic principles of the Constitution of the Republic of Lithuania;
- a copy certifying that the person is a deportee or political prisoner;
- If a person hold a citizenship of another state he shall submit a written application for the renunciation of the citizenship of another state held when he is granted citizenship of the Republic of Lithuania.

All documents must be processed according to the conditions laid down by law.

* * *

According to the paragraph 3 of Article 14 of the Law on Citizenship, *a person who, after contracting a marriage with a citizen of the Republic of Lithuania, has resided in the territory of the Republic of Lithuania for over a year may, in case of death of his spouse, be granted citizenship of the Republic of Lithuania after he has resided in the territory of the Republic of Lithuania* **for five years**, provided that there are no reasons on the ground whereof citizenship of the Republic of Lithuania shall not be granted and provided that the person meets the conditions established in subparagraphs 1, 2, 5 and 6 of paragraph 1 of Article 12 of the Law on Citizenship, that is:

- has passed the examination in the state language*;
- at the time of submission of the application has a document certifying his right to habitually reside in the territory of the Republic of Lithuania;
- has passed the examination in the basic provisions of the Constitution of the Republic of Lithuania*;
- is a stateless person or is a citizen of a state under the laws of which he shall lose citizenship of the said state upon acquiring citizenship of the Republic of Lithuania or notifies in writing of his will to renounce citizenship of another state held by him after he is granted citizenship of the Republic of Lithuania**.

Upon granting citizenship of the Republic of Lithuania the rights and obligations of the citizen of the Republic of Lithuania shall arise only after the person takes the oath to the Republic of Lithuania. The applications for granting citizenship of the Republic of Lithuania shall be submitted to the President of the Republic of Lithuania via the migration service.

The following documents shall accompany the application to grant citizenship of the Republic of Lithuania under the paragraph 3 of Article 14 of the Law on Citizenship:

- a copy of the person's identity card;
- a copy of the birth certificate;
- a copy of the marriage certificate;
- a copy of the document certifying the Republic of Lithuania citizenship of the spouse;
- document certifying the right of residence in the Republic of Lithuania at the moment of submission of this application;
- a document certifying that the person has been living in the territory of the Republic of Lithuania for the period referred to in paragraph 3 of Article 14 of the Law on Citizenship;
- a document evidencing that the person has passed the examinations in the state language and basic principles of the Constitution of the Republic of Lithuania;
- a copy of the death certificate of the spouse;
- If a person hold a citizenship of another state he shall submit a written application for the renunciation of the citizenship of another state held when he is granted citizenship of the Republic of Lithuania.

All documents must be processed according to the conditions laid down by law.

————

* *The requirement shall not be applied to persons who are 65 years of age or over, persons who have been established 0-55% capacity for work and persons who have reached pensionable age and who have been rated as having high- or medium-level special needs according to the procedure laid down by legal acts, also to persons ill with grave chronic mental illnesses.*

** *The requirement shall not apply to citizens of foreign states who have refugee status in the Republic of Lithuania.*

Sophie van Bijsterveld

IMMIGRATION AND RELIGION IN THE NETHERLANDS

1. Introduction

In the Netherlands, immigration has a strong impact in the area of religion. The religious map of the country has changed considerably over the last forty years due to immigration. Also, at least in part because of immigration, especially of Muslims, the issue of religion has again come into the limelight, socially, culturally, and politically. Furthermore, religion gives rise to new debates and dilemmas in the relationship between religion and the state, and religion and law.

This report deals with the relation between religion and immigration in the stricter sense: religion related to immigration, as such. Apart from demographic developments and related public policies, it deals with three specific issues relating to religion that occur in the context of immigration. They are the issue of 'church asylum', pastoral care for asylum seekers, and admission to and residence in the country for religious purposes.

The law relating to immigration, including asylum law, and the acquisition of citizenship are among the most detailed and complex areas of law. Not only is national law in relation to these topics complex in itself,[1] but there is also an international dimension. Bilateral and multilateral treaties exist, European policies and laws have been developed, and human rights treaties are relevant to these areas as well. In addition, the domains mentioned are characterized by change. In the context of this report, it is impossible to outline the relevant law, and the developments that have occurred over the past few decades and current developments, in any concrete detail. Therefore, they will be dealt with in this report in broad, general outlines for the purpose of highlighting the specific aspects relating to religion.

2. Immigration: General statistics

The discussion on immigration and on whether the Netherlands is a country of immigration is politically sensitive. To avoid such discussion, it is

---

[1] In the Netherlands, the law in these fields is established at the national level.

best to turn to statistical data. Statistically Netherlands provides data on the development and composition of the population. These data give a good basic overview of developments in the Netherlands over the past century.

As the figures in the Annex illustrate, significant immigration began from the 1970s onwards. The presuppositions at the time were that immigration was a temporary matter and that immigrants (guest workers) would return to their country of origin after a number of years. What in fact happened was the opposite. In the slipstream of primary immigration, family unification and family building led to further immigration.

Immigration figures, as such, do not present a full picture of the impact in terms of religious demography. As regards religious affiliation, first generation immigration also impacts upon further generations. A uniform and well-defined notion of religious adherence does not exist.

As far as Christian denominations are concerned, each church has its own criteria for membership and these may differ widely from one church to another. These, in turn, may differ from affiliation or (non-) affiliation as experienced by believers or non-believers themselves. There is no census, so figures on religious affiliation as presented in statistical surveys tend to be quite vague. Depending on the way they are composed, they may also differ quite significantly from one to another. A recent statistical survey mentioned 58% of the population regarded itself as having a religious affiliation, of this 29% comprises Catholics; 19%, comprises one of the larger protestant denominations, which has been united since 2004 to the Protestant Church in the Netherlands (two large reformed churches and the Lutheran Church in the Netherlands); 5% are Muslim; and 6% are affiliated with another religion or belief.[2]

The mood towards immigration has changed in the course of the last decade. It is difficult to pinpoint the reasons for the growing unease with immigration. However, the extent of immigration, especially from non-Western countries is an important factor. Behind this lies a general feeling about the inadequacies of past and present liberal attitudes, or perhaps even indifference towards integration and to cultural, religious, socio-economic, and educational differences. From 'respect for the cultures of origin', the attention has shifted to 'integration'.[3] This is reflected in politics and it has an impact on government policies as well. Although in

---

[2] See Centraal Bureau voor de Statistiek, *Religie aan het begin van de 21ste eeuw*, Heerlen 2009, p. 14 and p. 7.

[3] The annual 'Integration reports' provide valuable information on integration and the 'state of play'. For 2009, see the 'Jaarrapport integratie 2009, *Kamerstukken II*, Bijlage 2009-1010, 31268, no. 25.

discussions on religion and immigration, Islam usually features prominently, it must also be realized that a large number of immigrants are
adherents of other religions, including a large number of Christians.

Until about a decade ago, religion was by and by a 'blind spot' in
discussions on immigration and integration. By the turn of the millen-
nium, the religious dimension was rediscovered, in society in general,
and in the context of immigration. As a result, discussions on immigration and integration are to a considerable extent framed in terms of religion. From having been underrated, religion now runs the risk of being
over-emphasized. This is not just a matter of academic interest. A dis-
proportional focus on religion can also lead to an inadequate policy
response to integration issues.[4]

3. Immigration: Two tracks

There are two different immigration tracks: the application for asylum
and a regular application for residence.[5] The details of immigration law
are quite complex.[6] The general trend over the past number of years has
been a tightening of immigration policy. In 2008, a new immigration policy was developed. Accordingly, a Bill to this effect has recently been
introduced in the Lower House of Parliament. 'Selective immigration', on
the one hand, aims at facilitating certain forms of immigration for specific
(notably highly qualified) personnel; on the other hand, it aims to be more
strict as regards enforcement and illegal immigration. In this context, the
law and policy on admission and residence 'for religious purposes' (see
below, Section 7) is going to undergo some modification as well.

4. Nationality and citizenship

To stimulate integration, a so-called *inburgeringsexamen* has been introduced by law (Civic Integration Act (*Wet inburgering*)). This translates
more or less with 'civic integration exam'; in the Dutch language, it has
the connotation of both 'integration' and 'citizenship'. This obligation

---

[4] See among others, Sophie van Bijsterveld, *Overheid en godsdienst. Herijking van
een onderlinge relatie*, 2nd edn., Nijmegen: Wolf Legal Publishers 2009.
  [5] No data were available about the grounds for applying for asylum (such as fear for
prosecution on grounds of one's religion).
  [6] The basic law dealing with immigration is the Aliens Act 2000 (*Vreemdelingenwet
2000*), *Kamerstukken* II, 2008-2009, 30 052, nos. 1-3 (*Voorstel van Wet modern migra-
tiebeleid*).

exists for those immigrants who already live in the Netherlands, and are between the ages of 18 and 65. The law details further criteria. Among those excluded, are those, among others, who have already obtained citizenship, or who hold EU citizenship or the citizenship of a country of the European Economic Area, or Switzerland; those who have obtained certain professional qualifications in the Dutch language, or have attended a Dutch school for a number of years as compulsory education. The law also deals with many specifics such as the provision of courses and the organization of the exams. For our purpose, it is noteworthy that a specific category of those who are obliged to take the exam are 'religious workers', including religious teachers.

Not only are those who already reside in the Netherlands obliged to undergo a 'civic integration exam', but so also are certain categories of persons still living in their country of origin but who plan to emigrate to the Netherlands, for example for the purpose of family reunification. A basic mandatory test has been introduced (*Wet inburgering in het buitenland*). One of the categories, obliged by law to take such a test are *geestelijke bedienaren*, a term which is hard to translate. In English, the word 'clergy' or 'religious workers' might do.

The inclusion of 'religious workers' was specifically motivated at the time of the enactment of the laws. Their (potential) impact on their social environment was mentioned; also their role as an interface between their environment, and public authorities or social institutions was mentioned, as well as the undesirability of a 'religious worker' who would be less civically integrated into his environment. In a rather unexpected way, this underscores the fact that religion is not just a private matter, either on the part of believers or on the part of institutions and clergy or religious teachers.

In order to make naturalization more than just the acquisition of a passport, a 'naturalization ceremony' has been introduced. This event aims at conveying the message that achieving Dutch citizenship is something special. In this context, it must be mentioned that recent figures show that out of a total population of nearly 16.5 million people in the Netherlands, about 1.1 million people have more than one nationality.

5. Church asylum

Legally speaking, church asylum does not exist in the Netherlands. The Dutch Code of Criminal Procedure contains an Article prohibiting officers of the law from entering a church building during a service, unless they are pursuing an offender who has been caught red-handed. This provision has been copied in the General Act on Entry into Dwellings (*Algemene Wet op het binnentreden*). The origin of this provision is old. There was little discussion when it was included in the General Act.

'Church asylum' has occasionally been granted by churches to asylum seekers whose application for asylum had been rejected by the highest court. There have been a few cases of church asylum notably in the 1980s. In some instances, church services were conducted in order to prevent the official authorities from entering the premises. In other cases, the public authorities refrained from entering the premises in order to avoid confrontation. 'Church asylum' can only have a temporary character; can never be a long-term solution. It is many years since 'church asylum' actions were publicly reported. The practice of 'church asylum', which was always controversial in society and politics, and within the churches themselves, seems to have become quite rare these days.

Opinions about such action differ. Some think it is a welcome initiative. Others are of the opinion that the Dutch legal procedures regarding asylum, including access to the courts, is such that churches in a democratic state should not interfere.

6. Pastoral care for asylum seekers

In the 1990s, the question of structured religious pastoral care for immigrants in asylum seekers' centers was raised by the joint churches. They addressed the state about this issue. The number of asylum seekers, as well as the organizational set-up of asylum seekers' centers with limited movement for its residents, justified the provision of chaplaincy services comparable to chaplaincy services in, for instance, penitentiary institutions. The specific problems at stake required special attention. Furthermore, the concentration of asylum seekers' centers in a few locations in the country meant a heavy burden on available local pastoral resources. The state, however, was not inclined to set up such facility. As a result, pastoral care of asylum seekers is provided within the regular existing facilities. In this context, it must be mentioned that – apart from various publicly -facilitated services – a considerable number of volunteers are active in asylum centers, perhaps not for pastoral assistance, but for social and practical activities.

7. Admission and residence 'for religious purposes'

A specific policy exists for admission and residence for religious work-ers (*geestelijke bedienaren*).[7] The crux is that the admission or residence in the country is 'for religious purposes'.[8] The concept, therefore, is not an ecclesiastical/theological notion.

Given the degree of detail in the law and policy involved, a general sketch will be given of the basic outlines only. The general rule is that the foreign Nationals (Employment) Act (*Wet Arbeid Vreemdelingen*) applies.[9] However, a few adjustments have been made. For religious workers from third-world countries, it is not necessary to establish whether sufficient 'prioritized supply' is available, no notice needs to be given of a vacancy to the official 'Centres for Work and Income', and the requirement of competitive salary is modified to 'minimum wage'. With respect to the religious organization that wishes to employ the for-eign religious worker, a formalized test takes place to ensure that no public order problem exists. The individual himself must be of age and have a work permit, a permit for temporary stay, and a valid passport; he must also not pose a threat to public order or national security. For family reunification, the ordinary rules apply; this is also the case in respect of rights of those family members to enter the labour market. Of the 68, 570 applications for regular resident permits in the year 2008, 1% concerned applications for 'religious purposes'.[10]

At present, the Dutch migration law is in the process of being revised.[11] The main objects are to introduce a more focused and selective immigra-tion policy, and to streamline the administrative procedures. The new law will introduce the so-called 'referent', a contact (usually the employer) with specific duties and obligations; churches and other religious organi-zations wishing to employ a religious worker can function as such. To referents who have obtained a prior, general 'recognition', a simplified and accelerated procedure is available. According to the government, this is not likely to have practical effects for churches and other religious

[7] See, for instance, the English summary of the report of the Advisory Committee on Migration Affairs (*Adviescommissie voor Vreemdelingenzaken*) on this topic at: <http://www.acvz.org/publicaties/S_A16_ENG.pdf >.

[8] See specifically *Kamerstukken II*, 2005-2006, 19 637, no. 1051 (11 May 2006); it contains the Cabinet reaction to proposals of the Advisory Committee on Migration Affairs.

[9] This law is subject to revision: *Kamerstukken II*, 2009-2010, 32 144, nos. 1, 3.

[10] *Kamerstukken II*, 2009-2010, 32 052, no. 7, p. 4.

[11] See the Modern Migration Policy Bill, *Kamerstukken II*, 2008-2009, 32 052, nos. 1-3; see also *Kamerstukken II*, 2007-2008, 30 673, no. 10, a document which outlines the new policy.

organizations, given the relatively small number of cases which each organization is likely to be involved with.

8. Conclusion

In recent years, a variety of quite specific dimensions of religion in relation to immigration law policy have emerged. In this report, particular issues of 'church asylum', pastoral care for asylum seekers, and admission and residence in the country for religious purposes was discussed. The latter issue has given rise to the development of new law and policies. They include not only (criteria for) admission into the country, but also the introduction of obligatory civic integration programmes for immigrant clergy, both from abroad (prior to their stay in the Netherlands) and in the Netherlands. The current revision of immigration policy, although not specifically aimed at immigrant religious workers, has some inherent consequences for these workers.

ANNEX – The growth of the Dutch population over the last hundred years

Total popul. Per January (x 1.000)	1900	1910	1920	1930	1940	1950	1960	1970	1980	1990	2000	2009
Total	5 104	5 858	7 754	7 825	8 834	10 027	11 417	12 958	14 091	14 843	15 865	16 486
Total Non Dutch	53.0	70.0					107.0	212.1	473.4	641.9	651.5	719.5
Maroccan							0.1	17.4	71.8	148.0	119.7	70.8
Turks							0.1	23.6	119.6	191.5	100.7	92.7
Surinams									145.7	219.0	302.5	338.7
Dutch Antillians									36.2	71.2	107.2	134.8
Pop. growth												
Immigr.	28	35	42	67	20	71	45	91	113	117	133	–
Emigr.	25	35	63	57	26	51	58	57	59	57	61	–
Net Migration Balance	3	0	-21	10	-7	20	13	33	53	60	72	–
Tot. Growth	75	87	34	103	89	174	139	162	118	118	123	–

These figures are from the update by the Statistics Netherlands in December 2009.[12]

[12] http://statline.cbs.nl/StatWeb/publication/?VW=T&DM=SLNL&PA=37556&LA=NL

MICHAŁ RYNKOWSKI

IMMIGRATION AND RELIGION IN POLAND

1. General remarks

Immigration in Poland both an old and recent phenomenon. From the beginning of its statehood until the 18th century, the Kingdom of Poland (together with the Grand duchy of Lithuania as the Republic included both Nations) welcomed thousands of settlers, mainly of German, Dutch and Scottish origin, but also Jews, Italians and Armenians[1]. In the 19th century the situation changed: Poles became a nation of emigrants, due to a number of reasons. Between 1795 and 1918 the state did not exist. Every national uprising was followed by significant political emigration (1830, 1863), and at the end of 19th century the economic emigration to Germany, France, the USA and Brazil began. The new born country (1918) faced two world wars, an economic crisis between them, and a communist regime after 1945 which was never considered a dream destination. The only significant group of migrants who settled in Poland in 1950. were Greeks (approx. 12,500 persons) who had to leave their own country. On the other hand, Poles who were born and had lived in the eastern part of Poland, which in 1945 unexpectedly became the Soviet Union, had to leave their homes and move to Poland with new borders. For a number of years they felt like refugees, though they lived in their own state.

After 1989, Poland has slowly become an attractive destination for migrants, but figures can not be compared with those of other states. On top of that, a number of immigrants do not perceive Poland as a country of final destination. According to research carried out by the Main Statistic Office (GUS), only in 2019 will Poland become a country of net-immigration, where the number of persons incoming will be greater than the numbers emigrating.

A particular feature of Polish immigration law is repatriation – which is a massive return of Poles deported by the Soviet Union to Kazakhstan

---

[1] K. Iglicka, The revival of ethnic consciousness: the case of Poland, in: A. Górny, P. Ruspini (eds.), Migration in the New Europe, Basingstoke 2004, p.131.

and other Soviet Republics during World War II. The legal basis for this is a special statute, adopted on 9 November 2000[2]. The status of a repatriate is granted to a person, where one of the parents, grandparents or two great-grandparents used to have Polish nationality, and the interested person speaks the Polish language and has links with Polish traditions and customs (See: Karta Polaka – a Charter of Poles, statute dating from 7 September 2007, published in OJ 2007, No. 180, it. 1280). This statute refers only to persons whose ancestors were deported to Russia and/or Soviet Union (as Poles used to say under the communist rule, "persons who have been travelled" – this is grammatically incorrect, both in English and in Polish, but underlines the passive tense of unwanted "travel" to Siberia). Thus, it does not refer to people of Polish origin living in the USA, Brasil or any other state.

2. Legal sources

Legal sources and various forms of legal status that may be granted to foreigners under Polish law correspond to the requirements of international law and EC law.[3] The basic legal acts are:[4]

- A statute from 13 June 2003 concerning foreigners, consolidated version OJ 2006 No. 234 it. 1694
- A statute from 13 June 2003 concerning protection granted to the foreigners in the territory of Poland, cons. version OJ 2009 No. 189 it. 1472 from 22.10.2009. This statute implements directives 2001/55 and 2003/9).
- A statute from 15 February 1962, on Polish citizenship, cons. version OJ 2000 No. 28, item 353; a new statute has been adopted on 2 April 2009 by the Sejm and Senat, but has not yet been signed by the President, who has sent the text to the Constitutional Tribunal (see below).
- A statute from 9 November 2000 on repatriation, cons. version OJ 2004, No. 53, item 532.

The legal situation of the EU citizens is regulated by a separate statute from 14 July 2006, OJ 2006, No. 144, it. 1043.

---

[2] Consolidated version: Official Journal 2004, No. 53, item 532.
[3] A. Weinar, Europeizacja polskiej polityki wobec cudzoziemców 1990-2003, Warszawa 2006.
[4] Free of charge and regularly updated collection of legal acts with their consolidated versions (all documents in Polish only) is available on the Sejm website: http://isap.sejm.gov.pl/

From the legal point of view, there are two basic categories of stay, which can be divided into more detailed subgroups:

a) persons coming from safe countries, including EU-Member States

- a right to settle, if the person has lived legally for 10 years (or has been for 5 years refugee);
- a long-term EU-residence, for persons who have been living legally in Poland for the last 5 years and have sufficient financial resources
- a stay for a defined term, which may be granted by the voivod among others also to persons joining families, or to clergy of churches and religious communities, functioning legally in Poland (art. 53a of the statute on foreigners)

The key organ for all these cases is the voivod (regional governor, appointed by the Prime Minister).

b) persons coming from countries which are not always regarded as safe:

(1) refugees – this status is granted only under the terms of the Geneva Convention relating to the Status of Refugees of 28.07.1951, as amended by the Protocol signed in New York on 3.01.1967
(2) there is subsidiary protection to those, forwhom the status of refugee can not be granted, who nevertheless need protection
(3) a tolerated stay, which may be granted only to persons who can not receive the status of a refugee, but who could be deported only to a country, where his/her life would be threatened or would be subject to torture, punishment, humiliation, etc.

These cases are dealt by the Foreigners' Office (Urząd do Spraw Cudzoziemców), which is supervised by the Minister of Interior and Administration. For the decisions taken by the Head of the Foreigners' Office the second instance is the Refugees Council (Rada do Spraw Uchodźców), composed of 12 persons appointed by the Prime Minister, from whom 6 must have a professional legal background.

Acquisition of the Polish citizenship is dealt with in part 4.

3. Statistics

Detailed statistics are presented below, but a couple of figures should be quoted in order to describe general trends. According to Eurostat statistics, in 2008 57000 inhabitants with citizenship other than Polish (both EU and non-EU citizenship), lived in Poland which is quite a limited number for a population of 38 million. Only Bulgaria, Lithuania, Malta, Romania and Slovakia have a lower number, but in terms of percentage rates, the Polish rate is the second lowest, after Romania.

Interestingly, the first research on immigration[5] covered years 1989-1996 and showed that 50 % of migrants settled in Warsaw and its suburbs, and that 50 % of all immigrants came from the states-successors of the old Soviet Union, mainly from Ukraine, Russia, Belarus and Armenia. These two basic statements have remained true also for the past 15 years. The voivod of Masovia, of which Warsaw is the capital, issues approx. 30 % of all decisions and permits. A significant number of permits are granted to Bulgarians, Vietnamese, Indians, Japanese, Koreans, and Turks. Vietnamese immigrants are actually the only group which is the subject of academic research.[6]

3.1. Immigration figures

(Data for 2008. In the second line, figures for 2003[7] in brackets.)
The selection of criteria and countries of origin presented in this table is subjective. It should illustrate, that the three neighbouring countries: Ukraine, Russia and Belarus generate the highest number of immigrants. The other important group are Asians: Vietnamese, Chinese and Indians. Immigration from African countries, although growing, is still minimal.

Country of origin	Application for status of refugee	Refugee status granted	Tolerated stay Granted	Applications for settlement	Permit to settle granted	applications for stay for defined term	Stay for defined term granted
Ukraine	40 (86)	0 (0)	1 (0)	1725 (878)	1685 (449)	9054 (8334)	8307 (7954)
Belarus	58 (57)	14 (10)	2 (0)	708 (206)	640 (121)	2591 (2432)	2380 (2365)
Russia	7760 (5563)	129 (211)	1486 (20)	278 (269)	255 (169)	1579 (1967)	1468 (1877)
Vietnam	65 (25)	0 (1)	1 (0)	177 (317)	162 (202)	2308 (1929)	2580 (1067)
Armenia	50 (104)	1 (0)	4 (0)	134 (247)	116 (118)	1694 (1913)	1452 (887)

---

[5] K. Głąbicka E. Kępińska, P. Koryś, B. Sakson: Imigracja do Polski w świetle urzędowych statystyk, Institute for Social Studies, Warsaw 1997;

[6] Teresa Halik, Migrancka społeczność Wietnamczyków w Polsce w świetle polityki państwa i ocen społecznych, Wydanie I, UAM Poznań;

[7] http://www.udsc.gov.pl/files/old_file/440426f016ddd_biuletyn_2003_2005.pdf

China	22	0	1	17	16	1391	1205
	(15)	(2)	(0)	(52)	(45)	(419)	(391)
India	0	0	0	39	26	1112	977
	(236)	(0)	(0)	(47)	(30)	(643)	(585)
Turkey	18	0	0	61	45	963	834
	(22)	(0)	(0)	(39)	(22)	(617)	(551)
Algeria	14	0	0	24	17	109	97
	(13)	(0)	(0)	(26)	(9)	(94)	(57)
Morocco	3	0	0	11	13	150	129
	(0)	(1)	(0)	(12)	(8)	(58)	(47)
Nigeria	24	0	1	47	32	731	598
	(15)	(0)	(0)	(12)	(3)	(138)	(119)
Moldova	19	0	0	18	24	541	514
	(21)	(0)	(0)	(24)	(10)	(270)	(248)
Sri Lanka	22	1	5	2	1	26	17
	(32)	(0)	(0)	(0)	(0)	(26)	(17)
Iraq	70	28	1	7	8	141	137
	(75)	(0)	(0)	(7)	(4)	(50)	(45)
Total	8517	186	1507	3890	3625	31467	28865
	(7825)	(243)	(24)	(3000)	(1735)	(31724)	(28563)

There is no doubt that illegal immigration also exists, mainly from the Ukraine, other former Soviet Republics and Vietnam. The situation is more difficult for illegal immigrants who are not white: one has to keep in mind that even in a middle-size Polish town a black person can not remain unnoticed[8].

As a majority of immigrants come from neighbouring countries, 20 % of immigrants possess a very good command of the Polish language, 25 % good, 25 % sufficient, and only 30 % insufficient[9]. Therefore, even if Polish is considered a difficult language, the linguistic dimension does not cause major problems.

3.2. Religious aspect of immigration

According to the statute on protection of foreigners (13 June 2003) the data on religion may be collected and treated, but in none of the statistics, questionnaires or documents is the question of religion actually mentioned. This issue arises only in judgments of administrative courts, which are briefly described in point 5.

---

[8] Author himself, living for 32 years in fourth biggest Polish city Wrocław (640,000 inhabitants) saw only once a woman in a headscarf and she seemed to be a tourist, not an inhabitant.

[9] Note of GUS (Central Statistic Office), 23 December 2008.

As mentioned, the major groups constitute Ukrainians, Russians, Belarusians and Armenians, almost all of them being Catholic, Orthodox or atheist, but even the latter have Christian roots. The exceptions in this respect are the Chechens seeking asylum, and Chinese immigrants. Surprisingly, quite a number of Vietnamese living in Poland are Catholic; in Warsaw there are masses celebrated in Vietnamese (parish of Lord's Birth, Kościół Narodzenia Pańskiego, Warszawa-Witolin). The Catholic Church decided a couple of years ago to meet the expectations of foreign believers by establishing English speaking communities, which are available to all persons, who are not sufficiently familiar with the Polish language. In Warsaw, there are also masses in English, Italian, French, German, Lithuanian, Armenian and Korean.

There are hardly any Muslim immigrants, except for students from Arabic countries and some businessmen. According to Muslim sources there are some 20,000-30,000 Muslims in Poland, but official sources give much lower figures. Approx. 5000 of Muslims are Tartars, Muslims living in Poland for past 600 years.

4. Acquisition of Polish citizenship, test of citizenship

The current legal base is the above mentioned statute on citizenship dating from 1962, with amendments. Polish citizenship may be granted to persons who have a permit to settle for at least 5 years, are for 5 years long term residents of the EU, or have for 5 years a permit of permanent stay. A person married to a Polish citizen may apply for citizenship after 3 years. Each application is treated by the wojewoda (voivod, the local governor, appointed by the Prime Minister, representing the government in the region), who submits the application to the President, who according to Art. 137 of the Constitution grants citizenship. This statute does not foresee any test for acquisition, receiving citizenship is merely a question of time. In particularly deserving cases, citizenship can be granted even if the 5-year–term is not observed, and it has been applied a couple of times to various outstanding sportsmen.

The new statute on citizenship was adopted on 2 April 2009 and has been accepted by both Chambers of the Parliament (Sejm and Senat). The President of Republic has not yet signed the statute – he addressed the Constitutional Court asking to verify the legality of the act (case Kp 5/09, in January 2010 still pending). The president claims that the competences of the voivod has been extended too broadly.

Interestingly, the new statute does not prescribe any deadline as required for acquisition of the citizenship, and in fact, it seems to be one of the most liberal citizenships acts in Europe. A new element of application is information on the command of the Polish language, but there is no form or certificate needing to be attached. The second option is the decision of the President, confirming Polish citizenship: the persons must have lived for 3 years on the basis of a permit to settle or as a long-term resident of the EU. In this case, a certificate confirming command of language, as foreseen by the law on the Polish language, must be attached, or a certificate from a Polish school.

5. Asylum – some statistics

The current legal base is quite new; it is a statute from 13 June 2003 on the protection of foreigners. The Foreigners' Office (Urząd do Spraw Cudzoziemców) publishes on its website regular and exhaustive statistics[10]. In 2008, 8500 persons from 62 states applied for refugee status, which was granted according to the Geneva Convention to 186 (129 from Russia, 28 from Iraq, 14 from Belarus), subsidiary protection to 1074 (1057 from Russia) and tolerated stay to 1507 (1486 from Russia, 5 from Sri Lanka). Despite the enormous figures of immigrants coming from Ukraine, only 40 applied for refugee status, and this status was granted to none of them.

A number of judgements of the courts concerning application of refugees, referred to the religious dimension:[11]

1. the status of refugee in the case of a female citizen of Turkmenistan was refused: she claimed to be persecuted because of her religion. According to the data of the American Secretary of State, the authorities of Turkmenistan did not allow the persecuted person to leave the country at all, and the applicant legally crossed the border of Turkmenistan in 2002 and in 2004; the court underlined that the status of refugee is granted if the given person will be persecuted; the general condition in the country (limited freedom of religion) is not sufficient reason to grant refugee status (judgment of the Voivodship Administrative Court, 2.02.2006, V SA/Wa 1717/05, not published).

[10] http://www.udsc.gov.pl/files/statystyki/2008.xls
[11] Interesting collection of judgments on foreigners edited in Polish by Jacek Chlebny: Cudzoziemcy [Foreigners], Warsaw 2007.

2. the rude behaviour of neighbours towards the Jehovah witnesses in Armenia does not constitute sufficient basis for granting refugee status (judgment of the Voivodship Administrative Court, 13.01.2005, V SA/Wa 1239/04, not published; similar judgment: Chief Administrative Court, 31.08.2005, II OSK 682/05, not published)
3. a change of religion may constitute a major threat to the life of a person, who lives in a country where Islam is the state religion (judgment of the Voivodship Administrative Court Warsaw 11.10.2004, V SA 2914/03, not published)
4. the status of refugee was refused in the case of a Nigerian citizen who claimed he was persecuted and was afraid of witchcraft; the Court found out, that this person had had a safe stay in the territory of Ukraine before coming to Poland, and had many times crossed the Nigerian border (judgment of Voivodship Administrative Court, Warsaw, 11.05.2004, case V SA 4723/03, not published);
5. in the case of another Nigerian, whose father was a member of secret sect, who had killed members of his own family, the Chief Administrative Court underlined the need to carry out research on real threats. The Court challenged the decision of the authorities, which had not even investigated what was the name of the alleged secret sect (Chief Administrative Court, 29.01.2003, case V SA 1494/02, published in ONSA 2004, No. 2, item 57).
6. An obligation to pray in public or to behave or to wear clothes according to one's religion may violate human rights (the case of an Afghan citizen, a Muslim, who was forced to pray in public, and who was punched whenever he committed an error while reading the Koran aloud – Chief Administrative Court, 24.09.2000, V SA 1781/99, ONSA 2001, No. 4, item 176).

6. Miscellaneous

As immigration to Poland is very limited, a number of issues frequently discussed in other European states remain unknown in Poland. As examples, polygamous marriages of immigrants or honour killings can be mentioned. Also questions of conflict or of potential conflict between the Polish legal system and the internal legal system of churches and religious communities are unknown. The Polish press merely reports cases of fake marriages, which became problematic in early years of memberships of the EU. They were contracted mainly between Vietnamese young men and Polish girls from rural areas. The price of a fake marriage was approx. 5.000 Euros. In 2008, the public prosecutor_in Lublin managed to trace 22 persons involved in such marriages; the majority of them voluntarily accepted the suggested penalty[12].

Also cases where clergy helped illegal immigrants or cases of so-called "church asylum" are not known, or at least are not spectacular. On the other hand, the state security forces do not intervene and do not enter ecclesiastical premises: even during the times of Martial law (1981-1983), the police forces (infamous ZOMO) basically refrained from entering churches. There is no legal basis for non-intervention (church asylum), but it is treated as customary law.

The Polish labour market is open to all citizens of the EU, including Bulgarians and Romanians and also to citizens of Germany and Austria, who have upheld restrictions in the labour market towards Poles. There are no quotas on employment of citizens from other states, nevertheless they have to apply for a stay permit combined with the working permit.

As immigrants constitute a small group, they are not referred to in political discussions, neither seen as a potential threat nor as a potential factor to development.

7. Summary

Poland has been in recent decades a country of emigration rather than of immigration. In the last two decades small groups of immigrants have arrived, mainly from Ukraine, Russia and Belarus, followed by citizens of Vietnam and Armenia[13]. The statistics on immigration available, are regularly updated and are quite detailed[14]. Data on religious affiliation of foreigners is not collected (exception: procedures concerning protection of immigrants), since it is not collected for Polish citizens. Nevertheless data on religious affiliation is not irrelevant in individual cases, where applicants ask for asylum.

It can be concluded that the religious dimension of immigration does not pose (so far) any major problems.

[12] Gazeta Wyborcza, Lublin, 28.01.2008.
[13] E. Kępińska, D. Stola, Migration Policy and Politics in Poland, in: A. Górny, P. Ruspini (eds.), op. cit., p. 159.
[14] Website of Foreigners' Office: www.udsc.gov.pl contains a number of very useful information and is regularly updated.

Nuno Piçarra – Francisco Borges

IMMIGRATION AND RELIGION IN PORTUGAL

1. The facilitation and promotion of immigration and the granting of asylum

1.1. Immigration

I. Historically, Portugal has been mainly a country of emigration. Even today, there are large communities of Portuguese emigrants all over the world.

After the independence of the Portuguese colonies in Africa, in the 1970's, and the accession of Portugal to the European Union, in 1986, with the concomitant economic growth, the status of Portugal as a "country of immigration" became more relevant. In 2008, there were 440,277 immigrants legally resident in Portugal and 72,826 applications for a residence permit. Of these, 40,584 were applications for the renewal of an existing residence permit.[1]

Due to particular historical links and to the very important linguistic factor, the immigration from Portuguese speaking countries, mainly Brazil, became dominant. In 2008, there were 106,961 Brazilian citizens legally resident in the Portuguese territory, corresponding to 24% of the community of immigrants legally resident in Portugal.

Cape Verde, Angola and Guinea-Bissau have respectively 51,352 (12% of the immigrant population legally resident in Portugal), 27,619 (6%) and 24,391 (6%) immigrants legally resident in Portugal.

However, there is also a very significant influx of immigrants from Eastern Europe, with a leading position taken by Ukraine, with 52,494 immigrants (12% of the immigrant population legally resident in Portugal). In 2008 the Ukrainians were, after the Brazilians, the most significant community of immigrants legally resident in Portugal. Other important communities from Eastern Europe are Romanians (meanwhile European citizens), with 27,769 immigrants (6%), and Moldavians, with 21,147 (5%).[2]

---

[1] *Report on Immigration, Borders and Asylum of the Immigration and Borders Service*, 2008, pp. 21-22 & 35-36, available online at www.sef.pt.

[2] *Report...*, pp. 27-29.

II. Portuguese legislation on immigration changed substantially in 2007, when Parliament adopted Law 23/2007, of 4 July, the so-called Aliens Act. This Act aims to promote legal immigration, by simplifying procedures for obtaining a visa, and eventually a residence permit, and diminishing the number of public authorities involved in such procedures.

III. Although the conditions that must be fulfilled in obtaining the residence visa are strict and demanding, some provisions of the Aliens Act bring flexibility to those conditions. For example, the previous six categories of a long-term visa are concentrated in one general and comprehensive category: the residence visa [Article 58(1)]; the visa for the purpose of obtaining a residence permit for taking up an independent professional activity may be granted to a third-country national who holds just a written proposal for a contract for the supply of services with character of self-employment [Article 60(1)(a)]; a temporary stay visa for the purpose of providing dependent professional services of a temporary nature is provided; and research and highly qualified assignments have a simplified legal regime (Articles 56, 57 and 61).

IV. Law 23/2007 foresees important limitations to the refusal of entry of a foreigner to the Portuguese territory. Such limitations aim to protect those who were born in the Portuguese territory and reside here regularly and those who have children in their charge who hold Portuguese nationality, or who are nationals of a third country, but legally reside in Portugal (Article 36).

The fight against illegal immigration is articulated with the protection of human rights. Under certain conditions, the granting of a residence permit to victims of human trafficking, or of an action facilitating illegal immigration is provided (Article 109).

The Aliens Act acknowledges a right of family reunion with relatives who have legally entered the national territory and depend on or live in cohabitation with the holder of a valid residence permit. Legal permanence in the Portuguese territory as a condition of obtaining family reunion is not required [Article 98(2)].[3]

V. Decree-Law 67/2004, of 25 March, guarantees the right to health care and proper education to minors in irregular situations. The right to health care is broader: according to Order 25.360/2001, of 16 November,

---

[3] See infra 3.IV.

of the Ministry of Health, such right is extensive to any person, legally resident or not in the Portuguese territory.

VI. A mention should be made of extraordinary regularizations in the last two decades. Although qualified by the Portuguese Government as absolutely exceptional and unrepeatable, the effect that such regularizations has had on the flow of migration is undeniable. This is confirmed by the ever growing figures of each successive regularization.[4]

VII. Law 23/2007 includes a new provision, Article 88(2), which is not considered as an extraordinary regularization in itself. According to this provision, a residence permit for carrying out a subordinated professional activity may in exceptional circumstances be granted even if the applicant does not hold a residence visa, provided that he/she holds a work contract or has a labour relation, has legally entered the national territory, is registered in the Social Security System and accomplished all his/her correspondent obligations.

The mechanism provided by Article 88(2) of Law 23/2007 allows successive Governments to adapt themselves to fluctuations in the economy and to concrete social problems of each period, through different political options concerning immigration, more liberal or more conservative, without legislative changes.

VIII. Linked closely to the subject of immigration is the issue of the acquisition of Portuguese citizenship and, more specifically, of naturalisation. The legislation on this subject, like the one related to aliens, was modified recently. As a matter of fact, the Organic Law 2/2006, of 17 April, substantially amended the Nationality Act (Law 37/81, of 3 October).

IX. According to Article 6(1) of the Nationality Act, a subjective right to naturalisation depends on the following requirements:

(a) to be of legal adult age or emancipated according to the Portuguese law;

(b) to have legally resided in Portugal for a period of six years;

(c) to have sufficient knowledge of the Portuguese language;

(d) to have no convictions for having committed a crime that carries a prison sentence of three years or more according to Portuguese law.

---

[4] See *Report...*, pp. 18-21.

Residence in the Portuguese territory and knowledge of the Portuguese language are considered as sufficient indicators of an effective link to the national community.

X. The 2006 reform added another category of individuals who have a subjective right to naturalisation. Such category includes minors who were born in Portugal and meet the following conditions [Article 6(2)]:

(a) sufficient knowledge of the Portuguese language;
(b) no conviction for having committed a crime which carries a prison sentence of three years or more according to Portuguese law;
(c) to be in one of the following situations:
– one of the applicant's parents has legally resided in Portugal for a period of 5 years prior to the application or
– the applicant has completed in Portugal the first cycle of compulsory education.

XI. In addition to the subjective right to naturalisation, the Nationality Act maintains the existence of a discretionary naturalisation. According to Article 6(5), the Government may grant naturalisation to second-generation immigrants, provided that they have been residing in Portugal for the last ten years prior to the application.

Article 6(6) foresees other possibilities for discretionary naturalisation, applicable to foreigners who previously held Portuguese citizenship, who are descendants of Portuguese citizens, members of communities of Portuguese origin, or who have provided notable services to the Portuguese State or to the Portuguese community. These individuals are exempted from fulfilling the requirements regarding the period of residence, and knowledge of the Portuguese language.

XII. The number of applications for naturalisation has risen following the adoption of the Organic Law 2/2006, of 17 April. In 2008, of the 45,466 requests for acquisition of Portuguese citizenship, 34,326 concerned naturalisation. This is probably a consequence of the 2006 legislative reform, which favoured the residence-based mode of acquisition through naturalisation.

Citizens from Portuguese-speaking countries constitute the large majority of applicants acquisition of the Portuguese citizenship, although there is also a significant number of applications from Eastern European States. Cape Verde (9,926), Brazil (8,391), Guinea-Bissau (4,589) and Angola

(4,463), followed by Moldavia (4,449), São Tomé and Príncipe (2,193) and Ukraine (1,567), are the most significant nationalities of origin.[5]

1.2. Asylum

I. Portuguese legislation on asylum was also substantially modified in 2008, in order to be consistent with the European legislation on the subject, namely Directives 2004/83/EC, of 29 April ("Qualification Directive"), and 2005/85/EC, of 1 December ("Procedures Directive"). Law 27/2008, of 30 of June, transposed these directives to the Portuguese legal order. According to its preamble, it establishes «the conditions and procedures for granting asylum or subsidiary protection and the status of asylum, refugee and subsidiary protection».

II. The previous legislation on the subject (Law 15/98, of 26 March) was, in general, less favourable from the point of view of the third-country national concerned. For example, the broad concept of persecution actor was not explicitly accepted, and the rules concerning family unity had a more limited scope.

However, the greatest improvement of Law 27/2008 is a better definition of the relevant legal concepts and a more coherent organization of the whole system. Furthermore, the discretion of the competent authorities in the assessment of applications for international protection was limited and the legislation has become more accessible to its potential beneficiaries. For example, the obligation of the competent authorities to consider certain facts and circumstances when assessing applications is now legally guaranteed; the scope of subsidiary protection status and its content are clearly regulated; and the social rights guaranteed to refugees are explicit in Law 27/2008 and not left to general legislation.

Law 27/2008 is, in general, in line with the Directive 2004/83/EC.[6] Concerning the refugee and subsidiary protection statuses, the Portuguese legislation is more favourable to third-country nationals than the Directive 2004/83/EC.

III. The number of applications for international protection is not very significant in Portugal. In 2008, there were only 161 requests for the granting of refugee status (in 2007 there were 224). The applicants came

---

[5] *Report...*, pp. 80-81.
[6] See *infra* 2.2.I.

from Africa (71 applications), namely from the Democratic Republic of
Congo, Guinea-Conakry and Nigeria; from Asia (44 applications),
mainly from Sri Lanka; from Latin-America (30 applications), namely
from Colombia; and from Eastern Europe (16 applications), *e.g.* from
Bosnia-Herzegovina. In 2007, Colombia, Bosnia-Herzegovina, Guinea-
Conakry and the Democratic Republic of Congo were the most representative nationalities, in this order.

In 2008, only 12 refugee statuses were granted (1 in 2007), mainly to
nationals of African countries. However, it is interesting to note that 70
residence permits for humanitarian reasons were granted (28 in 2007),
mainly to nationals of African countries, but also to South-American,
Asiatic and Eastern European nationals.[7]

2. The limitations and restrictions to immigration and asylum

2.1. Immigration

I. Although Law 23/2007 is intended to strengthen legal immigration[8],
third-country nationals cannot easily comply with the conditions established by such Law.

According to Article 77 of Law 23/2007, in order to obtain a residence permit the third-country national must fulfil the following conditions:

«(a) Hold a valid residency visa, granted for one of the purposes
established in the present Act as grounds for the concession of a residence permit;

(b) Be Aware of any fact that is known by the competent authorities
that should be an obstacle to granting that visa;

(c) Be present in Portuguese territory;

(d) Possess means of subsistence, such as defined by the administrative rule referred to in Article 52(1) (d);

(e) Have guaranteed lodgings;

(f) Be registered for Social Security, whenever applicable;

(g) Not have been convicted for any crime punishable with a prison
sentence of more than one year;

(h) Not be serving a ban from entry into the national territory, following a removal measure from the country;

---

[7] *Report...*, pp. 79-80.
[8] See *supra* 1.1.II.

(i) Absence of any alert in the Schengen Information System for purposes of refusing the entry;

(j) Absence of any alert in the Immigration and Borders Service's Integrated Information System for purposes of refusing the entry, pursuant to Article 53.»

II. This regime must be articulated with Article 59(2) of Law 23/2007, which establishes a global quota to be approved by the Government, after a preliminary assessment of the Permanent Commission for Social Conciliation, indicating the availability of job offers in the correspondent period.

This quota is explicitly directed towards the regular process of immigration provided by Article 77, which demands a residence visa. However, Article 88(3) states, surprisingly, that this restriction also applies to exceptional granting of a residence permit provided by Article 88(2).[9]

Resolution of the Council of Ministers 28/2008, of 15 February, established the quota of 8500 workers for the period between the adoption of the resolution and 31 December 2008. In 2009, Resolution of the Council of Ministers 50/2009, of 16 June, established a quota of just 3800 workers. The Government justified this reduction on account of the economic crisis.

III. It was stated above that one of the main purposes of Law 23/2007 is to promote legal immigration. In order to achieve this objective, the Aliens Act aims to fight illegal immigration, e.g. through the strengthening of the sanctions applicable to those who exploit irregular migrants, the criminalization of sham marriages and the protection of the victims of human trafficking.

2.2. Asylum

I. As stated above, the legislation on asylum is, in general, in line with the Directive 2004/83/EC.[10] However, it is less favourable than the Directive from the point of view of the third-country national regarding the grounds for cessation, exclusion and termination of the refugee and subsidiary protection statuses. For example, the commitment of any intentional crime punishable with more than 3 years imprisonment is a

---

[9] See *supra* 1.1.VII.
[10] See *supra* 1.2.II.

ground for exclusion of international protection. The situation in cases of common crimes committed with a political objective is not explicitly regulated.

In any case, asylum and subsidiary protection can be refused whenever their granting results in danger or confirmed threat towards the internal or external security or public order of the Portuguese State.

3. The religious dimension of immigration and asylum

I. In Portugal, the majority (88%) of the population declares itself Catholic.[11] Immigration, naturalization and asylum have not significantly altered this situation. Naturally there are other religious communities: according to the available data there were in 2007 35,000 Muslims, 700 Jews and a Hindu community of approximately 7,000 persons. Around 4% of the population identifies itself with various Protestant denominations. With increasing immigration from Eastern Europe, namely from Ukraine, there is also a relevant Orthodox community.[12]

II. Article 41 of the Portuguese Constitution guarantees freedom of conscience, religion and worship. In particular, paragraph 2 states that «no one shall be persecuted, deprived of rights or exempted from civic obligations or duties because of his convictions or religious observance» and paragraph 4 states that «churches and other religious communities shall be separate from the State and free to organise themselves and to perform their ceremonies and their worship».

Article 13(2) states that «no one shall be privileged, favoured, prejudiced, deprived of any right or exempted from any duty on the basis of (...) religion». According to Article 15(1), «foreigners and stateless persons who find themselves or who reside in Portugal shall enjoy the same rights and be subject to the same duties as Portuguese citizens».

Consequently, the public administration is constitutionally forbidden to consider religion as a relevant element when assessing applications for immigration or for asylum. For the same reason, Portuguese legislation may not contain exemption clauses for clergy or pastors related to the above mentioned quota for the employment of Non-EU citizens.

---

[11] See *Anuário Católico de Portugal*, 2009, available online at www.ecclesia.pt.
[12] See United States Department of State, *2007 Report on International Religious Freedom - Portugal*, 14 September 2007, available online at: http://www.unhcr.org.

III. Since 2001, there has been specific legislation on religious freedom (Law 16/2001, of 22 June). Article 5 establishes the principle of cooperation between the State and the different churches and religious communities, always on an equal basis. According to Article 2(2), discrimination between different religious communities is forbidden.

Article 13(1) of Law 16/2001 states that anyone imprisoned, placed in a detention centre or in a hospital has a right to religious assistance. Article 13(3) establishes that the State has the duty to provide the necessary conditions for the possibility of religious assistance as provided by paragraph 1. Special tax benefits for the different religious communities are provided by Article 32.

In Portugal, there are no examples of churches giving asylum to third country nationals. The legality of such an action would be uncertain.

IV. The Portuguese State has not explicitly transposed Article 4(4) of the EU Directive 2003/86/EC, of 22 September ("Family Reunion Directive"). However, polygamous marriages are forbidden by both the Civil Code (Article 1601) and the Penal Code (Article 247). Furthermore, Article 99(1) (a) of Law 23/2007 only considers one spouse as a family member for the purpose of family reunion. The public administration (no court decisions are known) considers that the formal recognition of a second marriage violates the international public order of the Portuguese State [Article 1651(2) of the Civil Code].

However, this does not imply that some social benefits cannot be granted to a second spouse and to her children, in order to comply with the constitutional principle of equality (Article 13), without the formal recognition of a second marriage. As a matter of fact, the application of the international public order provision implies an adaptation to the specific characteristics of the concrete situation under evaluation. The condition of the least advantaged has to be considered in every case.

Jana Martinková

IMMIGRATION AND RELIGION IN SLOVAKIA

From the viewpoint of modern history (the last three centuries), Slovakia had been a country of emigration rather than of immigration. Emigration used to be one of the typical attributes of population development, with primarily economic and social roots. After the collapse of communism in 1989, the migration situation in Slovakia started to alter radically. The exchange of persons between the Slovak and Czech Republics (once dominant) decreased in favour of rising migration flows from and to other countries. Slovakia has become a transit country, slowly beginning to transform into a country of immigration recently, especially after its accession to the European Union in 2004.[1]

Residence of aliens

Currently, this area is regulated by Act No. 48/2002 Coll. on the residency of aliens. This Act distinguishes three kinds of the residence of aliens on the Slovak territory (temporary, permanent and tolerated residence), sets special provisions for EEA nationals, and provides for the possibility of an administrative expulsion of an alien. The decision-making authority in all these matters is vested in the state police.

A **TEMPORARY** residence permit can be granted for up to 2 years, in the case of EEA nationals up to 5 years, for the purpose of enterprise, employment, study, special programmes (e.g. academic, artistic or sport activities), family reunification, or fulfilment of official duties by civil units of armed forces. There is no legal entitlement to this permit. The application may be denied e.g. if

---

[1] For more details, see Boris Divinský: Undocumented Migration. Counting the Uncountable. Data and Trends Across Europe. Country report prepared for the research project CLANDESTINO, December 2008. Available at http://clandestino.eliamep.gr/wp-content/uploads/2009/02/clandestino_report_slovak-rep_final5.pdf

- the alien is a persona non-grata;
- there is a reasonable suspicion that during his/her stay, the alien would endanger the security of the State, public policy, health or the rights and freedoms of others and, on certain determined territories, also their nature;
- it can be assumed that the alien would constitute a burden to the social security system and to the health care system of the SR;
- there is a reasonable suspicion that the alien entered into marriage with the aim of obtaining a temporary residence permit;
- it concerns another spouse of an alien who was granted a temporary residence permit in the case of a polygamous marriage;
- the alien deliberately gave false or misleading data or submitted false or modified documents;
- granting a temporary residence permit is not in the public interest.

A **PERMANENT** residence permit is granted e.g. to an alien

- who is a spouse of a citizen of the SR with permanent residence on the territory of the SR or a dependent direct relative of a citizen of the SR with permanent residence on the territory of the SR;
- who is a child and fulfils further conditions specified by the Act;
- if it is in the interest of the SR.

The application can be denied for similar reasons as in the case of a temporary residence permit – and the permit can be granted even when the conditions stipulated by this Act are not fulfilled, provided that it is necessary for the provision of protection and assistance to a witness under a separate regulation, for reasons of special significance, or upon a proposal of the Slovak Intelligence Service due to security interests of the SR.

A **TOLERATED** residence permit can be granted up to 180 days e.g. to an alien

- when his/her departure is not possible and his/her arrest is not purposeful;
- who is a minor found on the territory of the SR;
- who is a victim of a criminal offence related to trafficking in human beings, provided that he/she is at least 18 years old;
- if it is required in order to respect his/her private and family life.

Since 2005, there are special provisions for EEA nationals and their family members. They require a valid ID card to enter the SR and to remain there for up to 3 months. If they wish to remain for longer, they must register as residents.

The Act also provides for a so-called administrative expulsion which can be imposed e.g. if an alien endangers the security of the State, public policy, health or the rights and freedoms of others and, on the determined territories, also their nature, or if he/she was sentenced in a final decision for a deliberate crime, and a punishment of expulsion was not imposed on him/her.[2]

No significant changes in this legal regulation are proposed at the moment.

The statistics of the Ministry of Interior[3] provides the following numbers:

Number of residence permits granted for the last 2 years

2007: Temporary residence – 4.199
Permanent residence – 10.588
Tolerated residence – 372
2008: Temporary residence – 6.615
Permanent residence – 9.689
Tolerated residence – 249

Note: The Ministry does not disclose the number of applications for residence permits submitted/rejected.

Overview of all types of residence permits granted per year for the last 5 years

2004 – 8.081
2005 – 7.595
2006 – 11.312
2007 – 15.159
2008 – 16.553

---

[2] However, both the Act on aliens and the Criminal Code prohibit administrative/ judicial expulsion of an alien to a country in which his/her life would be endangered due to his/her race, nationality, religion, belonging to a certain social group or due to his/her political conviction, or in which he/she would be in danger of torture, cruel, inhuman or humiliating treatment or punishment. It is not possible either to expel an alien to a country in which a death penalty was imposed on him/her, or if it is expected that such penalty could be imposed on him/her in the pending proceedings.

[3] See http://www.minv.sk/?rocenky

Overview of all types of residence permits valid as to 31 December of the relevant year for the last 5 years

2004 – 22.108
2005 – 25.635
2006 - 32.153
2007 – 41.214
2008 – 52.706 – this last number comprises 33.234 EEA nationals and 19.472 third- country nationals (in the latter group, more than one third is composed of immigrants from Ukraine and Vietnam; the other highly-represented countries are Russia, China, Korea and former Yugoslavian republics).

As for the religious dimension of immigration, given that the total number of inhabitants of Slovakia is currently more than 5.4 million, all legal immigrants amount to less than 1% of the population; moreover, those coming from prevailingly non-Christian (e.g. Islamic) countries represent only a tiny fraction of the whole immigrant group. Thus, it can hardly be said to date that immigration has significantly influenced the religious profile of Slovakia.

Acquisition of citizenship

According to Act No. 40/1993 Coll. on the citizenship of the Slovak Republic, citizenship may be granted to a person who

– has had a continuous permanent residence in the territory of the SR for at least 8 years;
– is of good character, as defined by this Act (e.g. the person has not been convicted of crime and is not being criminally prosecuted);
– proves his/her ability to write and speak in Slovak language, as well as a general knowledge of Slovak history, geography and its social and cultural development;
– carries out all his/her duties according to the Slovak legal order.

The first condition (the 8-year period of continuous residence) does not have to be fulfilled in some cases, e.g. if the applicant

– has been married to a Slovak citizen for at least 5 years;
– is found to be a person of significant importance for the SR in the area of economy, science, technology, culture, society or sport, or if it is in the interest of the SR for other reasons;

- has had a continuous permanent residence in the territory of the SR for at least 3 years before reaching 18 years of age;
- has been granted asylum status at least 4 years before he/she applied for Slovak citizenship.

The Ministry of Interior decides upon applications for citizenship. There is no legal entitlement to obtain a citizenship; if the Ministry denies an application, the applicant can submit a new one after two years.

According to the statistics of the Slovak Statistical Office,[4] there were 1.478 cases of citizenship granted in 2007. Given this number and its proportion to the total national population, naturalization can be viewed as even less of an influence upon the religious configuration of the country than immigration, described in the previous section of this report.

Asylum

This area is regulated by Act No. 480/2002 Coll. on asylum. It defines asylum as a protection of an alien from serious human rights violation by another state, as a result of its action or failure to act. The application for asylum is granted if the applicant

- has a well-founded fear of being persecuted on racial, national *or religious* grounds, for reasons of holding certain political opinions or belonging to a certain social group in the country of his/her origin and in view of this fear he/she cannot or does not want to return to that country; or if the applicant is persecuted for exercising political rights and freedoms in the country of his/her origin;
- on humanitarian grounds, even if the previous conditions are not met;
- for the purpose of family reunification, as further specified by the Act.

According to the Act, when assessing an application for granting asylum, it is irrelevant whether the applicant actually possesses the religious or other characteristic which causes his/her persecution, provided that such a characteristic is attributed to him/her by the persecutor.

---

[4] See http://portal.statistics.sk/files/Sekcie/sek_600/Demografia/Migracia/2009/Tab5_AJ_2007.pdf

The application is denied e.g. if

- the applicant, due to his/her incoherent, contradictory, improbable or insufficient statements, cannot be considered a credible person;
- the applicant represents a danger to the security of the SR or to society;
- there is ground for suspicion that the applicant has committed a crime against the peace, a war crime, or crime against humanity under international instruments, has committed a serious non-political crime outside the territory of the Slovak Republic prior to applying for asylum, or is guilty of acts which are in contradiction of the objectives and principles of the United Nations.

In the course of the asylum procedure, applicants are provided with accommodation, board or boarding-out allowance, basic sanitary products and other things necessary for living; they also receive urgent health care. They are not allowed to work until the decision on granting asylum comes into effect; however, there is one exception – where no final decision is made on the particular application for asylum within one year from initiation of the procedure.

As a rule, asylum status is granted for an indefinite period of time. However, it can be withdrawn, e.g. if the respective person is capable of returning to the country of his/her origin where the circumstances under which asylum was granted ceased to exist. Persons who are granted asylum have the status of permanent residents.

The competent state authority in asylum issues is the Ministry of Interior; its decisions can be appealed against to a court. The Ministry is also obliged to facilitate the asylants's integration into society, including provision of language training, and assistance in finding housing and employment.

Modifications of the Act on asylum took effect in January 2007, accounting for EU legislation. These changes introduced supplementary protection for foreigners (and their spouse and children) who were not granted asylum but may have been subject to grave persecution in their country of origin. Supplementary protection can be provided for a renewable period of one year; a person who is granted such protection has the status of a temporary resident. In addition, persons granted asylum are now entitled to a one-time subsidy amounting to 1.5 times the minimum living standard.

The amendment which entered into force in January 2008 was also a transposition of EU legislation. It laid down time-limits for court proceedings on asylum matters as follows: a regional court must decide on a legal remedy against a decision of the Ministry of Interior within 90 days, and the Supreme Court of the SR has to decide on an appeal against the decision of the regional court within 60 days.

In December 2008, another amendment to the Act on asylum entered into force, which is related to the duty of the state to provide free legal assistance to those applicants for asylum whose applications were rejected when submitting an appeal against the decision of the Ministry of Interior. Free legal assistance for third country nationals requesting international protection has been recently secured by the Centre for Legal Aid, an organization of the Ministry of Justice, financed from the state budget, in addition to numerous non-governmental organisations.

According to the statistics of the Ministry of Interior,[5] there is a significant drop in numbers between years 2007 and 2008. While in 2007, 2642 asylum applications were filed, only 909 applications were submitted in 2008. The number of applicants who were granted asylum increased slightly from 14 in 2007 to 22 in 2008, but the figure is still very low when compared with other EU Member States. In addition, there were 82 cases of supplementary protection provided in 2007 and 66 cases in 2008.

However, there are no official sources available indicating what role religion plays in asylum cases.

In the *European Commission against Racism and Intolerance Report on Slovakia (fourth monitoring cycle)*, adopted on 19 December 2008 and published on 26 May 2009, ECRI recommends that the Slovak authorities

- ensure that asylum seekers receive legal aid throughout the asylum application procedure, and that an effective appeal mechanism exists within this procedure;
- provide asylum seekers with the possibility of working in Slovakia earlier than the current one year after the beginning of the asylum procedure;
- continue improving conditions in detention facilities, and ensure that foreign nationals detained therein have access to complaints mechanisms, should they need them, and that they have confidence in them;

---

[5] See http://www.minv.sk/?statistiky-20

– take more measures to raise police officer's awareness of issues pertaining to racism and racial discrimination, and provide initial and on-going training to them on these questions;
– establish a long-term strategy for integrating refugees.[6]

As for churches giving asylum, there is neither a legal basis for, nor actual occurrence of, this issue in Slovakia.

Asylum seekers are free to exercise their religion; the Act on asylum even states that when placing an alien in an asylum facility, his/her religious and (inter alia) specific features shall be considered. Moreover, there are some non-governmental organisations with, at least in part, a church/religious background that are involved in providing assistance and counselling for asylum seekers in refugee centres, as well as in integration of recognised refugees into society – notably the Slovak Humanitarian Council, the Ecumenical Council of Churches in the SR or the Slovak Catholic Charity.[7] However, there does not seem to be any actual pastoral care or chaplaincy services provided specifically for the asylum seekers. This is definitely not regulated by law.

Principles of the united family, issues of polygamous marriage and forced marriage –and their bearing on immigration law and practice

For references to reunification of the Family in Slovak immigration law, see previous sections of this report. Polygamous marriage is also mentioned above. As for the issue of forced marriage, the Act on the residence of aliens states that a police department shall grant a temporary residence permit for the purpose of family reunification, among others, to an alien who is a spouse of an alien with a temporary residence permit or with a permanent residence permit, provided that the spouse is at least 18 years old. However, there are no official data available as regards the practical application of these legal norms.

Employment of Non-EU Citizens and religious exemption in this area

According to the Act No. 5/2004 Coll. on employment services, EU/ EEA citizens are not required to apply for a work permit if they want to

---

[6] See http://www.coe.int/t/dghl/monitoring/ecri/Country-by-country/Slovakia/SVK-CbC-IV-2009-020-ENG.pdf

[7] See Mária Grethe Guličová and Zuzana Bargerová: Organisation of Asylum and Migration Policies in the Slovak Republic. National Report for the European Migration Network, December 2008. Available at http://emn.sarenet.es/Downloads/download.do;jsessionid=1623A2E22F0D9111443EAE63036B8DEA?fileID=728

work in Slovakia. However, Slovak employers must notify the local Office of Labour, Social Affairs and Family about employing such foreigners. As for other nationals, they are obliged to apply to the local Office for a work permit before arriving in the territory of the Slovak Republic. The competent Office may grant the alien a work permit, provided that the vacancy could not be filled by a job seeker from the register of job seekers. In issuing the work permit, the Office shall consider the labour market situation. There is no legal obligation in issuing of a work permit. However, the Office shall – without taking into account the labour market situation – issue a work permit, inter alia, to an alien who is commissioned by a registered church or religious community to perform clerical activities.

Blaž Ivanc*

IMMIGRATION AND RELIGION IN SLOVENIA

1. Introduction

The aim of this article is to analyse how the Slovenian Asylum and Immigration Laws accommodate the constitutional guarantee of freedom of religion. The general legal protection of religion in Slovenia is determined by the new democratic Constitution from December 1991 (hereinafter: the Constitution)[1] and the new Religious Freedom Act enacted in February 2007 (hereinafter: the RFA).[2] Article 41 of the Constitution broadly protects the freedom of self-definition, and it refers not only to religious beliefs but also to moral, philosophical and other worldviews (hereinafter: the right to religious freedom). This Article gives assurance of freedom of conscience (the positive entitlement), the right of a person not to have any religious or other beliefs, or not to manifest such beliefs (the negative entitlement) and enshrines the right of parents to determine their children's upbringing in the area of freedom of conscience (Para. 3).[3] The provision of Article 41 of the Constitution has a distinguished position in the hierarchy of constitutional rights.[4] Also important for the

* Blaž Ivanc, PhD in Law, Assistant Professor, Faculty of Health Sciences – University of Ljubljana (Zdravstvena fakulteta – Univerza v Ljubljani), Poljanska c. 26.a, SI-1000 Ljubljana, SLOVENIA, EUROPE (Tel.:+386 1 300 11 69; Fax.: +386 1 300 11 19; E-mail: blaz.ivanc@zf.uni-lj.si).
   [1] The Constitution of the Republic of Slovenia (1991), Official Gazette RS Nos. 33/91-I, 42/97, 66/2000, 24/03, 69/04 and 68/06.
   [2] The Religious Freedom Act (Zakon o verski svobodi – ZVS), The Official Gazette of the RS, No. 14/07.
   [3] Art. 41 of the Constitution determines that: "(1) Religious and other beliefs may be freely professed in private and public life. (2) No one shall be obliged to declare his religious or other beliefs. (3) Parents have the right to provide their children with a religious and moral upbringing in accordance with their beliefs. The religious and moral guidance given to children must be appropriate to their age and maturity, and be consistent with their free conscience and religious and other beliefs or convictions."
   [4] Art. 41 also refers to other constitutional rights, such as, *e.g.*, the right to personal dignity and safety (Art. 34), the protection of the right to privacy and personality rights (Art. 35), the protection of personal data (Art.), the freedom of expression (Art. 39), the right of assembly and association (Art. 42), the right to conscientious objection (Art. 46) and the rights and duties of parents (Art. 54). See Orehar Ivanc, M.: *Commentary on the Art. 41 of the Constitution of the Republic of Slovenia)* in: Šturm, L. (eds.), *Komentar*

constitutional guarantee of freedom of religion is Art. 7 of the Constitution, which enshrines: (1) the principle of separation of the state and religious communities, (2) the principle of equality among religious communities, and (3) the principle of free activity (autonomy) of religious communities within the legal order.[5]

2. Legal provisions that facilitate or limit immigration

Several provisions of the Constitution determine the status and legal position of foreigners in the Republic of Slovenia and constitute a framework for further regulation by statutory law and by-laws. Aliens in Slovenia are, pursuant to Article 13 of the Constitution, entitled to enjoy – in accordance with international treaties – all the rights guaranteed by the Constitution and law, except for those rights that are – by the Constitution or by the law – granted only to citizens of Slovenia.[6] The Constitution empowers the legislator to impose some limitation on foreigners when they are exercising rights protected by the Constitution. The Third paragraph of Article 32 of the Constitution imposes limitations on the freedom of movement of aliens. Their entry into the country and the duration of their stay may be limited by statute. An exact legal regime concerning the entry and residence of aliens has been set up by the Aliens Act,[7] the State Border Control Act[8] and by the European Schengen Borders Code.[9] The third paragraph of Article 43 of the Constitution states that the law has to determine whether, and under which conditions, aliens will be entitled to vote. According to Article 47 of the Constitution the extradition of aliens shall only be permitted in cases covered by international treaties that are binding on Slovenia.[10] The provision of Article 79

Ustave Republike Slovenije (Commentary on the Constitution of the Republic of Slovenia), Faculty of Post-Graduate State and European Studies, Ljubljana, 2002, p. 444-459.

[5] Art. 7 of the Constitution: "(1) The state and religious communities shall be separate. (2) Religious communities shall enjoy equal rights; they shall pursue their activities freely.".

[6] Only Slovene citizens enjoy the right to vote (Art. 43), the right to participation in the management of public affairs (Art. 44), the right to petition (Art. 45), the right to social security (Art. 50) and the right to proper housing (Art. 78). See Jerovšek, T. *Commentary on the Art. 13 of the Constitution of the Republic of Slovenia)* in: Šturm, L. (eds.), *Komentar Ustave Republike Slovenije (Commentary on the Constitution of the Republic of Slovenia)*, Faculty of Post-Graduate State and European Studies, Ljubljana, 2002, p. 168.

[7] The Aliens Act – Official Consolidated Version, Official Gazette RS, No. 71/2008

[8] The State Border Control Act (Zakon o nadzoru državne meje – ZNDM-2), Official Gazette RS, No. 60/2007

[9] The Regulation (EC) No 562/2006 on Schengen Borders Code

[10] Orehar Ivanc, M.: *Commentary on the Art. 47 of the Constitution of the Republic of Slovenia)* in: Šturm, L. (eds.), *Komentar Ustave Republike Slovenije (Commentary on the Constitution of the Republic of Slovenia)*, Faculty of Post-Graduate State and European Studies, Ljubljana, 2002, p. 499.

of the Constitution provides that foreigners employed in Slovenia and members of their families, enjoy special rights, as determined by law. This constitutional provision is more comprehensively regulated in the Employment and Work of Foreigners Act.[11] The right of asylum is provided by Article 48 of the Constitution, which determines that the right of asylum shall be recognised for foreign nationals and stateless persons who are subject to persecution for their commitment to human rights and fundamental freedoms within the limits of the law.[12]

The organisation of asylum and migration policies and legislation in Slovenia has gone through several historical periods. In the period from 1945 to 1990 Slovenia experienced political and economic emigration. A large immigration of workers from other republics of the former Federal Republic of Yugoslavia to Slovenia is a characteristic of this period as well. In the period after the proclamation of the independent and sovereign State, in June 1991, Slovenia experienced a large influx of refugees mainly from Croatia, Bosnia and Herzegovina (between 60.000 and 70.000 in 1992). Acting on the basis of the Convention on the Status of Refugees (The Geneva Convention) of 1951, the Slovene authorities provided for temporary asylum, which was granted to 31.118 persons after registration procedure in 1993.[13] Their legal status was first regulated under the adoption of the Temporary Asylum Act, in March 1997. In year 1999, the first Resolution on Migration Policies was enacted in the National Assembly and a special Asylum Act, adopted in July 1999. The resolution was, then, replaced by a new Resolution on Migration Policies, in year 2002.[14] During the period between 1999 and 2004 Slovenia experienced high levels of illegal immigration.[15] In the period before entry into the EU, in May 2004, Slovenia harmonized its laws with EU law and from then is striving to implement and transpose the *Acquise Communitaire* into the Slovenian domestic law.[16] Since entry into the European Union, which denotes the beginning of the actual historical period, net migration into Slovenia has been increasing steadily: 6436 persons in

[11] Employment and Work of Aliens Act (ZZDT), Official Gazette RS, No. 66/2000, 52/2007
[12] Zalar, B: Commentary on the Art. 48 of the Constitution of the Republic of Slovenia) in: Šturm, L. (eds.), *Komentar Ustave Republike Slovenije (Commentary on the Constitution of the Republic of Slovenia)*, Faculty of Post-Graduate State and European Studies, Ljubljana, 2002, p. 502-505. More on Asylum Law in Chapter VI.
[13] *Slovenia National Report, The Organisation of Asylum and Migration Policies in Slovenia*, p. 9.
[14] The Resolution on Migration Policies, Official Gazette RS, No. 40/1999, the Resolution on Migration Policies, Official Gazette RS, No. 106/2002
[15] See Kogovšek – 2008, p. 418.
[16] Zavratnik Zimic, p. 76.

2005, 6267 persons in 2006, 14250 persons in 2007 and 19496 persons in 2008.[17] In 2007 more than three quarters (77.6%) of foreign immigrants migrated to Slovenia because of work and employment and seasonal work. The majority of 27504 workers who immigrated to Slovenia in 2007 were citizens of Bosnia and Herzegovina [12479], Serbia [6368] and the former Yugoslav Republic of Macedonia [3163]. 2646 immigrants to Slovenia were citizens of other EU Member States (790 citizens from Bulgaria and 451 from Slovakia). According to this trend Slovenia is becoming a country of immigration. The policy on migration is still subject to political deliberations. The Ministry of Labour, Family and Social Affairs has prepared a draft Strategy on Economic Immigration, which has to be sent to the Parliament. However, there is no political discussion on becoming a "country of immigration" that would provide for immigration of a large number of foreigners (such as is the case in Canada or Australia).

In principle, the constitutional right to religious freedom is guaranteed to foreigners in the same way, and to the same extent, as to citizens of Slovenia. The Resolution on Migration Policies and Immigration Laws entails only a few provisions directly referring to freedom of religion (e.g. a general prohibition of discrimination on the basis of religion or religious affiliation, as a ground for unlawful persecution of a person).

Statistics concerning applications for permanent and temporary residence permits

In a case where a foreigner has the intention to reside in Slovenia for a longer period than provided by the visa, he or she must apply for a residency permit. The permit for first residency can be issued only as a permit for temporary residence. A foreigner may apply for a permanent residence permit, if he or she uninterruptedly resided in Slovenia for five years on the basis of temporary residence permit and is fulfilling all the statutory conditions, and there are no reasons for rejection of the application.[18] In 2008 there were 32399 foreigners with permanent residence, and 39733 foreigners with temporary residence in Slovenia.

Table 1: Number of permanent residence applications, issued permits and non-issued permits

---

[17] Source of Data: Eurostat.
[18] See more in *Slovenia National Report, The Organisation of Asylum and Migration Policies in Slovenia*, p. 11–15.

Year	Applications for permanent residence permits	No. of issued permanent residence permits	Non-issued permanent residence permits (Terminated/Omitted/Rejected)
1998	1245	887	358 (-/-/-)
1999	2013	1954	59 (32/0/27)
2000	7359	6764	595 (492/1/102)
2001	2506	2031	475 (298/6/171)
2002	6639	5858	781 (435/46/300)
2003	4280	3686	594 (253/44/297)
2004	4453	4011	442 (152/24/266)
2005	5022	4666	356 (212/45/99)
2006	9290	9003	287 (178/12/97)
Total	42807	38860	3947 (2234/180/1362)

(Source: *Slovenia National Report, the Organisation of Asylum and Migration Policies in Slovenia*, p. 35; Ministry of Interior, Statistics on 29. 10. 2008)

The number of all valid permits for temporary residence on October 21st 2008 that were issued to foreigners amounted to 66.189 permits. Most foreigners with permits for temporary residence came from the Republic of Serbia (10.827), Republic of Macedonia (5.766), Croatia (3.522) and Bosnia and Herzegovina (3.062). The majority of the temporary residence permits were issued because of employment or work (43.356).[19]

Table 2: Number of temporary residence applications, issued permits and non-issued permits

Year	Applications for temporary residence permits	No. of issued temporary residence permits	Non-issued temporary residence permits (Terminated/Omitted/Rejected)
1999	24820	24539	281 (189/28/64)
2000	48324	45607	2717 (1380/96/1241)
2001	44452	42303	2149 (1061/141/947)
2002	38799	37054	1745 (943/68/734)
2003	41174	39800	1374 (772/116/486)
2004	37473	36276	1197 (740/78/379)
2005	39201	38188	1013 (652/96/265)
2006	39821	38305	1516 (1013/133/370)
Total	314064	302072	11992 (6921/708/4734)

(Source: *Slovenia National Report, the Organisation of Asylum and Migration Policies in Slovenia*, p. 27-29; Ministry of Interior, Statistics on 29. 10. 2008)

[19] *Slovenia National Report, The Organisation of Asylum and Migration Policies in Slovenia*, p. 27.

Table 3: Reasons for the issuance of temporary residence permits

Reason/ Year	No data	Family reunification on – foreigner of Slovene ethnicity	Employment and work	Stud-ies	Seasonal work	Daily migrants	Family reunification –Art. 36	Family reunification –Art. 37	Child born in RS	Settlement	Other rea-sons	Directed workers	Slovenian descent	Total
1999	9495		10787	337	152	495	1977	723	90	16	455	5	7	24539
2000	216		29640	923	1646	1950	6050	3157	255	94	1294	349	33	45607
2001	33		27603	1046	2733	2157	4932	1913	222	62	1003	560	39	42303
2002	13		20783	1152	5071	1187	4058	2261	260	36	946	1245	42	37054
2003	8		17912	1327	9270	1551	3824	2709	398	6	727	2021	47	39800
2004	1131	21	18100	1272	5149	1624	3900	1966	450	1	649	1990	23	36276
2005	1973	15	20471	1164	4696	848	4307	1529	465		586	2123	11	38188
2006	49		21885	1248	7101	1338	3744	66	276		470	2112	16	38305
Total	12918	36	167181	8469	35818	11150	32792	14324	2416	215	6130	10405	218	302036

A religious dimension to the temporary and permanent residence applications can be seen only in relation to the religious affiliation of immigrants applying for residence permit (see Chapter III).

3. Legal demands for the acquisition of citizenship

Legal requirements for the acquisition of citizenship by naturalization are determined by the Citizenship of the Republic of Slovenia Act (Hereinafter: the Citizenship Act).[20] According to Article 10 of the Citizenship Act, a person requesting naturalisation must fulfil the following conditions:

1. be 18 years of age;
2. have been released from current citizenship, or have proved that he/she will obtain release if he/she acquires citizenship of the Republic of Slovenia;
3. that the person has actually been living in Slovenia for 10 years, and continuously for 5 years prior to the submission of the application, and has the lawful status of an alien;
4. that the person has a guaranteed permanent source of income, at least an amount that enables material and social security;
5. that the person has a command of the Slovene language for the purposes of everyday communication, which he/she shall have to prove by a certificate verifying that he/she has passed a basic level exam in Slovene;
6. that the person has not been sentenced to a prison sentence longer than one year in the country of which he/she is a citizen, or in Slovenia for a criminal offence which is prosecuted by law, provided that such an offence is punishable pursuant to the regulations of his/her country as well as to the regulations of the Republic of Slovenia;
7. that the person's residence permit in the Republic of Slovenia has not been annulled;
8. that the person's naturalisation poses no threat to public order, security or defence of the State;
9. that the person has settled all tax obligations;
10. that the person submits a declaration that by obtaining citizenship of the Republic of Slovenia, he/she agrees with the legal system of the Republic of Slovenia.

---

[20] The Citizenship of the Republic of Slovenia Act (Zakon o državljanstvu Republike Slovenije – ZDRS), Official Gazette Nos.1I/1991-I,. 30/1991-I, 38/1992, 61/1992 Odl. US: U-I-69/92-30, 61/1992 Odl.US: U-I-98/91-21, 13/1994, 13/1995 Odl.US: U-I-124/94-8, 29/1995-ZPDF, 59/1999 Odl.US: U-I-89/99, 96/2002, 7/2003-UPB1, 127/2006, 24/2007-UPB2

According to Article 10 (Para. 3) of the Citizenship Act, the applicant must undergo a special test. The obligatory examination as to command of the Slovenian language (pursuant to Paragraph 1, Item 5 of Article 10) has to be taken by the applicant before the competent commission. The Commission is appointed by the Government and determines the criteria for the written and oral examination in the Slovenian language. Subsequently, the Ministry of Interior, as a competent authority, may, at its discretion, grant a person's request for naturalisation, if it is in compliance with the national interest. A central goal of the Resolution on Migration is the integration of foreigners into Slovene society. Thus, detailed rules were set up by the Decree on aliens' integration,[21] and the Rules on the Programmes for Integration of Foreigners.[22]

Article 40 of the Citizenship Act provided that a citizen of another republic of ex-Yugoslavia who had registered for permanent residence in the Republic of Slovenia on the day of the Plebiscite of the independence and sovereignty of the Republic of Slovenia on December 23, 1990, and has actually been living here, was able to acquire citizenship of Slovenia if within six months of entry into force of the Citizenship Act, he/she had filed an application with the administrative authority competent for internal affairs of the community where he/she has his/her permanent residence. 171.127 persons obtained Slovenian citizenship under the provision of Art. 40 of the Citizenship Act until the 31ˢᵗ December 2005. The total number of persons that gained Slovenian citizenship by naturalization in the period from 1991 to 2005, amounts 201.922 persons. A further 30.795 applicants obtained citizenship under the provision of Art. 10, and other provisions of the Citizenship Act. 12.469 applications were unsuccessful due to various reasons. During this period, on the basis of their own requirements, release or waiver, Slovenian citizenship has reduced by 4813.

Demographic changes in the religious configuration of the country due to naturalization

In 1971 most of the country's population were Slovenes (94.03%). In 1981 the number of Slovenes decreased to 90,52 per cent, and later on in the year 1991 further to 87,84 per cent.[23] At the time of the last cen-

---

[21] Decree on aliens integration (Uredba o integraciji tujcev), Official Gazette RS, No. 65/2008.

[22] Rules on the Programmes for Integration of Foreigners (Pravilnik o programih za integracijo tujcev), Official Gazette RS, No. 25/2009

[23] See Kržišnik-Bukić, V. (Ed.), Klopčič, V., Komac, M., *Albanci, Bošnjaki, Črnogorci, Hrvati, Makedonci in Srbi v Republiki Sloveniji – Položaj in status pripadnikov nekdanje Jugoslavije v Sloveniji* [Albanians, Bosnians, Montenegriners, Croats, Macedonians and Serbs – the Position and the Status of citizens of ex-Yugoslavia in Slovenia], p. 57.

sus in 2002, the share of Slovenes towards the total population was 83,06 per cent. In the period from 1991 to 2002, Slovenia experienced noticeable demographic changes in religious configuration. The percentage in membership of the majority Catholic religion has been decreasing (from 1.369.873 in 1991 to 1.135.626 in 2002). The number of persons belonging to Islam increased by 61% (from 29.361 to 47.488). The number of atheists increased by 135 per cent since 1991. However, a huge number of persons (307.973, or more than 15 per cent of total population) declined to give an answer concerning their religious affiliation. The question of religious affiliation has been highly controversial and the Constitutional Court has had to decide whether it was constitutional to collect such data. The Court decided that such a question can be part of a Census 2002 questionnaire, but it is not obligatory for a person to give an answer.[24] Thus, every person received a special explanation regarding this particular question. A highly-politicized debate over this issue most probably persuaded many religious people not to provide an answer.

Table 4: Religious allegiance in Slovenia – Census 1991 and Census 2002

Year/Religion	1991	2002
TOTAL	**1,913,355**	**1,964,036**
Catholic	1,369,873	1,135,626
Evangelical	14,101	14,736
Other Protestant	1,890	1,399
Orthodox	46,320	45,908
Other Christian	2,410	1,877
Islam	29,361	47,488
Jewish	199	99
Oriental	478	1,026
Other religion	269	558
Agnostic	…	271
Believer but belongs to no religion	3,929	68,714
Unbeliever, atheist	84,656	199,264
Did not want to reply	81,302	307,973
Unknown	278,567	139,097

[24] Decision of the Constitutional Court of the Republic of Slovenia (the *Census* case) No. U–I–92/01 (February 2002) (Act on the Census of the Population, Households, and Housing in the Republic of Slovenia in the Year 2001).

Table 5: Population by religion and ethnic affiliation, Slovenia, 2002 Census

Ethnic affiliation	Total	Religion											
		Catholic	Evangelical	other Protestant	Orthodox	other Christian	Islam	Oriental	other religion and Agnostic	Believer but belongs to no religion	Unbeliever, atheist	Did not want to reply	Unknown
TOTAL	1964036	1135626	14736	1399	45908	1877	47488	1026	928	68714	199264	307973	139097
Slovenes	1631363	1086650	13752	1046	3583	1506	2804	762	721	62809	186055	255857	15818
Italians	2258	1507	z	-	9	23	z	z	z	117	331	212	44
Hungarians	6243	5016	524	158	z	8	8	z	9	65	159	259	z
Roma	3246	1663	-	Z	67	6	868	z	z	287	99	163	87
Albanians	6186	363	-	Z	8	8	5237	z	z	74	97	286	108
Bosniacs	21542	107	-	-	318	6	19923	z	z	151	328	328	377
Montenegrins	2667	87	5	-	1193	z	634	z	z	76	463	172	31
Croats	35642	29942	24	51	201	51	30	13	22	682	2089	2199	338
Macedonians	3972	128	7	Z	2623	14	507	z	z	97	294	227	70
Muslims	10467	18	-	-	14	z	9328	-	z	238	251	374	237
Germans	499	214	125	7	z	z	z	z	-	27	71	41	z
Serbs	38964	381	22	43	32665	54	53	9	9	751	2952	1412	613
Others declared	3933	1081	164	35	725	15	445	149	84	230	513	424	68
Yugoslavs	527	38	-	-	167	-	55	5	-	32	158	57	15
Bosnians	8062	353	z	Z	1213	19	5724	z	z	97	259	247	144
Regionally declared	1467	1041	20	Z	6	z	15	z	z	70	157	128	19
Ethnically undeclared	12085	1682	25	36	1273	103	721	33	28	1973	3062	3003	146
Did not want to reply	48588	2593	31	6	1254	40	817	19	17	614	1405	41441	351
Unknown	126325	2762	33	9	579	15	308	14	20	324	521	1143	120597

(Source: Statistical Office of the Republic of Slovenia, 2002 Census, http://www.stat.si/popis2002/en/rezultati/rezultati_red.asp?ter=SLO&st=57)

As already stressed, 201.922 persons who were citizens of other republics of ex-Yugoslavia gained Slovenian citizenship in the period from 1991 to 2005, by naturalization (46 per cent of Bosnians/Bosniacs, 37 per cent of Croats and 13 per cent of Serbs). Naturalized citizens of other republics of ex-Yugoslavia, and new immigrants of Serbian, Montenegrin, and Macedonian nationality were/are mostly members of the Orthodox religion, and immigrants from Bosnia and Herzegovina and Kosovo were/are members of the Islamic religion (Muslim). According to the above table persons affiliated to Bosnians, Bosniacs, Albanians and Muslims constitute a population pertaining to Islam. Persons affiliated with Serbian ethnicity in Slovenia are affiliated with the Orthodox religion. Equally, numerous is the Croat ethnic group (35.642 persons) which affiliates with the Catholic religion. Noticeably, for as many as 174.913 persons (9 per cent of total population) there are no data on their ethnic affiliation because they declined to answer, or data is unknown from other reasons. As for religious affiliation, the number is substantially higher: 447.070 persons (22 per cent of total population) who gave no answer, or of unknown religious affiliation. Thus, the full impact of naturalization on Slovene religious demography cannot be fully estimated, and will have to be more closely analysed at the next census.

4. Legal regulation of asylum

During the period from 1991 until 2009 Slovenia experienced major development in the field of Asylum Law. The Asylum Act, adopted in July 1999, was changed four times (in December 2000, in July 2001, in September 2003 and in February 2006),[25] and finally replaced by the International Protection Act (hereinafter: the IPA), which was adopted on 21st November 2007.[26] The provision of Article 2 of the IPA, which determines the right to international protection, first provides for refugee status (Para. 2), that would be granted to a third country national, who,

[25] The main cause for changes of the Asylum Act was harmonisation with European migration policy directives, such as the Council Directives 2003/86/EC (Directive on Family reunification), 2003/109/EC (Directive on Long-Term Residents) and 2004/81/EC (Directive on Victims of Human Trafficking).

[26] The International Protection Act transposed new provisions of the Council Directives 2004/83/EC (Qualification Directive), 2005/85/EC (Procedure Directive) and 2003/9/EC (Directive on Reception Conditions) into the Slovene domestic law. The Temporary Protection of Displaced Persons Act, which was enacted in June 2005 as a consequence Council Directive 2001/55/EC transposition (Directive on Temporary Protection), would apply for the needs of granting temporary protection to a larger number of displaced persons. See *Slovenia National Report, The Organisation of Asylum and Migration Policies in Slovenia*, p. 27.

owing to a well-founded fear of being persecuted for reasons of race, religion, nationality, political opinion or membership of a particular social group, is outside the country of nationality and is unable or, owing to such fear, is unwilling to avail himself or herself of the protection of that country, or a stateless person, who, being outside of the country of former habitual residence for the same reasons as mentioned above, is unable or, owing to such fear, unwilling to return to it. Secondly, Article 2 of the IPA provides for status of subsidiary protection that might be granted to a third country national or a stateless person who does not qualify as a refugee but in respect of whom substantial grounds have been shown for believing that the person concerned, if returned to his or her country of origin, or in the case of a stateless person, to his or her country of former habitual residence, would face a real risk of suffering serious harm (Para. 3).[27] Thus, the status of subsidiary protection provides a humanitarian right of residence, when, according to a strict interpretation of the law, asylum could not be granted.[28]

Table 5: the number of asylum or international protection applications (from 1995 to 2007):

Year	Number of applications	Recognized status	Rejected applications	Terminated procedures
1995	6	2	4	10
1996	35	0	0	5
1997	72	0	8	15
1998	337	1	27	13
1999	744	0	87	237
2000	9244	11	46	831
2001	1511 (incl. The renewed applications after an appeal at the Admin. Court)	25	97	9911
2002	640	3	105	619
2003	1101	37	123	964

[27] According to the provision of the Art. 28 of the IPA serious damage depicts death penalty or execution, torture or inhumane or degrading treatment or punishment of the applicant in the country of origin or serious and individual threat to a civilian's life or person by reason of indiscriminate violence in situations of international or internal armed conflict.

[28] See *Slovenia National Report, The Organisation of Asylum and Migration Policies in Slovenia.*

2004	1208	39	317	737
2005	1674	26	661	1120
2006	579	9	561	288
2007	434	9	276	238

(Source: *Slovenia National Report, The Organisation of Asylum and Migration Policies in Slovenia*, p. 21; Ministry of Interior, Statistics on 29. 10. 2008)

Year	Asylum Applications	1st instance Decisions	Rejected
1996	35	-	-
1997	70	-	-
1998	335	-	-
1999	745	-	-
2000	9245	-	-
2001	1510	-	-
2002	650	740	120
2003	1050	1195	145
2004	1090[p: provisional]	1035	325
2005	1550[p]	1785[p]	665
2006	500[p]	900[p]	570
2007	370[p]	540[p]	270

(Source: Eurostat)[29]

The number of applications for asylum or international protection, reached its peak in 2004 with 1674 applications, and has been decreasing since then (579 applications in 2005, 434 applications in 2006 and 370 applications in 2007). The religion of the applicant often, is, not an important feature. On 29 October 2008 there were 51 persons with refugee status under the Geneva Convention, 49 persons who have been granted asylum for humanitarian reasons, and 17 persons enjoying subsidiary protection.[30]

The Human Rights Ombudsman highlighted several problems regarding asylum law and procedures; the IPA has lowered the standards and

[29] Available at: http://epp.eurostat.ec.europa.eu/tgm/table.do?tab=table&init=1&plugin=1&language=en&pcode=tps00021
http://epp.eurostat.ec.europa.eu/tgm/table.do?tab=table&init=1&plugin=1&language=en&pcode=tps00163; http://epp.eurostat.ec.europa.eu/tgm/table.do?tab=table&init=1&plugin=1&language=en&pcode=tps00164

[30] Ministry of Interior, Statistics on 29. October 2008. See *Slovenia National Report, The Organisation of Asylum and Migration Policies in Slovenia*, p. 30.

narrowed the scope of legal remedies available to the applicant. The law only provides for free legal aid in proceedings at the Administrative and Supreme Court. The Constitutional Court in the decision No. U-I-95/08-14, Up–1462/06-39 ruled that applicants for asylum may during the procedure reside at a private address, even if the Asylum home or its branch office facility were not fully occupied (which was a statutory precondition).[31] The announced revision of the IPA in the year 2009 will strive to correct some of the deficiencies.

5. The (legal) institute of church asylum

In Slovenia there are no examples of churches or religious communities giving asylum. The asylum law and the state church law do not provide for a legal institute of church asylum. Since there is no legal basis for church asylum, the state can only address the matter in accordance with the positive state law. Until now, churches and other religious communities have not been engaged in cases of civil disobedience in regard to asylum seekers and illegal immigrants.

6. Pastoral assistance to immigrants

Pastoral assistance to immigrants is a matter of state concern only when a person (illegal immigrant or asylum seeker) is placed in an institution of a closed type. The Centre for Foreigners in Postojna (as an institution that restricts individuals' freedom of movement) accommodates:

A. *foreigners that are illegally staying in the Republic of Slovenia*: 1. Foreigners who do not leave the country within the prescribed time limit and cannot be immediately deported from the country (Arts. 56, 93.z of Aliens Act), 2. Foreigners whose identity is unknown (Art. 56 of Aliens Act), 3. Foreigners under the deportation order (Arts. 50, 93.z of Aliens Act), 4. Unaccompanied minors (Art. 60 of Aliens Act), 5. Foreigners illegally staying in Slovenia waiting for deportation pursuant to a bilateral agreement until they are extradited to foreign security authorities (accommodated up to 48 hours; Art. 5 of the Rules on special residence conditions and movement of foreigners in the Centre and requirements and procedures for enforcing lenient measures), 6.

---

[31] The Human Rights Ombudsman Annual Report for year 2008, p. See also the Decision No. U-I-95/08- 14, Up–1462/06-39 of the Constitutional Court from 15th October 2008, Official Gazette RS, št. 111/2008.

foreigners in deportation procedures or foreigners who have not left Slovenia, and have reapplied for asylum (Art. 56 of the International Protection Act); and

B. *applicants for international protection*: 1. Applicants for international protection whose movement is restricted by decisions pursuant to the International Protection Act (Art. 51), and 2. Applicants for international protection, issued on a decision based on Council Regulation (EC) – Dublin procedures (Art. 51).[32]

The Religious Freedom Act lacks concrete provisions with regard to ensuring pastoral assistance for illegal immigrants. However, the right of access to religious assistance is an element of the constitutional right of religious freedom. The right of churches and religious communities to have free access to persons placed in any kind of state institution of a closed type has been regulated by special state – church agreements as envisaged by Article 21 of the RFA.[33] Special state – church agreements have been signed with the Holy See, the Evangelical Church in the Republic of Slovenia, the Pentecostal Church in the Republic of Slovenia, the Serbian Orthodox Church, the Islamic Community in the Republic of Slovenia and the Buddhist Congregation Dharmaling, and they all entail a specific provision with regard to ensuring pastoral assistance in all institutions of a closed type.[34] Since the RFA does not entail concrete provisions with regard to ensuring pastoral assistance to illegal immigrants, the issue of financing such pastoral assistance is not regulated by the statute. As the RFA enables the employment of the necessary number of priests in the army, in the police, in prisons, in hospitals and in social

---

[32] URL: http://www.policija.si/portal_en/organiziranost/uup/CenterZaTujce/naloge. php

[33] Article 21 of the RFA provides that for the purpose of implementing individual provisions of the Constitution of the Republic of Slovenia or the law, the state may conclude agreements with the registered churches or other religious communities. Such agreement shall be concluded with the supreme authority of the church or other religious community in the Republic of Slovenia or the supreme authority of the church or other religious community with an international legal personality who is competent for the matter under his/her autonomous rules.

[34] See: Art. 11 of the Agreement between the Republic of Slovenia and the Holy See signed on 14 December 2001, Art. 9 of the Agreement on the Legal Status of the Evangelical Church in the Republic of Slovenia signed on 25 January 2000; the Art. 9 of the Agreement on Legal Status of the Pentecostal Church in the Republic of Slovenia signed on 17 March 2004; Art. 9 of the Agreement on Legal Status of the Serbian Orthodox Church signed on 9 July 2004; Art. 10 of the Agreement on Legal Status of the Islamic Community in the Republic of Slovenia signed on 9 July 2007; Art.10 of the Agreement on the Legal Status of the Buddhist Congregation Dharmaling signed on 4 July 2008.

welfare institutions performing institutional care,[35] there are no reasons to treat other closed-type institutions, such as Centre for Foreigners, in a different way. Spiritual assistance to illegal immigrants is (or will most likely be) provided by those priests that are already employed by the Police or other state institutions.[36] The Human Rights Ombudsman, which monitors all the institutions of a closed type, criticized the fact that there is no special place intended for religious activity in the Centre for Foreigners. In 2008 a "room for silence" was constructed in the Centre for Foreigners, which now serves as a place for meditation and a place where religious ceremonies of various religions can take place.[37]

7. Principles of the united family

The Resolution on Migration Policies stressed the importance of the principles of the united family and considers them to be one of the basic elements of immigration policies.[38] With the adoption of amendments to the Aliens Act (2005), and with the enactment of the IPA (2007) Slovenia transposed the provisions of the Council Directive 2003/86EC of 22 September on the right to family reunification, into its domestic law.

Article 36 of the Aliens Act explicitly guarantees the right to family reunification (2005).[39] The law provides that aliens who reside in the Republic of Slovenia on the basis of a permanent residence permit, and aliens who have resided for the past year in the Republic of Slovenia on the basis of a temporary residence permit which was issued for a period of at least one year, shall be granted (under the conditions of and in accordance with the Aliens Act) the right to reunion, preservation and reintegration of the family with immediate family members[40] who are

---

[35] Ivanc, B: *The financing of Religious Communities in The Republic of Slovenia – Legal Aspects*, in: Basdevant- Gaudemet, B. and Berlingò, S. (Eds.): *The financing of Religious Communities in the European Union*, Peeters, Leuven – Paris Dudley, MA, 2009, p. 303-312.
[36] See also the Jesuit Refugee Service website (http://www.rkc.si/jrs/).
[37] See Annual Report for year 2008 of the Human Rights Ombudsman, p. 74.
[38] Chapter VI of the Resolution on Migration Policies.
[39] Bešter, p. 163.
[40] The alien's immediate family members are:
- the spouse;
- the alien's unmarried children (minors);
- the spouse's unmarried children (minors);
- the parents of minor alien;
- the alien's or the spouse's unmarried children who have reached the age of majority and

aliens.[41] The principles of the united family are enshrined in the provision of Article 17 of the IPA, which determines that a person under international protection may apply for reunification with his family members. The responsible authority shall issue a decision granting the family members equal status with the person lodging the request, if the criteria for reunification have been fulfilled. In order to be unified with one's family 4794 foreigners immigrated to Slovenia in 2007.[42]

Polygamous marriage and forced marriage cases

In the case of polygamous marriage, the relevant provisions of domestic law are identical with the provision of Art. 4 (Paras. 4 and 5) of the Council Directive 2003/86/EC which determines that the competent authority may grant international protection, or issue permission for temporary residence, only to one spouse. Other members of the sponsor's family may be considered as family members only exceptionally, if the circumstances so require. This approach has been adopted by the national legislator with the enactment of the Aliens Act (Arts. 36 Para. 1-4, Art. 93k Para 1) and the International Protection Act (Art. 17). There are no statistical data on immigration-related cases in which the problem of forced marriage was exposed. In principle, forced marriage cannot have legal effects.

8. Legal restrictions for the employment of Non-EU Citizens

On the basis of Article 5 (Para. 2) of the Aliens Act and the Resolution, a quota for the employment of Non-EU Citizens has been imposed by the Governments' Decree, laying down a work permit quota for a max. 24.000 permissions for year 2009, to limit the number of aliens in the labour market, and a Decree on restrictions and prohibition of employment and work of aliens. Art. 5 (Para. 6) of the Employment and Work of Aliens Act sets a general rule that the annual quota may not surpass 5

– the alien's or the spouse's parents whom the alien or spouse is obliged to maintain in accordance with the legislation of the state of which he/she is a national (Art. 36 Para. 3 of the Aliens Act).

[41] Special provisions of the Aliens Act regulate the right to family reunification for family members of Slovenian nationals and of EU citizens. See Arts. 93.k. – 93.n. of the Aliens Act.

[42] *Intercultural Dialog in Slovenia*, Statistical Office of the Republic of Slovenia, Ljubljana, January 2009, p. 73.

per cent of the labour force in Slovenia (as determined by the Statistics Office of the Republic of Slovenia). In statutes and by-laws there are no exemption clauses for clergy or pastors.

9. Conclusion

In principle, the constitutional right of religious freedom is guaranteed to foreigners in the same way and to the same extent as to the citizens of Slovenia. The Resolution on Migration Policies and Immigration Laws entail only a few provisions directly referring to the freedom of religion (e.g. a general prohibition of discrimination on the basis of religion or a religious affiliation as a ground for unlawful persecution of a person). Despite the fact that the Religious Freedom Act lacks concrete provisions on pastoral assistance to illegal immigrants, the right of access to religious assistance is an element of the constitutional right of religious freedom. The right of churches and religious communities to have free access to persons placed in any kind of state institution of a closed-type has been regulated in special state – church agreements and has been secured in practice. The Slovenian Asylum and Immigration Laws should ensure the constitutional guarantee of freedom of religion in a more comprehensive manner. The Religious Freedom Act and a number of executive regulations should be reviewed with this in mind.

Bibliography

Bešter, R.: *Pravni okvir, relevanten za integracijo imigrantov v Sloveniji* [*Legal framework, relevant for integration of Foreigners in Slovenia*], Razprave in gradivo, No. 58, Ljubljana, 2009, p. 161-195.

Debelak, S., Gregori, N.: *Pravna in institucionalna usklajenost slovenske migracijske politike z merili Evropske unije*, VI. Dnevi javnega prava, Inštitut za javno upravo, Portorož, 5.-7. Junij 2000, p. 321-330.

Orehar Ivanc, M.: *Commentary on Arts. 41 and 47 of the Constitution of the Republic of Slovenia)* in: Šturm, L. (ed.), *Komentar Ustave Republike Slovenije (Commentary on the Constitution of the Republic of Slovenia)*, Faculty of Post-Graduate State and European Studies, Ljubljana, 2002, p. 444-459, 499.

Ivanc, B: *The financing of Religious Communities in The Republic of Slovenia – Legal Aspects*, in: Basdevant- Gaudemet, B. and Berlingò, S. (Eds.): *The financing of Religious Communities in the European Union*, Peeters, Leuven – Paris Dudley, MA, 2009, p. 303-312.

Jerovšek, T. *Commentary on Art. 13 of the Constitution of the Republic of Slovenia)* in: Šturm, L. (ed.), *Komentar Ustave Republike Slovenije (Commentary on the Constitution of the Republic of Slovenia)*, Faculty of Post-Graduate State and European Studies, Ljubljana, 2002, p. 168.

Kržišnik-Bukić, V. (Ed.), Klopčič, V., Komac, M., *Albanci, Bošnjaki, Črnogorci, Hrvati, Makedonci in Srbi v Republiki Sloveniji – Polo€aj in status pripadnikov nekdanje Jugoslavije v Sloveniji [Albanians, Bosnians, Montenegriners, Croats, Macedonians and Serbs – the Position and the Status of citizens of ex-Yugoslavia in Slovenia]* Inštitut za narodnostna vprašanja, Ljubljana, December 2003

Kogovšek, N. *Slovenia* [Country report] in: *Comparative Study of the Laws in the 27 EU Member States for Legal Immigration – including an assessment of the Conditions and Formalities Imposed by Each Member State for Newcomers*, European Parliament International Organization for Migration, February, 2008 (URL: http://www.iom.int/jahia/webdav/shared/shared/mainsite/law/legal_immigration_en.pdf)

Zalar, B: *Commentary on Art. 48 of the Constitution of the Republic of Slovenia)* in: Šturm, L. (ed.), *Komentar Ustave Republike Slovenije (Commentary on the Constitution of the Republic of Slovenia)*, Faculty of Post-Graduate State and European Studies, Ljubljana, 2002, p. 502-505.

Zavratnik Zimic, S.: *Migration Trends in Selected EU Applicant Countries* Volume VI – Slovenia: The Perspective of a Country on the "Schengen Periphery",

International Organization for Migration, Ljubljana, 2003 (URL: http://www.iom.int/jahia/webdav/site/myjahiasite/shared/shared/mainsite/published_docs/serial_publications/IOM_VI_SI.pdf)

Other sources:

Ministrstvo za notranje zadeve, Mirovni inštitut (Ministry of Interior, Peace Institute) *Slovenia National Report, The Organisation of Asylum and Migration Policies in Slovenia*, European Migration Network, July 2009 (URL: Http://emn.sarenet.es/Downloads/prepareShowFiles.do;jsessionid=D5048FB9FC46727315B0BD561AA8C8EA?directoryID=114=

Intercultural Dialog in Slovenia, Statistical Office of the Republic of Slovenia, Ljubljana, January 2009

CARMEN GARCIMARTÍN

IMMIGRATION AND RELIGION IN SPAIN

1. Background

Spain became a country of immigration in the second half of the XX century, instead of a country of emigrants, as it had been in the first half.[1] Since the early nineties, there have been more foreigners living in Spain than Spanish living abroad, and the percentage of foreigners living in Spain has grown increasingly in the first years of this century. By March 2009, 10.3 % of the Spanish population were legal immigrants.[2] Opportunities for better living conditions, more job opportunities, especially in certain fields (agriculture, construction, housekeeping, etc.) and family reunification, have been key elements in the development and stabilization of immigration.[3]

The tendency seems to be changing because of the economical crisis and the high unemployment rates, but there are no statistical data available yet.[4]

---

[1] Spain is expressly tagged as a "country of immigration" in a Report of the Spanish Secretary for Immigration and Emigration (See the *Strategic Plan for Citizenship and Integration 2007-2010*. An executive summary of the Plan is available in English in http://www.mtas.es/es/migraciones/ Integracion/PlanEstrategico/Docs/PECIingles.pdf). The Report assesses the transformation of Spain into a country of immigration, and it estimates that this situation is going to endure for several generations (see p. 6). A new Bill, currently in the Parliament, regulates the compromise of the Government to accept a yearly quota of refugees to settle in Spain. However, all this is not enough to consider Spain a settlement country, in the sense Australia, New Zealand, Canada or USA are considered.

[2] That means 4.495.349 persons of a total of 46.661.950. If we consider also foreigners without residence permit that are registered in a county register, the total number of immigrants becomes as high as 5.598.691 (Spanish Institute for Statistics, January 1st 2009). Numbers of immigrants can be found in http://extranjeros.mtin.es/es/Informacion-Estadistica/. Other statistical data are available in http://www.ine.es.

[3] Until 1998, almost half of the foreigners living in Spain were retired people or students. This pattern had radically changed. See *National Report on Immigrants (ENI-2007)*, directed by REHER, DAVID-SVEN, p. 8.

[4] An early study can be found in a Report from the Organization for Economic Co-operation and Development, *International Migration Outlook*, 2009 edition (summary available in http://www.oecd.org/dataoecd/5/20/43176823.pdf.)

We must distinguish between two kinds of immigrants, in terms of juridical regime: EU citizens and non-EU citizens. EU citizens are free to enter, work and live in Spain without restrictions.[5] The only reasons for preventing them from entering or expelling them are public order, public health and security reasons.[6] Immigrants from other countries must satisfy certain requirements, which vary depending on the country.

Immigration in Spain follows several patterns. The biggest group come from the EU; 16 % of the immigrants are from Romania, and 22 % from other EU countries.[7] 18% of the immigrants come from Andean America (former colonies of Colombia, Bolivia, Peru and Ecuador), which shares a history and language with Spain. Morocco has fewer cultural links with Spain, but it is only a short distance away from the Spanish shore. So, 15.2 % of immigrants come from that country, and a much fewer proportion from other Sub-Saharan countries.

Regarding the applications for residence, we can distinguish EU immigrants and non-EU immigrants with or without residence permits but recorded in a county register. Until the Act of 2000, the difference between the two latter numbers was not significant (around 29.000 immigrants registered in the county registers without residence permits). But since that year, being registered in the county records makes the immigrant eligible for medical assistance and regularization. Owing to this incentive, the difference between the two totals rose up 1.750.000 by 2005.

As a matter of interest, I will take into account all categories of immigrants, other than illegal. No official statistics regarding applications are available; only the number of visa or permits granted can be obtained.

---

[5] The same provisions apply to citizens from countries that are parties to the Agreement on the European Economic Area (Iceland, Liechtenstein and Norway) and citizens of the Swiss Confederation (Information provided by the Secretary for Foreign Affairs). All information from this Secretary, unless otherwise cited, can be found in http://extranjeros.mtin.es/es/NormativaJurisprudencia/Nacional/RegimenExtranjeria/Regimen-General.

[6] Royal Decree 240/2007, of February 16th, on the entry, free movement and residence in Spain of nationals of Member States party to the Agreement on the European Economic Area, article 15.

[7] Since January 1st 2009, restrictions to nationals from Bulgaria and Romania based on the terms of the Acts of Accession of these States to the EU are not in force.

	Total immigrants	E.U. citizenships	Non E.U. citizenships	
			Temporary	Permanent
2008	4.473.499	2.132.400	1.372.044	969.056
2007	3.979.014	1.621.796	1.505.629	851.589
2006	3.021.808	929.713	1.457.564	634.531
2005	2.738.932	780.841	1.526.251	431.840
2004	1.977.291	672.250	917.513	387.528

Source: Spanish Secretary for Immigration and Emigration and author

According to the Law, there cannot be any discrimination in granting permits or anything else on account of the applicant's religion[8]. In practice, a religious dimension to immigration does not seem to exist. If we look at the three main countries of origin, people from Andean America are for the most part Catholics, Romanians are Orthodox and Moroccans are Muslims.

2. Legal regulation of immigration and citizenship

Since the Act on the rights and freedoms of foreigners in Spain was enacted (2000), there has been an increase in control of immigration, and a toughening of conditions for coming to live in Spain.[9] Following certain amendments, a new Bill for modification of the Act, currently in Parliament, continues the same trend.[10]

The rights and benefits that legal immigrants enjoy in Spain are highly attractive for people from countries where these benefits do not exist, or are insufficient: right to children's free education, with access to the Spanish system of scholarships and aids; workers have access to the Social Benefits System and can send their income to their countries of origin -Social Benefits System comprises rights such as receiving a salary on retirement, disability, motherhood, widowhood or orphanage, medical assistance, etc.-; orphaning.

Programs to facilitate integration are not designed to call for further immigrants, but, in fact, they are a further stimulus in encouraging

[8] Act of December 22nd, 2000, article 23.
[9] Organic Law 4/2000, January 11th, regarding the rights and freedoms of foreigners in Spain, and their social integration. The Act was amended by the Organic Laws 8/2000 December 22nd, 11/2003 September 29th, and 14/2003 November 20th. Its regulation was approved by Royal Decree 2393/2004, December 30th.
[10] The Bill is available in http://www.intermigra.info/extranjeria/archivos/legislacion/ATT00176.pdf. A comment can be found in http://www.tt.mtin.es/periodico (12/18/2008).

immigration, since foreigners know they will not be left unassisted once they enter Spain.[11]

Conscious of this circumstance, the Government adopted various measures to avoid illegal immigration, and to control the number of immigrants. First, foreigners already in Spain, illegally or with a non-permanent visa, cannot obtain a work permit. Second, regularization has disappeared, a practice developed from 2000 to 2005, which enabled illegal immigrants to be legalised through a simple procedure (Nonetheless, it still remains possible to get residence through particular means where exceptional circumstances arise[12]).Third, the contingent -the number of foreigners needed to work in specific fields in Spain, defining the caps for each region and occupation-, tries to regulate the annual flow of immigrants.[13] In some cases, training may be offered, ranging from basic language and workplace safety to custom vocational training, with subsidies from the Spanish government.

People from countries that have signed an agreement with the Spanish Government regarding this issue will have preference in obtaining the visa. As an additional measure, in order to avoid illegal immigration from Morocco and Senegal, the Spanish Secretary of Labour co-operates directly with their counter partners in these countries in recruiting labour migrants, in exchange for help in preventing unauthorised departures. Development assistance in Africa is also linked to the policy of reducing irregular migration to Spain.[14]

Also, a special three-months visa in order to look for a job will be granted to those who meet certain requirements.

Once a person gets a work permit, and works for five years, permanent residence can be obtained. So, the Government fills the gap that exists within certain activities, and rewards immigrants who really contribute to the common good of the country.

Another measure must also be mentioned: the program of optional return, in favour of going back to the country of origin when the immigrant has a means of living there.[15]

---

[11] There is a Strategic Plan for Citizenship and Integration 2007-2010 currently in force (see note 1 above).

[12] Act of November 20th, 2003, article 31-3.

[13] Act of December 22nd, 2000, article 39.

[14] See International Migration Outlook, from the Organization for Economic Co-operation and Development, 2009 edition.

[15] Act of November 20th, 2003, additional disposition 8. The Bill of modification includes new ways to accumulate benefits and allowances to ease the return. However, according to the latest Report from the Organization for Economic Co-operation and

Foreigners can obtain Spanish citizenship through residence or special concession granted by the Government – assuming that they were neither born in Spain nor are related to Spanish citizens-.

In the first case, the prospective citizen must provide evidence that he had had legal residence in Spain for ten years. A shorter time is required if certain conditions occur. In regard to this it should be noted that Sephardies, that is, Jews of Spanish or Portuguese descent, can obtain citizenship if they can prove legal residence in Spain for just two years.[16]

All applicants must also prove good civic behaviour, and a certain level of integration into Spanish society. Nevertheless, no special test is required.

The Government can also grant citizenship in special circumstances. In such case the fact that the applicant speaks Spanish or other Spanish dialect, as well as any other fact which may prove his integration into Spanish "culture and life style", such as studies, may be involved in social or humanitarian activities, and so on.[17]

Spain is a non-denominational country. However, although Catholics are a majority (more than 75 % of the total population), being a catholic or a convert to this faith cannot be considered as proof of integration into Spanish society. However, belonging to any religious community in Spain can be considered a proof of integration. In fact, local authorities, in dealing with residence permits – not citizenship- consider certifications from a religious community to which the applicant belongs or collaborates with as proof of local integration.[18] Specific actions to integrate immigrants will be provided, but they are not compulsory, and are not considered as a test, but a means for a better integration.

The religious configuration of the country has changed in the last decade due to immigration. There are no official statistics on religious affiliation. It is not recorded as such, because the Spanish Constitution bans any request for a statement about it. The latest survey on religion from a public agency, the Centre for Sociological Research, found that 76.7 % of Spaniards are Catholics, 2% Islamic, 1.5% Evangelical, and 2% Orthodox, without a noteworthy representation of Jews.[19] Most of these non-Catholics are from non- Spanish origin.

Development (International Migration Outlook cited), this program was unsuccessful. Only 4.000 immigrants returned to their countries, instead of the 80.000 that could have done it.

[16] Spanish Civil Code, article 22.

[17] Statute of the Civil Register, article 220.

[18] See *Report on the plight of immigrants and refugees in 2008,* by the Spanish Secretary of Foreign Affairs, approved on October 14th, 2008, p. 62.

[19] See http://www.cis.es/cis/opencm/ES/1_encuestas/estudios/tematico.jsp

The change in society can be easily perceived if we consider the number of religious entities recorded in the Registry of Religious Entities in 1997, and the one documented ten years later:

Denomination	1997	2007
Evangelicals	719	1293
Islamic	74	406
Jewish	14	18
Orthodox	5	13

Source: Spanish Secretary for Relations with Religious denominations, and author

The main worshipers' countries of origin are as follows:

Evangelicals	Islamic	Jews	Orthodox
Ecuador	Morocco	Argentina	Rumania
Dominican Republic	Algeria	Chile	Bulgaria
Guatemala	Mauritania	Uruguay	Russia
Germany	Senegal	Colombia	
United Kingdom	Pakistan		

3. Regime of asylum

There have been some changes in the regulation of asylum during the past decade. The Law regarding the right of asylum and the plight of refugees was approved in 1984,[20] and since then it has been modified in 1994[21] and 2007.[22] However, several administrative acts have been enacted in these later years, to deal with particular issues regarding asylum.[23]

The total number of people seeking asylum in Spain has decreased in the last decade, as can be seen from the following chart:

Year	1999	2000	2001	2002	2003	2004	2005	2006	2007	2008
Total	8.405	7.926	9.490	6.309	5.918	5.401	5.254	5.297	7.662	4.516

Source: Spanish Secretary for Immigration and Emigration and ACNUR

---

[20] Act 5/1984 of March 26th. This Law was developed through the Royal Decree 511/1985, February 20th.

[21] Act 9/1994 of May 19th, developed through Royal Decree 203/1995 of February 10th.

[22] Act 3/2007, of March 22nd-

[23] Royal Decree 964/2001 of July 10th, regarding asylum due to humanitarian reasons or public interest; Royal Decree 1325/2003 of October 24th, about massive entrance of refugees; Royal Decree 2393/2004 of December 30th, adopting the Directive 2003/9/CE of the EU Council, January 27th.

Countries of origin in the latest year were Colombia (15%), Ivory Coast (10.8 %), Nigeria (7.8%), Algeria (7.2%). Percentages were similar in the previous years, with a gap in 2007, when almost 1,600 refugees from Iraq sought asylum in Spain. There are also significant numbers of refugees from Sub-Saharan countries.

It is also interesting to note that, according to the Office of Asylum and Refugees, about 80-85% of applications are submitted at the Police Stations in the country, 11-12% at the borders (mainly in Madrid Airport), and the others at Diplomat Missions abroad.

Once an asylum application is filed, asylum seekers have the right to have interpreters, legal counsel and medical assistance. Applicants can stay in Spain for up to sixty days while their application is pending. If asylum is granted, the refugee has the right to have social and health care, education and a work permit. Those who are denied asylum must leave Spain, usually within sixty days.

About 50 % of asylum applications are refused. The percentage of petitions granted and refused has been similar in last years. The main reasons for refusal are that grounds for obtaining asylum do not exist or do not seem reasonably authentic.

No official statistics regarding the frequency of seeking asylum on religious grounds can be found. The Courts widely recognized these claims: asylum was granted to Armenian Christian Iranians,[24] Baptists Nigerians,[25] and Sudanese who opposed the fundamentalist Islamic regime.[26] Nevertheless, a change in case law can be perceived in recent years. Two cases in 2003 denied asylum on religious grounds to Armenian Christian Iranians.[27] According to a report from the Spanish Embassy in Tehran, Christians are not persecuted in Iran, and they must not suffer greater restrictions than other citizens.[28] The latest case on this issue also denied asylum to an Armenian Jehovah Witness because it was not proven the cause for his leaving the country was religious persecution.[29]

If asylum cannot be granted according to a strict interpretation of the law, the refugee may be allowed to reside in Spain for humanitarian or

---

[24] High Court, S. May 31st 1999 and S. January 15th 2001.
[25] Supreme Court, S. January 11th 2001.
[26] High Court, S. January 16th 1994.
[27] Supreme Court, S. April 24th and May 8th 2003.
[28] See *Guide of the right of asylum*, by the Secretary of Labour and Social Issues, Madrid (2005), pp. 36-37.
[29] Supreme Court, S. March 27th 2009.

public interest reasons.[30] Residence will be granted especially when the person has had to leave his country because of political, ethnic or religious clashes, and does not meet the requirements for getting asylum in Spain. However, fewer favours are granted if no reasonable suspicion exists that the refugee's deportation will convey a risk to his life or physical integrity in his country of origin.[31]

There are no legal bases for churches giving asylum. Asylum is the protection granted by the Spanish Government to those foreigners who are considered refugees.[32] The granting of the benefits of asylum is exclusively within the powers of the state. No actions undertaken by churches, or any other entity, outside the framework of the law will have any consequences with regard to asylum and its benefits.

In dealing with this issue, the authorities take into account ACNUR and NGOs who aim at helping refugees. The task of these entities is to provide information, legal or social assistance and so on. Moreover, the authorities give foreigners who are seeking asylum, a brochure which contains information about these organizations.

4. Pastoral assistance for immigrants

We must distinguish between pastoral assistance offered by different denominations.

With regard to the Catholic Church, the principles of pastoral assistance are stated in a declaration from the Commission of the Bishops' Conferences of the EU. Briefly, there is no distinction between assistance to legal and illegal immigrants.[33] Structures and pastoral care are provided in the same way for both groups in Spain.

---

[30] Act 5/1984, article 17, modified in 1994.
[31] Royal Decree 2393/2004, article 31. This different status will disappear if the Bill for modification of the Act of 2000 is enacted.
[32] Article 13-4.
[33] "We are extremely concerned about the situations of people with irregular status, many of whom are victims of exploitation that denies their human dignity. We are also concerned about those who, although in regular situations, cannot live with their families. In her pastoral activity, the Church tries to take these serious problems constantly into consideration. A person who exercises his or her right to search for better living conditions by legitimate means should not be considered as a criminal simply for doing so". (Declaration of the Bishops of COMECE with regard to a Common Asylum and Immigration Policy of the European Union, March 30th, 2001). Pope John Paul II addressed several messages for the International Meeting of Migrations where he reaffirmed that illegal immigrants deserve the same pastoral attention as legal ones. See, for example, Message of July 25th, 1995. These messages can be found in http://www.vatican.va/roman_curia/pontificial_councils/migrants.

There are some specific structures for the religious assistance of immigrants: inter-cultural or inter-ethnic parishes; ethnic missions or chaplaincies; chaplains named to care spiritually for immigrants.[34] Personal parishes of Catholic Oriental Rites can also be constituted in a diocese. However, the faithful from these parishes belong to their oriental Rite of origin. This is the case with Ukrainian Catholics in Spain.

These structures are of a temporary nature, although they seem necessary in the actual stage of immigration. The ultimate target is the integration of immigrants into the country, and taking part in a common religious life is a way of doing so for Catholic immigrants.

The Catholic Church in Spain faces another challenge: the coordination and unification of models of spiritual assistance for immigrants. Dioceses are autonomous in the organization of the pastoral care of immigrants. Therefore, there is no one single model. Usually, a diocese organizes pastoral care according to its own practice, which varies greatly, for example, between dioceses in the South East and those in the North. They can also establish some kind of agreement with the dioceses of origin, whenever a high number of immigrants from a country come to live in a certain diocese.

Most Orthodox in Spain are immigrants. Therefore, parishes are geared mainly towards the religious assistance of immigrants. It is noteworthy that no agreement has been signed between these Churches and the State, perhaps because of the insignificant number of Orthodox who have migrated to Spain at the time the Agreements in force were signed (1992). Because of the close links between Catholics and Orthodox, it is not unusual that Catholic resources and facilities are borrowed by the Orthodox for worship.

Evangelicals have specific body for assisting immigrants. There is a Council for Religious Assistance in the Spanish Federation of Evangelical Denominations. Also, Diaconia is an evangelical entity dedicated to social assistance, but none of them have a special department or council for immigrants.

Religious assistance is a somewhat strange concept for Muslims. Consequently, no special targets regarding immigrants can be found, although one could say that everything -building and using mosques,

---

[34] See the Document approved by the Spanish Conference of Bishops on November 22nd 2007, entitled *The Catholic Church in Spain and Migrants* (available in http://www.conferenciaepiscopal.es/documentos/Conferencia/IglesiaInmigrantes.htm). It contains some reflections and practical guidance on behalf of the Holy See Instruction *Erga migrantes caritas Christi*.

religious education in public schools, and virtually all matters- stated in the Agreement is devoted to the assistance of Muslims from abroad.

Jews are a minority in Spain, and even a smaller immigrant group. Therefore, no particular spiritual assistance, other than general assistance, is provided for immigrants.

When immigrants are placed in a centre for foreigners, the exercise of their rights is guaranteed. Religious assistance is not expressly mentioned in the law, but it is an essential right. Then, the centre's authorities must allow access to a religious minister when requested, as happens in other public centres (penitentiaries, hospitals, and so on).

5. Family reunification

Spanish Law considers family reunion a right of foreigners residing in Spain. The applicant must demonstrate that he/she has an adequate home to house the family, and economic means to support them. In order to avoid fraud of law, it is not allowed to regroup the spouse if separated. Neither can there be reunion with a second husband or wife if a previous divorce is not recorded in reliable documents.[35]

According to the Law, only one spouse can be regrouped, even if the country of origin enables "other kind of families". It is an implicit statement referring to polygamous marriages, and it is in accordance with Article 4.4 of the EU Council Directive 2003/86/EC on the right to family reunification.[36] Nevertheless, Spanish law poses a problem when it says that only a spouse can be regrouped, without stating which spouse (generally the first) can be regrouped. This situation allows the husband to choose which of his wives will be regrouped. This difference between the spouses' rights could be considered against the public order of Spain. Moreover, the reunion of the second or further wife, mainly if the marriage was celebrated after the husband's residence in Spain, could be considered as a sign of not abandoning polygamy, and therefore, of not being willing to integrate in Spain.[37]

---

[35] Act January 11th, 2000, articles 16 ff, regarding rights and duties of foreigners in Spain.

[36] European Union: Council of the European Union, Council Directive 2003/86/EC of 22 September 2003 on the Right to Family Reunification, 3 October 2003. 2003/86/EC. Online. UNHCR Refworld, available at: http://www.unhcr.org/refworld/docid/3f8bb4a10. html [accessed 7 May 2009]. Article 4.4: "In the event of a polygamous marriage, where the sponsor already has a spouse living with him in the territory of a Member State, the Member State concerned shall not authorise the family reunification of a further spouse".

[37] See VARGAS, MARINA, *La reagrupación familiar de extranjeros en España*, Thomson, Navarra (2006), p. 236.

This limitation has an impact on family reunion, so long as Morocco continues to be a major country of origin for Spanish immigrants[38], and the first regarding in family reunion in Spain.[39] Morocco Mudawana[40] allows polygamy, although it is not common.

On the contrary, Spanish legislation does not take into account the limitation stated in Article 4.5 of the Directive, that is to say, establishing a minimum age for spouses -not higher than 21- to prevent reunion of forced marriages.[41] Even, the law excludes reunion of the foreigner's under age descendants if they are married.[42]

6. Immigration and religious ministers

Spanish authorities approve every three months a short list, or catalogue of jobs which are difficult to fill. Employers are able to recruit foreign workers to fill a position on this catalogue, for no more than five years (although eventually they might be renewed). For jobs not on the short list, employers must submit to a labour market test or "negative certification", giving evidence of insufficient employment demands. Once the foreigner gets the job, he must remain in the same sector and region for the first year, although he may change employer.

The Government can also approve, yearly, a quota or contingent of workers not living in Spain, taking into account the national employment situation. This situation will not be taken into consideration when workers come from a country with which Spain has signed a reciprocity agreement, or if special situations stated by the Law occur.[43]

---

[38] The same may be said regarding other mayor countries of origin that admit polygamy as well: Mauritania, Algeria, etc.

[39] According to the data from the Secretary of Foreign Affairs, from January 2005 until April 2008, 76.669 visas were issued to Moroccans due to family reunion. The next countries are Colombia with 37.763 visas and Ecuador, with 35.893. See "Family reunion" in the *Report on the plight of immigrants and refugees in 2008,* by the Spanish Secretary of Foreign Affairs.

[40] An equivalent to the Civil Code (2004).

[41] According to the *Report on the plight of immigrants and refugees in 2008,* 99 wives and 90 husbands, in a total of 5.938 persons regrouped because of marriage, were sixteen or under sixteen years old.

[42] Royal Decree 2393/2004, article 39.

[43] Act of December 22nd, 2000, article 38. As for now, work permits via quota or contingent has diminished from about 30.000 to 901 for 2009. Also, the regional shortage list or catalogue has decreased around 70%. Nevertheless, these are not as much Government restrictions as a decline on the job demand in Spain (see more in MOYA, DAVID, *La reforma de la Ley de Extranjería,* Workshop 04/22/2009, Real Instituto Elcano, Madrid (available at http://www.realinstitutoelcano.org).

All these limitations do not apply in certain circumstances. According to the Law, a work permit is not necessary for religious ministers and representatives of religious entities registered in the Register of Religious Bodies, whenever they strictly limit their activities to those of a religious nature,[44] do not receive a salary, and the religious entity assume their maintenance. However, the Royal Decree that develops the Law does not include "representatives", but only "religious ministers".[45] That poses a problem, because some persons devoting their time and work to religious entities are not in the category of religious ministers.

Another problem arises from the development of the Law: the R. D. 2393/2004 contains more detailed requirements for religious ministers in obtaining a visa. It does not mention "representatives" of the denomination, and applicants must have the category of being a religious minister or a contemplative according to the statutes of the religious denomination registered in Spain. So, fewer people will be able to obtain a visa as religious minister if this article is strictly enforced.

---

[44] Act of December 22nd, 2000, article 41.
[45] Royal Decree 2393/2004, article 68.

Lars Friedner

IMMIGRATION AND RELIGION IN SWEDEN

Since the 1960s, Swedish immigration legislation has focussed on limiting immigration to Sweden.[1] The main provisions prescribe that a permit is needed for *entry* into Sweden[2]. A visa[3] is normally required for entry, even if citizens from certain countries, i.e. EU and other EEA countries[4], do not need such a permit.[5] An alien requires a residence permit to stay in Sweden for a period exceeding the period for which a visa can be granted.[6] Such permits can be granted either temporarily[7] or permanently.[8] Citizens of EU or other EEA countries (and their family members) are in special circumstances (for instance when they are employed in Sweden) allowed to stay in Sweden without a residence permit.[9] To work as an employee in Sweden, an alien needs a work permit.[10] A work permit is not needed for citizens of EU or other EEA countries (and their family members), nor those who have been granted permanent residence permits.[11]

During 2008, no less than 70,000 persons were granted residence permits for Sweden.[12] The numbers for 2007, 2006, and 2005 were 66,708, 65,975, and 44,394 respectively. (These numbers do not include those already having a temporary residence permit who get the time limit extended.) There are no statistics giving the numbers of permanent and temporary permits respectively. Neither are there general statistics on

[1] www.migrationsverket.se
[2] Chapter 2, Section 3 Aliens Act (2005:716)
[3] The definition of a visa is "a permit to enter and stay in Sweden for a certain limited period." (Chapter 2, Section 3 Aliens Act)
[4] European Economic Area (EEA) consists of the EU countries, Iceland, Liechtenstein, and Norway
[5] Chapter 2, Sections 3, 8, and 10 Aliens Act; Chapter 3, Sections 1 and 8 and Chapter 4, Section 6 Aliens Ordinance (2006:97)
[6] Sw, *uppehållstillstånd*; Chapter 2, Section 5 Aliens Act
[7] Sw. *tidsbegränsat uppehållstillstånd*
[8] Sw. *permanent uppehållstillstånd*; Chapter 2,4 Aliens Act
[9] Chapter 2, Sections 3a and 3a:3-9 Aliens Act
[10] Sw. *arbetstillstånd;* Chapter 2,7 Aliens Act
[11] Chapter 2,8 Aliens Act
[12] The Swedish population on 28 February 2009 was a good nine million people (www.scb.se)

the number of applications for residence permits refused. As regards asylum, 8,276 permits were granted in 2008, and the statistics indicate that this means that 24 per cent of all applications considered by the Swedish Migration Board[13] that year were approved.[14] However, it should be noted that residence permit cases, after rejection by the Swedish Migration Board, can go on to appeal to the Migration Court[15] and from there to the Migration Court of Appeal.[16] Certain applications are also approved by decisions of these courts.[17]

A large number of immigrants to Sweden have traditionally come from neighbouring countries, especially Finland, but the biggest number of immigrants (from a single country) to Sweden during 2008 were citizens of Iraq.[18]

The requirements for becoming a Swedish *citizen* are that the alien prove his or her identity, is 18 years old, has a permanent residence permit[19], has lived in Sweden for five years,[20] and has had, and can be expected to have, an honest way of living.[21] Special provisions for citizenship apply regarding, among others, children[22], persons who have previously been Swedish citizens and for those who are married to or cohabit with a Swedish citizen.[23] There are no special tests for those applying for Swedish citizenship.

Immigration to Sweden in recent decades has undoubtedly changed the religious demography of Sweden. Although the national population records do not contain any data on religious affiliation, there are some statistics from the Swedish Commission for Government Support to Faith Communities.[24] The system of government support to faith communities started in 1971,[25] and within a few years some orthodox

---

[13] Sw. *Migrationsverket*
[14] www.migrationsverket.se
[15] Sw. *migrationsdomstolar*
[16] Sw. *migrationsöverdomstolen*
[17] Chapter 14, Section 3 and Chapter 16, Section 9 Aliens Act
[18] www.migrationsverket.se
[19] Citizens of EU or other EEA countries do not require a residence permit (Section 20, Swedish Nationality Act (2001:82))
[20] Only two years for citizens of Denmark, Finland, Iceland, and Norway; only four years for a stateless person or a person who is a refugee
[21] Section 11 §lagen om svenskt medborgarskap
[22] ibid. Sections 1-10
[23] ibid. Section 12
[24] Sw. *Nämnden för statligt stöd till trossamfund*
[25] *Ekström*, Staten, trossamfunden och samhällets grundläggande värderingar – en bakgrund in *Samarbetsnämnden för statsbidrag till trossamfund* (ed.), Samfunden och bidragen (Stockholm 2006), p. 11

churches were also entitled to support.[26] Since the late 1970s Muslim organisations have also been granted state support.[27] This development reflects the rise of immigrant faith communities in Swedish society.

A person who is a *refugee* or otherwise, has the right to obtain a residence permit in Sweden, if he or she actually is in the country.[28] The same right applies to an alien who has – through a decision of the Government – been received into Sweden within the framework of transfer to Sweden of those in need of protection.[29] The definition of a refugee is "an alien who is outside the country of the alien's nationality, because he or she feels a well-founded fear of persecution on grounds of race, nationality, religious or political belief, or on grounds of gender, sexual orientation or other membership of a particular social group and is unable, or because of his or her fear is unwilling to avail himself or herself of the protection of that country". According to this provision, such a person is regarded as a refugee, irrespective of whether the authorities of the country are responsible for the alien being subjected to persecution or those authorities cannot be assumed to offer protection against persecution by private individuals. If the alien is stateless, the provision applies to him or her, or if he or she is outside the country in which he or she has previously had his or her usual place of residence and is unable or, because of fear, unwilling to return there.[30] The definition of a person who "otherwise is in need of protection" is of an alien who is outside the country where the alien is a citizen (or a stateless person who is outside the country where he or she has previously had his or her usual place of residence), "because he or she feels a well-founded fear of suffering the death penalty or being subjected to corporal punishment, torture or other inhuman or degrading treatment or punishment, or needs protection because of external or internal armed conflict or, because of other severe conflicts in the country of origin, feels a well-founded fear of being subjected to serious abuses or is unable to return to the country of origin because of an environment disaster".[31] An application for a residence permit could be refused if there are urgent reasons not to grant a residence permit, in view of what is known about the alien's previous

[26] ibid. p. 12
[27] ibid.
[28] Chapter, Section 1 Aliens Act; the Swedish provisions are founded on the fact that Sweden has acceded to the international 1951 Convention on the Legal Status of Refugees
[29] Chapter 5, Section 2 Aliens Act
[30] Chapter 4, Section 1 Aliens Act
[31] Chapter 4, Section 2 Aliens Act

activities, or with regard to national security, if the alien before entry to
Sweden has stayed in (or has a special connection to) a country other
than the country of origin and is protected there against persecution and
against being sent to the country of origin or to another country where
he or she does not have a corresponding protection.

A person who "otherwise is in need of protection" could also have his
or her application for residence permit refused if, in view of what is
known about his or her criminal activities, there are special reasons not to
grant a permit.[32] Special provisions apply in the event of a mass influx.[33]

The provisions on asylum have been changed several times during the
last ten years. The rules on asylum due to gender or sexual orientation
were added in 2005.[34] The system of Migration Courts and a Migration
Court of Appeal was introduced through the new Act on Immigration[35],
also in 2005. Through a decision of the Riksdag, against the wish of the
Government, provisional rules were put in force providing the possibility
of a new trial for persons who have stayed in Sweden for a long time and
have not – for various reasons – left the country. These provisions on new
trials were aimed at families with children and at persons who could not
be forced to leave for their home countries due to the situation in the country.[36] These provisional rules were in force for a period of some months.

In 2005, as well, a change was made that improved the protection of
unaccompanied children arriving to Sweden.[37] In 2004, an amendment to
the Act on Immigration stated that greater regard should be given to
children's needs for their parents, when a criminal is ordered to leave
Sweden.[38] It was also decided in the same year that state grants to a
refugee could be reduced if the refugee did not cooperate in stating his
or her identity.[39] In 2002 special provisions were introduced for a situation of mass influx.[40]

---

[32] Chapter 5, Section 1 Aliens Act; the "Dublin Ordinance" – the Council's Ordinance (EG) no. 343/2003?? of February 18, 2003, on Criteria and Mechanisms to Decide
which Member State that has the Responsibility to Inquire an Application for Asylum
which a Citizen of a Third Country has Made in any Member State – also states that
refugees who have made an application for asylum in another EU member state (or Norway or Iceland) can be sent to that state for decision on asylum
[33] Chapter 21, Sections 1-9 Aliens Act
[34] SFS 2005:1239
[35] Sw. Aliens Act
[36] Act (2005:762) amending the Aliens Act (1989:529)
[37] SFS 2005:432
[38] SFS 2004:515
[39] SFS 2004:407
[40] SFS 2002:1111

As mentioned, applications in cases concerning immigration have – since 2006 – been handled by Migration Courts and the Migration Court of Appeal.[41] The decisions of the Migration Court of Appeal are published,[42] which means that the practice of the state authorities can now easily be followed. Among the decisions of the Migration Court of Appeal are that the fact that a person is stateless is not *per se* a reason for asylum,[43] that the Swedish Migration Board – in the proceedings at the courts – has to prove that the alien had an opportunity to move to a safer place within his or her own country (if this is the reason for refusing an application for asylum),[44] and that that the need of protection of an alien who has stayed for a long time in a country other than his or her home-country shall be examined also in relation to the other country.[45] The decisions give the impression that the practice of the authorities closely approximates to the intent of the Act on Immigration.

According to the published cases, the question of religion has not been an issue, so far.

Beside the provisions for asylum, an alien can also be granted a residence permit "if at an assessment of the situation of the alien there exist such extraordinary distressing circumstances that he or she ought to be granted the right to remain in Sweden".[46] When this clause is taken into consideration, the alien's health, his adaptation to the Swedish society and the situation in his home-country is to be especially examined.[47]

According to Swedish law, there is no "church asylum", nor are churches or other religious communities arranging "asylum" outside the framework of the law. There are, however, examples of priests and other church employees (as well as active church lay people), who have taken part in actions of "civil disobedience", i.e. hiding people that are turned away from the country through decisions of state authorities.

There is no specially organised pastoral care for legal or illegal immigrants. The normal activities of churches and other religious communities regarding pastoral care also apply to immigrants.

---

[41] Chapter 14, Section 3, Chapter 16, Section 9 Aliens Act
[42] www.rattsinfosok.dom.se/lagrummet
[43] MIG 2008:21
[44] MIG 2009:4
[45] MIG 2008:40
[46] Chapter 5, Section 6 Aliens Act
[47] ibid.

The Act on Immigration was amended in 2006[48], due to new EU Council Directives. Since then, a residence permit in Sweden is granted to an alien who is married to or cohabits with (or who intends to marry or to cohabit with, if the relationship appears to be serious and there are no special grounds for not granting a permit) a person who has been granted a residence permit to settle in Sweden.[49] Also unmarried children (under 18 years of age) who have a parent with a permanent residence permit or have a parent who is married to (or cohabit with) a person with a permanent residence permit in Sweden, are granted a residence permit. The same provisions apply to a person who is a parent to an unmarried child who has arrived unaccompanied in Sweden[50] and, also, to a person who is in some way a member of the family of a person who has a permanent residence permit, if the person was part of the same household and there was a special relationship of dependence between the relatives, already existing in the country of origin.[51] Special arrangements for residence permits exist for foreign children who are adopted in Sweden, an alien who is entitled to visiting his or her children in Sweden, persons who are of Swedish origin, and persons who have stayed in Sweden for a long time with a residence permit. If exceptional reasons apply, any person who has a "special tie" with Sweden can be granted a residence permit.[52] So far, there have been no reported court cases concerning polygamous or forced marriages, although such situations are not entirely unknown among Swedish immigrants.

Since 2008, provisions concerning work permits have been broadened, so that such a permit can be granted to an alien who has been offered employment in Sweden, provided that it makes it possible for him or her to earn his or her living, and the salary (and other employment benefits) is not worse than the benefits that follow from Swedish collective agreements or practice.[53] The residence permits granted will last no longer than two years and can be extended only once for a maximum period of four years.[54] There are no quotas, and there are no special provisions for clergy or pastors.

---

[48] SFS 2006:220
[49] Chapter 5, Sections 3-3a Aliens Act
[50] Chapter 5, Section 3 Aliens Act
[51] Chapter 5, Section 3a Aliens Act
[52] Chapter 5 Sections 3-3a Aliens Act
[53] Chapter 6, Section 2 Aliens Act
[54] Chapter 6, Section 2a Aliens Act

DAVID MCCLEAN

IMMIGRATION AND RELIGION IN THE UNITED KINGDOM

United Kingdom immigration law is of daunting complexity and, as in many other states, is highly controversial: in the European elections of June 2009 two seats were won by the British National Party which campaigned on an anti-immigration platform.

1. Facilitation or limiting immigration

The United Kingdom is, and has been for many years, a country to which migrants are attracted. The English language, the traditional links with former colonies, a stable political system with a developed welfare state, and (at least until very recently) relative prosperity have all encouraged immigration. The British often speak of their 'crowded island', and by European standards it does have a relatively high population density; there is a degree of public unease at the strain perceived to be created by large-scale immigration. So, legislation is essentially directed to limiting rather than facilitating immigration. Progressively tighter immigration controls have been introduced and the legislation has often been criticised by the churches and has sometimes run into trouble in both Parliament[1] and the courts.

The main instrument governing immigration into the United Kingdom is known as 'the Immigration Rules'.[2] The Rules are made by the Home Secretary under a broad power in section 3(2) of the Immigration Act 1971. Unusually, the approval of the two Houses of Parliament is *not* required: if a statement of changes to the Rules is disapproved by a resolution of either House, the Act merely requires the Home Secretary to 'make such changes or further changes in the rules as appear to him to be required in the circumstances'. There are many other legislative provisions in the form of Acts of Parliament and statutory instruments,

---

[1] For example, the Government was defeated in the House of Commons (in which it has a large majority) on 29 April 2009 on its refusal to make proper provision for Gurkha ex-servicemen to have the right to settle in the UK.

[2] Formally cited as HC (for House of Commons Paper) 395 (1994) as (much) amended; a consolidated version is maintained on the website of the UK Borders Agency.

and some changes seem to be made every year: the Borders Citizenship and Immigration Act 2009 is the latest in the series.[3]

The Rules do not limit the right to enter the United Kingdom of British citizens and of certain citizens of Commonwealth countries (those with the right of abode) and they do not apply to migrants from the European Economic Area or Switzerland (though there are some transitional restrictions on nationals of Bulgaria and Romania).

The points-based system

The Rules were much amended in 2008 by Statements of Changes, the later made in November 2008 and coming fully into effect on 31 March 2009; it was heavily criticised in the House of Lords but survived a motion for disapproval. The changes develop further the point-based system of immigration control first announced in 2006, based on the system used for many years in Australia. The changes were described by the UK Border Agency as 'the biggest shake-up of the immigration system for 45 years'.

Intending migrants need to pass a points-based assessment before they are given permission to enter or remain in the United Kingdom. The system consists of five tiers, each with its own points requirements:[4]

tier 1: highly skilled workers, for example scientists;
tier 2: skilled workers with a job offer, for example teachers and nurses;
tier 3: low-skilled workers filling specific temporary labour shortages, for example construction workers for a particular project [but this tier is currently suspended];
tier 4: students;
tier 5: youth mobility[5] and temporary workers, for example musicians coming to play in a concert.

Except for cases in tier 1 and youth mobility cases in tier 5, a migrant must by sponsored by a UK-based employer or educational institution; the sponsor must hold a sponsor licence. Obtaining a licence is a complex task: the application form runs to 35 pages and the guidance notes

---

[3] It was to have provided, *inter alia*, for some additional control on persons arriving in the UK, from another part of the 'Common Travel Area' (the United Kingdom, the Crown dependencies (the Channel Islands and the Isle of Man) and the Republic of Ireland); this proposal was defeated in the House of Lords and the current position (see Immigration Rules, r 12) remains unchanged.

[4] Immigration Rules, r 245ff.

[5] The youth mobility scheme is limited to Australia, Canada, Japan and New Zealand (Immigration Rules, App G) and replaced a much wider working holiday scheme much used by young people and having no such geographical limitation.

to 130. There are further processes before a certificate of Sponsorship is issued for a particular entrant.[6]

An example may make the nature of the 'points-based system' clearer. The rules applying to tier 2 migrants (other than those transferring within one company, to whom special rules apply) require an applicant for entry to score 50 points.[7] The points available are as follows:

if the prospective employment is in a 'shortage occupation'[8]:	50
if the job offer passes the Resident Labour Market Test[9]:	30
if the applicant has an appropriate sub-degree level qualification:	5
if the applicant has a Bachelors or Masters degree:	10
if the applicant has a PhD:[10]	15
if the applicant's prospective earnings are from £17,000-20,000[11] a year:	5
if the applicant's prospective earnings are from £20,000-22,000 a year:	10
if the applicant's prospective earnings are from £22,000-24,000 a year:	15
if the applicant's prospective earnings are above £24,000 a year:	20

A student seeking entry under tier 4 to attend a course of study in central London must produce a sponsorship letter from the educational institution[12] and show that he or she has (and has had for the past 28 days) money to cover the fees for the course and £7,200[13] for living costs.[14] A lower amount suffices where the student is to live elsewhere in the country. There has been much concern at the existence of bogus colleges set up solely for immigration purposes, providing no or minimal tuition but providing certificates of success in return for a large fee.

The intended effect of the new Rules is to reduce the overall level of immigration. It seems likely that this will indeed be the result but statistics are not yet available to demonstrate the full effect. The pattern of immigration in recent years is indicated in Table 1:[15]

---

[6] The rules governing sponsorship are not set out in the Immigration Rules but are set administratively by the UK Borders Agency.

[7] Immigration Rules, r 245ZB and App A, paras 59-84.

[8] The list changes from time to time, but in 2009 included certain engineering and healthcare posts, veterinary surgeons, teachers and social workers.

[9] Essentially this means that the job must be advertised to persons already settled in the UK and it be shown that no suitable person was found.

[10] No provision seems to be made for other forms of doctorate.

[11] £20,000 equalled €22,750 at the time of writing.

[12] Immigration Rules, App A, para 113ff.

[13] €8,200.

[14] Immigration Rules, App C, paras 1-13.

[15] All statistics quoted are derived from official Government publications: this Table is based on Table 2.03 in the Total International Migration tables published by the National Statistical Office.

Table 1: Total Net International Migration 1991 to 2007

United Kingdom

Country of birth   *thousands*

Year	All	United Kingdom	European Union	Commonwealth			Other foreign
				All	Old	New	
1991	+ 44	- 49	+ 9	+ 46	+ 6	+ 41	+ 38
1992	- 13	- 65	+ 10	+ 29	-	+ 29	+ 13
1993	- 1	- 67	+ 7	+ 36	+ 6	+ 30	+ 22
1994	+ 77	- 21	+ 7	+ 52	+ 7	+ 45	+ 40
1995	+ 76	- 62	+ 22	+ 59	+ 9	+ 50	+ 57
1996	+ 55	- 65	+ 24	+ 50	+ 9	+ 41	+ 46
1997	+ 48	- 62	+ 19	+ 53	+ 12	+ 40	+ 37
1998	+ 140	- 31	+ 23	+ 85	+ 43	+ 42	+ 63
1999	+ 163	- 41	+ 7	+ 97	+ 30	+ 67	+ 100
2000	+ 158	- 68	-	+ 106	+ 21	+ 86	+ 120
2001	+ 173	- 60	+ 5	+ 111	+ 37	+ 74	+ 118
2002	+ 154	- 98	+ 3	+ 101	+ 29	+ 71	+ 148
2003	+ 147	- 99	+ 10	+ 112	+ 27	+ 85	+ 123
2004	+ 244	- 117	+ 82	+ 167	+ 45	+ 122	+ 112
2005	+ 204	- 93	+ 91	+ 124	+ 25	+ 99	+ 83
2006	+ 191	- 136	+ 106	+ 133	+ 16	+ 117	+ 88
2007	+ 237	- 96	+ 125	+ 117	+ 12	+ 105	+ 91

The sharp increase in net immigration from the EU does of course reflect the enlargement of the Community (newly acceding States being removed from the 'other foreign' category). 'Old Commonwealth' means Australia, New Zealand, South Africa and Canada; 'New Commonwealth' means all 49 other Commonwealth countries. The pattern of inward immigration from the New Commonwealth has changed over the years: the large flow from the Caribbean in the late 1940s and 1950s has declined to some 15,000 a year; from countries in East and West Africa it reached a peak of 45,000 in 2004 and has since fallen to some 25,000 a year; from the Indian sub-continent there has been a marked increase, from about 30,000 a year in the 1990s, to 50,000 in 2000 and about 90,000 in the most recent years. All these figures pre-date the introduction of the points system.

Ministers of religion

There are special additional requirements for entry prescribed for ministers of religion:[16]

(a) that the applicant has been working for at least one year as a minister of religion in any of the prior 5 years or, where ordination is prescribed by a religious faith as the sole means of entering the ministry, has been ordained as a minister of religion following at least one year's full time or two years' part time training for the ministry; or
(b) if seeking leave to enter as a missionary has been trained as a missionary or has worked as a missionary and is being sent to the UK by an overseas organisation; or
(c) if seeking leave to enter as a member of a religious order is coming to live in a community maintained by the religious order of which he is a member and, if intending to teach, does not intend to do so save at an establishment maintained by his order;
and intends to work full time as a minister of religion, missionary or for the religious order of which he is a member, does not intend to take any other employment, can maintain and accommodate himself and any dependants adequately without recourse to public funds, and can produce an International English Language Testing System certificate issued to him to certify that he has achieved level 6 competence in spoken and written English.

These rules have attracted much criticism. In the debate on the changes to the Immigration Rules in the House of Lords in November 2008[17], Lord Avebury spoke as patron of the Buddhist Prison Chaplaincy Organisation, whose spiritual director, the Venerable Ajahn Khemadhammo, is also chair of the Theravada Buddhist Sangha UK and abbot of a monastery in Warwickshire which from time to time hosts visiting monks from Thailand. He said,

There has never been any problem with monks coming to Theravada monasteries here, but now abbots are having to plough through reams of paperwork to become sponsors, a severe distraction from their lives of meditation and teaching the Dharma. ... It looks as though monks can enter, either as ministers of religion under tier 2, or as temporary religious workers for up to 24 months under tier 5. Tier 2 requires fluent English, and that is not usually spoken by monks when they first arrive

[16] Immigration Rules, App A, paras 85-92.
[17] *Parliamentary Debates (Lords)* 25 November 2008, cols 1418ff.

from south Asian countries. But under tier 5, they are barred from engaging in many of the normal activities of monks, such as chanting at funerals, or any pastoral duties, including counselling. It may be very hard for monks to qualify at all if these restrictions are interpreted rigidly. ... The fees will hit small monasteries very hard. It costs £400 for the licence for tiers 2 and 5 and £175 for each certificate of sponsorship, plus the cost of the visa.

This was followed a few weeks later by a letter to the Home Secretary from the Archbishops' Council of the Church of England. It queried the requirement that ministers of religion admitted under tier 2 would be expected to have a higher standard of English[18] than anyone else in that category. Why did the conduct of worship require greater language competence than work as a hospital doctor? Why did the rules apply to contemplative orders and to those who were to conduct services and pastoral work in languages other than English? It is not known if any reply has been received.

2. Applications for temporary and permanent residence

Temporary admission

Statistics of applications for entry made initially to UK diplomatic posts abroad do not seem to be available. The official *Control of Immigration Statistics* focus on actual entry, or refusal of entry, to the UK. In 2007, excluding EEA nationals and asylum cases, 13,400,000 persons sought to enter the UK and 31,145 were refused entry and removed.[19] The great majority of entrants were temporary visitors or persons returning after a visit to another country and so not migrants at all. More relevant were the 358,000 students (and 16,700 dependants) admitted in 2007, an increase of 16% on 2006; 124,000 persons admitted as work permit holders or as their dependants in 2007, a reduction of 15% on 2006; 42,160 spouses and fiancé(e)s and 7,150 children admitted for a limited period with a view to longer-term settlement;[20] and 7,225 Commonwealth citizens with a grandparent born in the UK admitted in 2007 to take up or seek employment. Rather surprisingly there were 860 ministers of religion.

---

[18] i.e. equivalent to the Council of Europe level B2 as opposed to the usual Level C1.

[19] For these and the following statistics, see *Control of Immigration: Statistics 2007* (Home Office Statistical Bulletin 10/08), Table 2.2.

[20] Council Directive 2003/86/EC on the right to family reunification does not apply to the United Kingdom.

Permanent residency (settlement)

British citizens and limited categories of citizens of Commonwealth countries have the 'right of abode' in the United Kingdom. EEA and Swiss nationals and their families may (but are not obliged to) apply for confirmation of permanent residence after living in the United Kingdom for five years. Other non-EEA nationals must apply for indefinite leave to remain usually after five years lawful residence. For some, the points-based system will apply; family members of already-settled residents are admitted under easier rules.

Since 2007 applicants for indefinite leave to remain must demonstrate an adequate knowledge of the English language and (with some exemptions) pass the 'Life in the UK' test first introduced in 2005 for naturalization purposes.[21] The test consists of 24 questions based on the information contained in an official handbook *Life in the United Kingdom: A Journey to Citizenship* (2nd edn, 2007).

The 2007 statistics[22] show 89,725 applications for settlement, of which 77,845 were successful; including dependants 124,855 persons were granted settlement. Further information is difficult to obtain as the published statistics combine all post-entry decisions, most of which are applications for extension to a grant of temporary residence.

3. Citizenship

There are no fewer than six categories of citizenship: British citizenship, British overseas citizenship, British overseas territories citizenship, British national (overseas), British protected person, and a residual category of British subject. Only the first unequivocally carries the right to live and work in the UK, and the others are ignored for present purposes. Since 1983, the essential qualification for the acquisition of British citizenship is birth in the United Kingdom where at the time of birth one parent was a British citizen or legally settled in the United Kingdom.[23] Some persons with the other forms of citizenship may apply to register as a British citizen.[24] Others may apply for naturalization,[25] must pass

---

[21] Immigration Rules, r 33B.
[22] *Control of Immigration: Statistics 2007* (Home Office Statistical Bulletin 10/08), sections 4 and 5.
[23] British Nationality Act 1981, s.1(1).
[24] See British Nationality Act 1981, s.4ff (as amended).
[25] British Nationality Act 1981, s.6 and Sch.1.

the test on Life in the UK already mentioned and attend a citizenship ceremony at which they must take the traditional oath of allegiance[26] and a newly-coined 'pledge'[27].

In 2008, 156,015 applications for citizenship were made.[28] The principal previous nationalities of successful applicants were: India (9% of the total), Pakistan and Iraq (each 7%), Somalia (6%) and Zimbabwe, Afghanistan, Philippines, South Africa, Turkey and Nigeria (all 4%).[29] The application was refused in 8,735 cases, the main reason (31% of the total) being that the applicant was considered not to be of good character.

The effect of immigration on the religious configuration of Great Britain can be assessed by reference to the figures from the most recent census, taken in 2001:

Table 2: religious allegiance, great britain, 2001 (percentages of population)

	England	Wales	Scotland	Total for Great Britain
Christianity	71.74	71.90	65.08	**71.16**
Islam	3.10	0.75	0.84	**2.78**
Hinduism	1.11	0.19	0.11	**0.98**
Sikhism	0.67	0.07	0.13	**0.59**
Judaism	0.52	0.08	0.13	**0.47**
Buddhism	0.28	0.19	0.13	**0.26**
Other	0.29	0.24	0.53	**0.31**
No religion	14.59	18.53	27.55	**15.94**
None stated	7.69	8.07	5.49	**7.51**

The Census results contain an analysis of ethnic groups by religion. For example, almost 80% of Muslims identified themselves as of Asian or African descent; and the district with the highest proportion of Muslims

---

[26] I [name] swear by Almighty God that on becoming a British citizen, I will be faithful and bear true allegiance to Her Majesty Queen Elizabeth the Second, her Heirs and Successors, according to law.

[27] I will give my loyalty to the United Kingdom and respect its rights and freedoms. I will uphold its democratic values. I will observe its laws faithfully and fulfil my duties and obligations as a British citizen.

[28] For statistics, see *British Citizenship Statistics United Kingdom 2008* (Home Office Statistical Bulletin 09/09).

[29] Ibid, para 8, Table A.

in its population (Tower Hamlets, in Greater London) had a very large immigrant population. Of those religions without a long history in the UK, only Buddhism presents a rather different picture, with almost 40% of its adherents classifying themselves as White.

4. Asylum

Asylum applications

The UK applies the 1951 United Nations Convention relating to the Status of Refugees, as extended by the 1967 Protocol, in deciding whether to grant asylum. Persons who are found not to be refugees within the terms of the Convention may nonetheless be granted Humanitarian Protection (HP)[30] or Discretionary Leave (DL) for five years, after which they can apply for indefinite leave to remain.[31]

Asylum applications peaked in the years 1999-2002, where they averaged 75,000 a year.[32] They then fell sharply: 50,000 in 2003, 34,000 in 2004, and 25,000 in 2005. In 2007, 23,430 applications were made. The great majority were unsuccessful (73%); 3,800 were granted asylum and 2,335 HP or DL.[33] There were 14,055 appeals to the Asylum and Immigration Tribunal, 23% of which were successful. 12,705 former applicants were deported or left voluntarily during the year.

The process

Applications for asylum are considered by a 'case owner' within the UK Borders Agency. About a week after an initial explanatory meeting, the asylum interview is held at which the applicant is asked to explain his or her reasons for seeking asylum.[34] An interpreter is provided if needed; legal representatives may attend to assist the applicant. An asylum-seeker may be provided with financial support and accommodation in

---

[30] Immigration Rules, r339C.

[31] See Immigration Rules, r 327ff.

[32] *Asylum Statistics 2008* (Home Office Statistical Bulletin 11/08)

[33] In the first quarter of 2009, the refusal rate was only 59%. It is not clear if this represents a trend to a more generous approach.

[34] Although no longer used, interview questions once included, in an attempt to establish duplicity, such absurd questions as 'How many books in the Bible are there? How do you prepare a turkey for Christmas? What do the numbers 666 mean? Give the names of the thieves crucified alongside Jesus'. The present writer would fail such a test.

certain cases, has access to free health care from the National Health
Service, and is entitled to free legal assistance subject to means tests.[35]

That sounds very satisfactory but church groups concerned about the
treatment of asylum-seekers present a very different picture. They draw
attention in particular to the fact that asylum-seekers are prohibited from
obtaining employment and have no access to welfare benefits. The presence, according to official estimates by the National Audit Office, of at
least 283,500 persons in the UK who have been refused asylum but who
have not been removed points to the scale of the problem.

In 2008 the (Church of England) Children's Society published a
report[36] on child destitution amongst asylum-seeker families. It found
that the mother was often forced to resort to prostitution. The report
concluded that the main cause of destitution was lack of legal representation: legal aid for asylum-seekers was severely restricted, and did not
allow time to deal with the UK's complex immigration system. The
detention of children in Immigration Removal Centres has been of great
concern, notably in Scotland where the Church of Scotland has taken up
the issue of the conditions in such centres. In the previous year, the
Archbishops' Council joined the Still Human Still Here campaign, a
coalition of church, refugee, and asylum-seeker organisations concerned
about the welfare of asylum-seekers after their initial application to stay
has been refused. The campaign called on the Government to continue
financial support and accommodation, and to provide access to education and healthcare for refused asylum-seekers. It also wanted the Government to grant permission for them to work until they leave the country or are permitted to remain.

A recent study[37] of 56 destitute asylum-seekers, many of them Christians, from 20 countries, found that none were 'economic migrants', and
they included a surgeon, a lawyer, a civil engineer, a poet, and a painter.
Most were living on less than £5 a week. Two-thirds of them had been
tortured before they arrived in the UK. Although many asylum-seekers
sleep on the streets, in parks, on church floors, and on buses, they are not
included in the Government's homelessness statistics. Most are not eligible for housing or benefits, and they are not allowed to work. Many have
suffered physical and sexual attacks. The majority of those interviewed in

---

[35] Asylum Support Regulations 2000, S.I. 2000/704 as most recently amended by the
Asylum Support (Amendment) Regulations 2008, SI 2008/760.
[36] *Living on the Edge of Despair.*
[37] *Underground Lives* (Positive Action for Refugees and Asylum Seekers, March
2009).

the report said that if they were to return to their country of origin, they would be killed or tortured. One woman, from the Democratic Republic of the Congo, who was forcibly removed from the UK, was tortured when she arrived in Kinshasa. She escaped again to the UK and lodged a new claim for asylum, using her torture scars as evidence. The report says that the UK Borders Agency makes little effort to find out what happens to those whom it repatriates. Rejected asylum-seekers, it says, are

forced to live underground, enduring severe poverty, extreme hunger, mental and physical ill-health and multiple forms of abuse, as well as constant fear of being rounded up and deported. They walk down the same streets as UK citizens, but inhabit a terrifying, parallel universe.

The General Synod of the Church of England at its February 2009 group of sessions passed by 242 to 1, with 1 recorded abstention, a motion in these terms:

That this Synod, continuing to affirm scriptural teaching about care for vulnerable people, welcome for strangers and foreigners, and the Church's calling to reach out to the marginalised and persecuted, call upon HM Government:

(a)   *to ensure that the treatment of asylum-seekers is just and compassionate, and to that end to:*
(i)   *confer a right to work on all asylum-seekers,*
(ii) *declare an amnesty for so called 'legacy cases' that predate the Government's New Asylum Model, and*
(iii) *bring to an end the practice of detaining children and families in Immigration Removal Centres;*
(b)   *to find a practical and humane remedy to the intolerable situation of destitute 'refused' asylum-seekers who are unable to return to their country of origin because of personal safety, health or family reasons;*
(c)   *to investigate and report publicly on the quality of the legal services provided to asylum-seekers.*

There have been many instances of local churches providing shelter to asylum-seekers facing deportation, although it is recognised that there is no 'right of sanctuary' in a church and the most that can be done is to provide support, publicity and win time for legal steps to be taken. In a well-publicised case in 2001, a church in Cleethorpes gave shelter to a family from Kosovo. When they moved back to their home to await the outcome of an appeal, they were arrested at dawn and deported. In the following year 12 police, two in riot gear, broke into a mosque in the

Midlands to arrest and deport two asylum-seekers. Churches do what
they can to give pastoral support to individual families but there is no
systematic state programme.

Case-law

Most asylum decisions are taken by tribunals and not reported as fully as
court decisions. Some decisions, especially of the Asylum and Immigration Appeal Tribunal, are immensely careful and detailed, and are recognised as providing country-specific guidance to those making asylum
decisions.

   FS and others (Iran – Christian Converts) Iran CG[38] provides an
example. The Appeal Tribunal examined 87 pieces of documentary evidence, including eight substantial UNHCR, European and government
reports. The Tribunal drew careful distinctions between ethnic Christians, members of ethnic minority Churches (who were not persecuted,
at least as a general rule, but nonetheless suffered from societal discrimination and a second class status in the eyes of the state and its
institutions) and other Christians, often converts, who were members of
Protestant or evangelical Churches. They were subject to a legal regime
in which their conversion was at least theoretically punishable with
death, and the theocratic nature of the state enabled conversion to be
seen as both a religious crime against God and a political crime against
the very foundations of the state. There was no evidence, however, that
converts were unable to survive socially, for they had the support of
their Christian community. They are able to practise their religion, 'up to
a point'.

   But the Tribunal drew another distinction between those converts who
would simply attend Church, associate with Christians and study the
Bible, and those who would become leaders, lay or ordained, or pastors,
or who would actively and openly proselytise or who would wear in public outward manifestations of their faith such as a visible crucifix, including those who would be so overt in their discussions of their faith with
Muslims that they would be likely to be seen as proselytisers by the various forms of authorities in Iran. For the ordinary convert, who is neither
a leader, lay or ordained, nor a pastor, nor a proselytiser or evangelist, the
Tribunal would regard them as not at a real risk of persecution or treatment breaching Article 3. It would regard the more active convert, pastor,

[38] [2004] UKIAT 00303.

church leader, proselytiser or evangelist as being at a real risk. Where an ordinary individual convert had additional risk factors, they too might well be at a real risk. In the case of a single woman, lacking such economic or social protection which a husband or other immediate family or friends might provide, the difficulties she faces as a convert were significantly compounded.

The approach in that case was confirmed four years later in *SZ and JM (Christians – FS confirmed) Iran CG*[39] after an even more extensive review of documentary and other evidence.

Some cases do reach the higher courts. A decision of the Scottish courts, *Quin Shue Lin (correctly known as Chen Ri Lin) Ptr*,[40] illustrates the application of the principles governing the grant of refugee status. The petitioner, a national of China, sought asylum. In 1993 he was baptised a member of the True Church of Jesus, a Protestant church with places of worship in several parts of China. The petitioner's wife and her parents have also been baptised in that church. He was an active member of the church in Jiujiang with responsibility for the maintenance and decoration of the local place of worship. He was twice arrested and detained, once while attending a prayer meeting in the church and again at a prayer meeting in his own home. After his escape from detention on the second occasion, an arrest warrant and a circular depicting the petitioner and indicating that he was wanted by the Chinese police in connection with his escape from detention were issued by the Chinese authorities. He went into hiding in Guangshou; his wife moved to Fu Quin city in Fujian province, where she continues to be a member of the True Church of Jesus. The petitioner's claim for asylum was refused and after two unsuccessful appeals he sought judicial review in the Court of Session. He failed. The initial decision recognised that the petitioner had a well-founded fear of persecution on the ground of religion, but noted that the petitioner's wife had gone to another part of China, where the church was not persecuted, and that, therefore, the petitioner had the option of internal flight. For the petitioner it was argued that the internal flight option was not available in cases where the State is the agent of persecution, but this argument was rejected.

---

[39] [2008] UKAIT 00082.
[40] 2004 S.C.L.R. 608. See also an earlier Scottish decision, *Archer v Secretary of State for the Home Department*, 2001 Scot (D) 15/11 (Christian persecuted in Northern Nigeria; asylum refused on ground of possible internal flight to Southern Nigeria).

The relevance of the European Convention on Human Rights and especially article 9 on freedom of religion was considered in detail by the House of Lords in *Regina (Ullah) v Special Adjudicator; Do v Immigration Appeal Tribunal*.[41] There were two distinct cases, heard together. Mr Ullah was a citizen of Pakistan and an active member of the Ahmadiya faith. Members of his faith suffer from a degree of religious persecution from Muslim extremists, and Mr Ullah claimed that he was subjected to a variety of restrictions of religious freedom and social discrimination and had suffered harassment and attacks on himself and his family since he began preaching his faith in December 1998. Miss Do, a citizen of Vietnam, claimed asylum on the ground of her fear of persecution as the result of her religious beliefs as a Roman Catholic. There was evidence to support Miss Do's claim that her freedom to practise her religion was circumscribed in a number of respects; although she could return to Vietnam and practise her religion there, she would have to do so in reduced circumstances.

The Court of Appeal held, in effect, that only article 3 of the Convention could be relied upon in this context. The House of Lords disagreed. After a full analysis of the European case-law, it held that issues might exceptionally be raised where the anticipated ill-treatment would infringe other articles of the Convention, in particular, articles 2, 5, 6, and 8, and did not rule out such a possibility in respect of article 9;[42] but also held that reliance on such articles required presentation of an exceptionally strong case such that the actual or threatened treatment would amount to a flagrant denial or gross violation of the relevant right, facts not present in the two cases before the House.

Most asylum decisions necessarily turn on questions of fact, often difficult to assess. The published country-specific guidance examining the background to the most common types of asylum claim from particular countries. For example that on Pakistan, revised February 2009, examines claims by Ahmadis, examining the 'internal flight' option, and by women, and summarises relevant tribunal decisions. The guidance on Vietnam contains four pages assessing the position of minority religious groups, with reference both to the formal legal position and the realities in each part of the country.

---

[41] [2004] UKHL 26, [2004] 2 AC 323.

[42] The House noted *Razaghi v Sweden* (Application No 64599/01) (unreported) 11 March 2003 which suggested that article 9 was irrelevant in this context, but held that the judgment was not clear on the point

5. Conclusion

Citizenship has limited significance in English and Scottish law as compared with the position in many countries in the civil law tradition. That may explain why it is not the subject of much debate. Immigration and asylum issues, on the other hand, are highly controversial. Given that the United Kingdom has net immigration approaching a quarter of a million a year, and some 25,000 asylum applications a year, there are very real pressures on the administrative and legal systems. The continued reductions in Commonwealth immigration, largely to balance the free movement of EU nationals, cause concern especially to the many UK residents whose origins lie in other Commonwealth countries. The problem of the 'refused asylum-seeker' seems to defy solution.

PRINTED ON PERMANENT PAPER • IMPRIME SUR PAPIER PERMANENT • GEDRUKT OP DUURZAAM PAPIER - ISO 9706

N.V. PEETERS S.A., WAROTSTRAAT 50, B-3020 HERENT